To Andrea & Peter
with love

The Needs ABC Therapeutic Model for Couples and Families

A Guide for Practitioners

Tom Caplan

Routledge
Taylor & Francis Group
New York London

Routledge
Taylor & Francis Group
270 Madison Avenue
New York, NY 10016

Routledge
Taylor & Francis Group
27 Church Road
Hove, East Sussex BN3 2FA

© 2011 by Taylor and Francis Group, LLC
Routledge is an imprint of Taylor & Francis Group, an Informa business

Printed in the United States of America on acid-free paper
10 9 8 7 6 5 4 3 2 1

International Standard Book Number: 978-0-415-87305-5 (Hardback) 978-0-415-87306-2 (Paperback)

Library of Congress Cataloging-in-Publication Data

Caplan, Tom.

The needs ABC therapeutic model for couples and families : a guide for practitioners / Tom Caplan.

p. ; cm.

Includes bibliographical references and index.

Summary: "The Needs ABC Therapeutic Model for Couples and Families: A Guide for Practitioners shows readers how to successfully tailor a therapeutic approach to meet the needs of couples and families. It has been preceded by Needs ABC (Acquisition and Behavior Change), a model for group work and other psychotherapies published in the UK by Whiting and Birch. Beginning clinicians will come away from this book with concrete, practical skills and expanded theoretical base for their practice, and they'll be able to apply their new knowledge directly and in ways that will help them create long-lasting change in clients who present with difficult behaviors. The book explains the concepts and theories behind the Needs ABC approach and provides tangible methods with which to perform as a Needs ABC therapist or integrate aspects of the Needs ABC approach into the reader's own therapeutic techniques. Practitioners will find that the Needs ABC model complements cognitive-behavioral, integrative, and other therapeutic models, as well as general guides to couples and family therapy"--Provided by publisher.

ISBN 978-0-415-87305-5 (hardcover : alk. paper) -- ISBN 978-0-415-87306-2 (pbk. : alk. paper)

1. Couples therapy. 2. Family therapy. I. Title.

[DNLM: 1. Couples Therapy--methods. 2. Family Therapy--methods. WM 430.5.M3 C244n 2010]

RC488.5.C362 2010
616.89'1562--dc22

2010018616

Visit the Taylor & Francis Web site at
http://www.taylorandfrancis.com

and the Routledge Web site at
http://www.routledgementalhealth.com

For my children and their children

Contents

Preface: The Evolution of the Needs Acquisition and Behavior Change Model

The thought manifests as the word.

The word manifests as the deed.

The deed develops into habit.

And the habit hardens into character.

So watch the thought and its ways with care.

And let it spring from love, born out of concern for all beings.

Buddha

The Needs Acquisition and Behavior Change (Needs ABC) model emphasizes working with what clients are asking for in their interpersonal relationships rather than focusing without exploration on the "bad" behaviors that ultimately bring them into the treatment setting. It also proposes that the way clients feel when they are frustrated in the realization of their relational goals will predict either more or less useful strategies for relational problem solving.

This model evolved and developed as a result of my experience working in a number of treatment settings. My background in psychotherapy initially had a strong focus on group work along with an active private practice where I worked with individuals, couples, and families. I started learning about groups as a treatment modality when I did my master's placement in the School of Social Work at the McGill Domestic Violence Clinic. At that time, the clinic was directed by two professors, Judy Magill (who passed away shortly after my graduation) and Annette Werk. They both commented that, even though I had a lot to learn, my style seemed to be very encouraging to the clients—men who were perpetrators of abuse—and seemed to help them to discuss their problem more openly and honestly. Interestingly enough, this was the same style I used in all my work; it was just the way I did things, though I wasn't sure exactly *what* I was doing. At the McGill Clinic, we did a lot of feelings work ("reaching for feelings"), and when I graduated and Annette, who surely felt a void with Judy's passing, asked me to join the supervision team, I began to take my position seriously. Harle Thomas, a former student just a few years younger than myself, encouraged me to present at the next Group Work conference as he had done the previous year. The subject of my first paper, "Safety and Comfort, Content, and Process: Facilitating Open Group Work for Men Who Batter" (Caplan & Thomas, 1995), which I wrote and copresented with Harle, was the beginning of the deconstruction of what was to become my Needs ABC Model.

When I started working at the McGill Domestic Violence Clinic in 1980, the therapeutic approach we used involved a twofold methodology: (1) the use of "process-oriented" interventions (looking past the concrete content of what a client was saying to what was implied in what was being said—or *meta message*); and (2) reaching for feelings (helping clients express how they were feeling with regard to what they were saying, often with the use of a "feelings chart"). In the men's group, composed of male perpetrators of domestic violence, the chart had no "anger" column in an attempt to help them to recognize other relevant emotional components to what they had said—that fear or sadness, for example, could possibly be hidden behind their anger and that an understanding of this would be very helpful in addressing their less than useful behaviors. We had no specific explanation of *why* this was important, but it was recognized that when the men were able to connect with these "softer" emotions they were also better able to communicate with their partners.

In those days, the interpretation of the meta message, or the overall impression given by the client through his narrative, was quite general and concrete. For example, if a client stated that he was angry at his partner for scolding him about the way he tied the garbage bag for pick-up, the intervention used would be something like, "It must be pretty scary to be criticized by your wife," with the focus more on the appropriate emotion than on anything else. The concept used was fairly simple: the facilitator would think about any emotion other than anger, with "fear" and "sadness" being favorite picks; any less dramatic or "dangerous" emotion would do. They then would do a "reaching for feelings" exercise with the group or group member, using the aforementioned chart. There was no thought about what else might be implied in the client's statement.

Even though I had a fairly good handle on Family Systems Theory, Cognitive Behavioral Therapy (CBT), "feelings work," and the traditional social work skills (e.g., joining, mirroring, paraphrasing), I was exceedingly interested in learning all I could about therapeutic models and strategies. As time went on, my work gradually came to be influenced by Michael White's Narrative School, especially his concepts of therapist "curiosity" and "externalization of the problem," which allowed clients to look at what they were doing with more objectivity (White & Epston, 1990); de Shazer (1985, 1991) and De Shazer et al.'s (2007) Solution-Focused Therapy, where the "Magic Question" is a point of interest with regard to what the client was hoping to happen that would be curative for the situation at hand; and especially Greenberg and Johnson's (1988) Emotionally Focused Therapy (EFT). I had taken a workshop with Leslie Greenberg, who seemed to validate the concept of various levels of emotional states he had described as *primary*, *secondary*, and *tertiary*. This led me to consider that there were, in fact, different levels of emotions and that some emotions were more easily expressed than others, depending on the context. This was also the precursor to my definition of various levels of relational needs. Because I sensed that parts of each of these models, including the ones I had initially been taught, provided opportunities to help clients in ways a monolithic model never could, I began to integrate these into my work with groups and with my individual, couple and family work. This led me, eventually, to become interested in the Integrative Psychotherapy movement and to develop my model.

In winter 1982, I was facilitating a domestic violence men's group because one of my students who was supposed to have run the group that evening was unable to do so. I was already acquainted with most of the men and with their presenting issues because of the use of videotape in our supervision sessions. At that point in time, I had coined the concept of *universal themes* as a way to help link clients together for potential discussion during the group's "working phase." These were, quite simply, themes such as "feeling criticized," "getting closer," "ability to trust," and "taking responsibility." All these seemed to be common themes often expressed by members of these groups that could be "universally" understood by all group members, whether any given theme was a salient issue for them in particular. In other words, even if a client did not have issues with criticism, he could still understand someone who did. I began the group with my usual injunction: "Please sign in by telling the group how things have been going for you since we last met with regard to the problem that brings you here." The first client, James, said that he felt better now that his girlfriend had stated her appreciation for his coming to the group. I responded, "I guess there is good news and bad news for you. The good news is that you seem to be gaining your partner's trust little by little. The bad news is that you have to hold yourself to a higher standard if you want to continue to do so"—highlighting trust and responsibility-taking. Robert, the next in turn, continued, while consulting the feelings chart, by saying, "It does feel a little scary to think I will have to continue to be careful of how I react when things happen that I find disturbing." We continued around the circle until we arrived at Philippe, who was second from last. Philippe stated that his wife was always telling him what to do and that even when he did do something it "was wrong, always wrong." I intervened by saying, "I guess it's a little sad to think that nothing you do seems to work and that she seems to be keeping you at a distance"—highlighting feelings of inadequacy and being "pushed away." He responded, "That's really not what I need … to feel like a 'screw-up' all the time.… She never gives me what I need."

After the sign-in was completed, I seeded the group discussion with an intervention that combined some of the universal themes that I had gleaned, including "inadequacy" and "distancing." About 20 minutes went by with what seemed to be a fairly lively discussion about these and other themes when Philippe, addressing George—who had praised his partner for "actually being all he had ever needed in a relationship" again—stated, quite emphatically, "My wife only criticizes; she never gives me what I need." At this point, I started to wonder, "What's with all of this neediness all of a sudden?" reflecting back to Philippe's sign-in. With that, Alex, a client who often seemed to fancy himself a group "co-therapist," responded, "Well, what the heck do you need—to always have it your way?" Anticipating a diatribe from Philippe, I readied myself to intervene. However, to my surprise, Philippe responded, almost sadly, "All I want from her is to feel that I can do something right. When we were first married I felt I could do no wrong. As soon as our first child came along I couldn't even powder Jenny right." The group seemed to grow strangely silent, perhaps because everyone had expected more of a set-to than what had actually transpired. At this point, I considered how to link the clients together based on what Philippe had said and then intervened by stating, "It seems to me that a number of you also feel sad about not being able to measure up to others' expectations." (I prefer to make my interventions as general as possible to broaden the relational need scope—in this case using *others'* expectations instead of *partners'*.) With this, the group seemed to light up, as if everyone had suddenly given himself permission to talk about issues he usually found too difficult to access. Jonah began by stating, "Between his boss and his wife" he also could do nothing right. Robert also exclaimed that he had often struggled with living up to his girlfriend's "high standards," and Nicholas disclosed that "even though it doesn't bug me that much, sometimes I have to give up trying and ask my wife to do it the way she wants instead."

In effect, it suddenly became clear to me that the dysfunctional behaviors being displayed by these men were attempts at getting specific needs met within the context of their relationships—that the themes actually represented their *relational needs*. The challenge, therefore, was to help these men *acquire* these needs appropriately, and, once acquired, the behavior they had exhibited would no longer be necessary—the *behavior* would *change*. As well, the dramatic difference in affect (sadness vs. anger) that Philippe used in expressing to the group what he "needed" from his wife seemed to make the other group members sit back and listen. This emotion was definitely more productive in describing what Philippe wanted relationally and, based on the group members' participation following my intervention, more potentially productive in problem solving. The day after that group, in my home office, I employed an existing list of "universal themes" I had used when writing previous journal articles to see if I could match them to specific needs the clients had with regard to their relationships. Some of these "relational needs" seemed quite simple to conceptualize: for example, "trust" was a need for "loyalty"; feeling inadequate or criticized was a need for "competence." For others, to describe succinctly what a client wanted from his partner was more difficult; "reliability" was easy to understand intuitively but more difficult to explain concisely, for example. The lack of reliability was eventually described in part as having a "conditional relationship," or the need for an unconditional relationship. In the end, it continued to appear evident that the "engine" that drove a path of success or failure to relational problem solving was still the emotional component. However, defining the themes as client-specific relational needs seemed to clarify why less productive emotional states existed in clients who came into the clinic, why they were not getting what they wanted relationally from their partners, and why they were employing strategies that were only further frustrating their attempts to acquire these needs.

As time went on, I began experimenting with my individual (adult and adolescent) and couples private practice clients to determine whether my hypothesis of unmet needs driving less productive emotions and, in turn, dysfunctional or less productive behaviors was valid for my clients in general. I was happily surprised to find that not only did it fit their therapeutic profile but that it also seemed to give them something tangible to work with, making it possible for meaningful progress to be made. Furthermore, individuals who wanted to feel more competent or respected by others (e.g., partner, employer, parent) had to recognize that it was *their* responsibility to choose appropriate strategies to fulfill these needs, an issue that was so important in terms of treatment outcome. Again, as a client, understanding concretely what I was looking for in my relationships with others made the planning of need-acquisition strategies much simpler and, potentially, more accurate. On the other hand, as a therapist, by allying with the client around their relational needs, I seemed to make them feel more understood, less defensive, and more prepared to examine other options. Finally, an examination of a client's family of origin relationships—the formation of their primary relationships—seemed to help clients understand more clearly why these needs were so powerful that they often predicted destructive dysfunctional behaviors when they were not being met. These insights often empowered the client by helping them to understand that they could meet their relational needs if they used more advantageous means. At the same time, in particular with couples, these concerns were, in reality, a legacy from past relationships and were not necessarily about the clients as people but who each reminded the other of.

Over the next nine years, Harle and I presented at every annual group work conference in North America, modifying and improving the model, and I began to field contracts to teach my model to local agencies as well. Eventually Harle and I parted ways, leaving behind 10 articles on the model. As I began to write more about the model on my own, the reality of what I was doing began to crystallize. I was not asking the clients to think about what they were *doing* but what they were hoping to *achieve* by doing what they were doing. This distinction was to prove enormously important in terms of helping clients not just to understand their problems but to move beyond them and into a new, more productive set of behaviors. What I was hearing from my clients was what they needed from others—to feel more important or competent or available and so forth. When they didn't get what they wanted, they seemed to have feelings—anger, sadness, or whatever—that only perpetuated the problem that had brought them into therapy in the first place.

It dawned on me that focusing on what clients *were doing* rather than *why* they were doing it only reinforced these negative feelings and often made things worse in the longer term. Who likes to be reminded of their shortcomings? It is embarrassing and shameful.

One can unhesitatingly say that beating one's wife, gambling the family savings away, or drinking to the point of losing one's job are truly shameful acts. However, while such behavior is surely an embarrassment, and much more, that is not the issue here. Because most of us actually understand on an intellectual level the difference between "right" and "wrong" (an understanding that produces the shame in the first place), our model is about helping clients examine their behavior with no holds barred and to examine what might work better for all concerned. For clients to challenge their *modus operandi* and to replace it with something more functional, they must see the counselor as an ally rather than as someone who will continue to punish them for their transgressions. In essence, they must clearly understand what the problem actually is and why they use the behaviors they do to try to get it solved. This will potentially lead them toward remorse and making amends more readily than a directive would. By understanding the etiology and nature of the problem, it becomes easier to construct a new set of behaviors related to the underlying relational needs. At this point, they can work toward finding better ways of getting what they want in a more socially responsible manner. For example, take the case of an adolescent who has been cutting classes and smoking dope throughout the day. If, even in the nicest way, his therapist comments on his dope smoking or class cutting, she immediately becomes "one of them." If, however, the adolescent describes being pressured to achieve higher standards than he feels capable of and the therapist comments on his need to be accepted for who he is and supported in finding his way to appropriate expectations, he will immediately think, "Boy, this person gets it when nobody else has." Or take the couple who comes into the therapist's office: the woman complains that, even though she works full time as an emergency room doctor, she feels "like the hired help," and the man belligerently asserting that, despite being a full partner in a prestigious law firm, every time he tries to help she criticizes. If one focuses on the way she criticizes rather than her need to feel important to him or tries to help him to negotiate some form of attention giving (to her) rather than validate his feeling unacknowledged for his expertise around the house, the therapist is simply colluding in the perpetuation of resentments rather than supporting the potential for needs-getting strategies that remove the "finger pointing" and support the clients in the careful examination of how to take responsibility for getting their needs met properly.

With all of this in mind, and having continued to expand my experience of a client acquiring her or his relational needs that, in turn, ultimately predicted a behavior change, and while continuously refining the same, I decided to write a second book on the model. In this volume, the focus is on couples and families and how the Needs Acquisition and Behavior Change model is an excellent choice toward finding a way to help these clients to move functionally forward in their lives and away from an emotional landscape in which therapy is necessary; our goal as therapists is to help our clients reach the stage whereby therapy is no longer necessary at all.

Please remember while reading this book that the examples are truncated excerpts taken from suitably disguised cases and do not necessarily represent the reality of the time frame involved in accomplishing the outcomes described. As all therapists know, progress can be slow, and it can also be uneven. It should also be understood that, even though the revelation of the relational needs does help enormously with the work ahead, some therapies can take longer than others. As well, in the real world, some clients do not succeed in remaining in therapy long enough to resolve their issues. Having said all that, I know from my own experience that the Needs ABC model for therapy can be an excellent tool to use in helping couples to find the equilibrium and happiness that they need to progress through life in the context of a happy and fulfilling personal relationship.

The Needs ABC Model was originally developed by the author at the McGill Domestic Violence Clinic, which, though predominantly offering treatment in groups for the men who perpetrate this abuse and support for the women who are the survivors, also provides affected couples with therapy (when it is safe and appropriate to do so). The clinic also serves as a training arena for future therapists. It uses an integrated therapeutic approach combining observation and elucidation of client process, using concepts also described in cognitive-behavioral and motivational, narrative, and emotion-focused models, blending these and other previously described approaches in an adaptable *modus operandi* that can be made to suit the needs of any therapeutic unit, including individual, couples, and group therapy.

When clients decide to attend therapy, or indeed when they are mandated to do so, the underlying reason is the implication that they have a problem to be solved with respect to the way they approach relationships, one way or another. The specifics of their problem will always be different, but the bottom line is that they are having difficulties relating to others or dealing with fundamental aspects of themselves. Even clients who come readily or even eagerly to therapy will not find it easy to explore, probe, and discuss the very topics that make them most uncomfortable, ashamed, or unhappy. Accepting our vulnerabilities and weaknesses seems to be a fundamental aspect of being human. However, key to emotional wellness is the acquisition of a good understanding of our relational needs—what they are, how we have been trying and failing to achieve them, and how we could do better with this goal. Clients who become enabled to see their own vulnerabilities and relational needs are not weakened; on the contrary, becoming able to express these needs as a susceptibility ("There are times when I doubt your feelings for me, because I was never able to rely on my parents for emotional support") can pave the way to meaningful, productive problem solving. Recognizing and accepting our weaknesses make us all stronger, as human individuals, as couples, and as families.

Acknowledgments

In writing this book, I want to especially thank a number of people. It goes without saying that Annette Werk got the ball rolling by inviting me into McGill, and for this I am ever grateful. As well, the Association for the Advancement of Social Work with Groups (AASWG) has continued to be a strong supporter of my work through all of my developmental stages of article writing and presenting at its various conferences. Of special note is the late Roselle Kurland who had taken a special interest in my therapeutic approach and who was a constant source of encouragement and validation. Tim Kelly and David Whiting of the London-based *Groupwork* journal worked with me patiently and diligently while I was getting my "sea legs" writing my first book.

Two others deserve special mention. First is my editor, Deirdre Nuttall, who has helped me with what I considered to be the monumental task of organizing the plethora of articles I had written—with or without the help of others, some published and some not—into a coherent tome. And, finally but most importantly, is Barbara, my friend, wife, and ally. I now realize why many authors also thank their partners. Putting up with the many hours spent away from them either writing or at conferences takes a special dedication and unconditional relational regard.

I am fortunate indeed.

1

Introducing the Needs ABC Model

The Needs Acquisition and Behavior Change (Needs ABC) model, an integrative model within the broader school of cognitive behavioral therapy, focuses on client relational needs and the emotions predicted by them rather than on specific client behaviors. The model assumes the following:

1. The need described in the themes embedded in clients' narratives drives their emotions.
2. These emotions drive behavior.
3. Meeting needs through appropriate behavior results in eliminating the inappropriate behavior.

In addition, three important goals govern the Needs ABC model:

1. Safety: Allying with clients around their relational needs will help clients to feel understood and to trust the process of therapy. This helps participants to begin experiencing a sense of safety that can lead to greater participation and self-disclosure.
2. Ownership: Once a sense of security has been developed, the next goal is for clients to take responsibility for their part in the problem and to collaborate with the therapist and other family members in the development of appropriate restorative strategies.
3. Understanding: The facilitator should assess and illuminate clients' relational needs and emotional states during the therapeutic process and do the following:

a. Help clients to understand the evolution and reason for having these important relational needs that color their functioning.
b. Help clients to understand how these needs predict how they feel.
c. Help clients to understand why they behave in the dysfunctional ways that they do.

In its development, the Needs ABC model was influenced by the work I carried out in other clinical settings with substance abuse, gambling, and other behavioral problems. Needs ABC was designed to minimize client–therapist contextual resistance and to form, as quickly as possible, a positive therapeutic alliance with those in attendance (Henry & Strupp, 1994, pp. 51–84; Nichols, 1987, pp. 272–296). Joining with the client sooner rather than later would help engage the client in the collaborative problem-solving process earlier in the course of therapy, allowing more opportunity for the "practicing" and refining of strategies while maintaining client engagement (Warzak, William, Parish, & Handen, 1987).

Our focus here is on couples. By extension, we will also be discussing adolescents in the context of their relationship with their parents, the impact of couples' problems on their adolescent children, and how the same adolescents can be assisted in engaging in the therapeutic process and supported on their journey toward becoming mature adults who will, in turn, be able to form healthy couples. We will refer to a large number of case studies, which are fictional accounts of therapy based closely on my clinical experience and on the very real problems that my clients have brought into therapy. For brevity, the actual time frame involved is not necessarily represented. It should also be understood that, in the real world, some clients do not manage to remain in therapy for long enough to resolve all their presenting issues.

In addition to my book *Needs ABC: A Needs Acquisition and Behavior Change Model for Group Work and Other Psychotherapies* (Caplan, 2008b), you might want to explore Doel and Sawdon (1999) and Yalom (2005).

In this book I have tailored an application of this approach to couples and families as a unit and to adolescents as individuals who are reluctant to present for therapy in general. As we are aware, for parents, children approaching adolescence can be a difficult period which can even signal the onset of serious relational difficulties in parental couples and families that, up until that point, have experienced relatively straight-forward, happy relationships.

In general, couples and family therapy first emerged in the 1950s as positive, proactive methods of helping clients build on their personal strengths and on their strengths as a family unit or as couples (Nichols, 2007, pp. 7–34). Continually over the course of the intervening years since, new and adapted models of family therapy have emerged, such as structural family therapy, with a focus on creating change, and narrative therapy, with a focus on the way people tell their life stories. All couples therapy models seek to provide couples having difficulties in their relationships with the ability to access more functional behavior and a happier interpersonal situation, although the methods used can vary considerably.

For obvious reasons, couples and family therapy are closely interlinked. Like couples therapy, family therapy seeks to help the people involved to improve their interpersonal relationships by working on dysfunctional behaviors and, generally, by understanding better the reasons behind these behaviors (Nichols, 1987, pp. 65–72). It usually does not attempt to blame or scapegoat any individual in particular but instead explores the patterns of behavior that have emerged from the group that is the family.

Distinguishing the Needs ABC Model

Therapy has, over the course of its relatively short history, been offered to couples by practitioners from quite a wide range of theoretical backgrounds. No therapeutic approach arises out of thin air. Instead, therapists learn and build on work that has already been carried out by their predecessors by adapting their style and approach to their own personalities, to the specific needs of their clients, and to their cultural and temporal environment. Different styles of therapy can all work, given certain circumstances and the willingness on the part of clients and therapist alike to engage with each other and to commit to therapy. However, the peculiar flexibility of the Needs ABC model, which combines concepts also found in the teachings of various well-known practitioners of group, individual, and couples therapy (the more important of which we will shortly discuss) with the author's own approach and therapeutic innovations derived from experience in all of the aforementioned modalities, makes it especially adaptable to a wide range of situations and circumstances.

The Needs ABC approach focuses on isolating and putting into practice useful, pragmatic solutions to the problems facing the individual. As in the case of Teyber's (1997) approach, "A primary working goal for the therapist is to provide validation throughout each session by grasping the client's core messages and affirming the central meaning in what the client says" (p. 44). Needs ABC therapists also believe that without an understanding of the unmet needs that lie behind dysfunctional behaviors and the emotions they predict, it is difficult to create lasting change. At the same time, one must also work hard at choosing new reactions, new ways of behaving, while re-creating one's personal narrative and, in the context of couples therapy, one's relationship with one's partner.

The Needs ABC model uses an integrated therapeutic approach combining observation and elucidation of a client's relational process and incorporates some concepts also described in cognitive-behavioral, motivational, solution-focused, narrative, and emotion-focused models. The overriding premise of this model is that a client's unmet relational needs—in this case, in the context of them as one element of a couple—will predict a more or less useful emotion and that a less useful emotion will predict a less functional problem-solving strategy. If the relational need is defined and a more productive emotion is determined, treatment planning can be done around a more appropriate acquisition of the need. Once the need has been acquired with a more useful emotional approach, clients will no longer experience the emotional need to exchange in the destructive behaviors that brought them to therapy; a functional relationship will ensue, and more appropriate problem-solving techniques will be assimilated.

But what makes the Needs ABC approach different from the many other models available to therapists? While it draws on the wisdom and experience of many therapists and therapeutic writers, acknowledging a considerable debt to clinicians working with a range of models, the

Needs ABC model is distinguished by its emphasis on *the relational needs behind maladaptive behaviors and the emotions they provoke* rather than on the behaviors themselves and by its flexibility in terms of application to clients in a range of personal and therapeutic settings. In the context of providing therapy, it provides a unique approach that helps clients understand the origins of their problematic behaviors individually and in the context of their presenting problems and formulate more constructive ways to react to stress. By deemphasizing behavior and emphasizing emotion and need, it becomes easier for clients to access the reasons that lie behind their problems and to work constructively toward solutions. All of this is very important when it comes to counseling people on how to heal the way they interact with the most important people in their lives.

For example, a man may consistently present with "anger" and express himself using angry words; self-exploration may reveal the more strongly felt sentiment lying beneath the anger as a deeply felt sense of hurt because he cannot get as close as he would like to the people he cares for, particularly his life partner. The way he reacts to this anger (hurt) is likely to be problematic and may relate to the way he reacted as a child when he attempted to have his relational needs met in the context of his family of origin. Similarly, a woman might present with "sadness" and express herself using sad words but might discover that the underlying emotion is really anger at a lack of validation in her personal relationship. Accessing her anger may then help her to assert herself, whereas feeling sad only might maintain her position of perceived impotence and victimhood. Of course, while anger and sadness are, respectively, stereotypical expressions of emotion by men and women, these examples could equally well be reversed.

Throughout this book, we will be looking in detail at how the Needs Acquisition and Behavior Change model can be employed in a range of contexts. However, to set the scene, let's have a quick look at how the basic model translates into therapy. Please consider that the following is only a brief overview and that we will be looking more deeply into how to use the model effectively as we progress. The following story shows how one woman's frustration with her father's forgetfulness can be related to what we will refer to as the universal themes—those easily described and understood and to which

I find it useful to use a nonstereotypical emotion, or scenario, when I sense that a stereotype is extant and inhibiting problem resolution. For example, if a woman tearfully relates her concern that her partner does not feel she can contribute financially to the household, I might say, "I guess it's infuriating to think that you might make a larger contribution that he does now." This will highlight her relational need to feel *competent* in the eyes of her partner while suggesting a more active or motivating emotion, which could help her to become more assertive with regard to the acquisition of her relational needs.

people can easily relate—of *betrayal, abandonment,* and *powerlessness.* Although her partner has not experienced the same specific problem as she, he can relate to the universal themes embedded in her narrative. As you read the following, please bear in mind that only *her* relational needs will be highlighted to more clearly understand how to develop and articulate an appropriate therapeutic statement:

Janette was a 35-year-old mother of three who had married Will, her "childhood sweetheart," right after she graduated from high school. She had been going out with Will since the age of 14 and decided to "go all the way" at the age of 17 when she was in her last year of high school. She and Will had enrolled in separate colleges, each some distance away from their home town, and it was not clear if they would be able to remain together. At the time, Janette felt that she was offering Will "a gift."

Shortly after graduation, Janette was dismayed to discover that she had become pregnant, since she had originally wanted to go to law school. Despite some misgivings, she decided to keep the child with a promise from Will that he would do his utmost to support her financially as well as share in the parenting. Janette's parents had been against her keeping the child and had told her emphatically, "If you decide to keep the child you will have to take care of it! Don't expect anything from us."

Though disappointed that she would have to put her education on hold, Janette took her parents' words as a challenge. They had never been that supportive and had divorced around the time that she began to date Will. In the meantime, Will seemed to work longer hours and become less involved with both Janette and their infant. Because the young couple did not have much financial support from their parents, Will had also forgone college and instead worked in a series of blue-collar jobs he felt were beneath him as someone who had graduated high school with grades high enough to attend "any college he wanted."

Janette convinced Will to have another child and gave birth to their second just after their first child turned 2. Janette always had always wanted a "large family" (she was an only child) and felt that taking care of two would be as easy as caring for one and that, since she had decided to be a mother, she might as well "do it properly."

In the meantime, Will became less and less available, using the financial commitment of providing for his family as an excuse, and when Janette became pregnant with their third, against her husband's wishes, Will admitted to being unfaithful with one of his co-workers and asked for a divorce [loyalty].

Janette was devastated. She had been so busy with her children that she had lost all contact with her friends. In fact, part of her secretly feared that if she did not attend to her children she might "lose" them as well [reliability]. Her mother had moved to Europe and remarried, and her father had never been reliable because of his drinking and partying—especially since his wife had left. Janette also began to drink, and it was only a matter of time before child protection services were called in and she was given an ultimatum to get help for her drinking or lose custody of her children. Janette sought help at a government-funded substance abuse treatment facility close to her home town, in their outpatient department, so she could continue to be with her children while dealing with her substance abuse problem.

Since Will continued to distance himself from his role as "father" and to remain absent from his children's lives [reliability], Janette tried to enlist her father for some emotional and practical support.

In fact, Janette's dad had been able to babysit on several occasions without incident. However, there were also several occasions when he was unavailable because of his drinking [loyalty].

During one of Janette's and Will's therapy sessions she recounted her devastation [power] at her father letting her down once again [loyalty].

Averting her eyes from the gaze of her partner and their therapist, Janette began to talk:

"My father said he was going to go shopping with me yesterday but called at the last minute to tell me he was having 'just one more drink with the boys.' He never made it. I have decided that I don't have a father anymore" [power]. As she finished speaking, her voice began to break but she bit her lip to avoid crying.

On hearing the story, Will muttered that Janette's father is "no good" and that she is "better off without him" [loyalty].

Far from being reassuring, these comments seemed to make Janette feel worse. She sank into a morose silence and contemplated her feet on the carpet, apparently reluctant to say any more or to engage further with the discussion.

On listening to Janette's story, and knowing something of her background, the therapist could rely on the following schematic to formulate a process-oriented intervention for the couple, focusing for now on Janette's needs.

The therapist listens to Janette's story and tries to think about how she is feeling about what is being said (putting herself in the client's shoes, so to speak). In this case, the therapist's initial reaction concurs with Will's—that Janette's father is extremely selfish in choosing his friends over his daughter [loyalty]:

- The therapist then thinks about what Janette actually wants (client need) or does not yet have (needs-deficit). For example, the show of frustration could represent her anger at feeling that no matter what she says, she will never be able to trust her father [loyalty]—or for that matter, Will.

- Or the statement might also represent Janette's frustration with other important relationships in her life, such as her relationship with her mother, in which she felt abandoned [reliability].
- The therapist constructs a hypothesis about what she perceives as Janette's relational need and its emotional component. Janette is afraid of completely losing Will the way she lost her father, emotionally and concretely.
- Or Janette perceives herself as never being able to have a reliable relationship with anybody. The therapist formulates a needs-based, emotion-focused, statement reflecting the process in Janette's story, taking into consideration her stage of development in therapy. There are least three possibilities for what Janette is missing in her relationship(s): feeling that she needs emotional reliability, or being able to trust in important relationships, or both. The therapist knows that these unmet needs for loyalty or reliability are common and that once they are identified, Will should be able to recognize when he has also had these feelings in relationships and whether he been able to successfully deal with them.

Understanding "where Janette is coming from" should make it easier for Will to gain insight into her and his own emotional needs in the context of their relationship.

This schematic can be used to formulate the following theme-based, emotion-focused intervention based on the universal themes of respect or abandonment and is typical of a Needs ABC intervention:

It seems that Janette is pretty upset that her father has more loyalty for his friends than his daughter.

He could also add:

It must be frustrating to feel so disconnected at times, just when you think you are getting close [reliability].

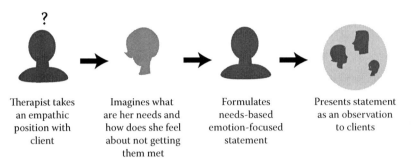

| Therapist takes an empathic position with client | Imagines what are her needs and how does she feel about not getting them met | Formulates needs-based emotion-focused statement | Presents statement as an observation to clients |

Figure 1.1   The formation of a needs-based emotion-focused statement.

Because clients often relate their emotional states to others inadequately, understanding the underlying, more productive emotion embedded in a narrative is used to help clients to understand their emotional needs in relationships more clearly. A productive emotion is one that is more "useful" in problem resolution, potentially leading to a better outcome at the time of the relational interchange. In other words, a productive emotion is one that predicts a better resolution to the problem at hand at the time of the relational interchange. For example, a man's expression of "fear" or "sadness" should cause a less defensive reaction in his partner than if he expresses his relational concerns from a position of anger. A "secondary" (Greenberg & Johnson, 1998), less productive emotion (like "anger" in the previous example) is often presented because it is more culturally acceptable in the situation at hand and therefore is more easily expressed, although it may, in effect, worsen the predicament. When Janette tearfully describes her father's disloyalty, she may well be sad (the less productive emotion) but is also most probably angry (the more workable "primary" emotion) (Greenberg & Johnson). Whereas sadness and despair may be immobilizing, anger can be motivating. If Janette can recognize her resentment, she will be more likely to motivate herself to become more assertive with her father and, ultimately, in other relationships, particularly with Will. Adding the more appropriate emotional component to the interpretation of process, the therapist can formulate a statement reflecting a more productive emotional component of the process in the client's story, taking into consideration the client's stage of development in therapy, as follows:

- Suggested less productive emotion: "sadness"
- Suggested more productive emotion: "anger"

The therapist constructs a more specifically emotion-focused process statement and makes it to the couple, saying:

> It seems that Janette is pretty angry that her father has more loyalty for his friends than his daughter.

He could also add:

> It must be infuriating to feel so disconnected at times, just when you think you are getting close.

Using this combination of techniques, therapists can also guide their clients toward productive relational problem-solving strategies. For example, the therapist and the couple collaborate on the following action plan through role-play:

- With the use of a feelings chart, ask both Will and Janette to distinguish between the presenting emotion and the more empowering emotion in Janette's narrative.
- From a list of relational needs, ask them to suggest what they feel is Janette's unmet need.
- Problem solve, or role-play, possibilities for the expression of the more useful emotion in ways that will functionally describe the unmet relational need.

When using this provided intervention map, it is important to *identify* and *ally* with the client's expressed emotions while *supportively challenging* ineffective behaviors—in this case, Janette's drinking. The following dynamic helps to explain the significance of the aforementioned:

- The needs deficit (client's relational need) drives the emotion—that is, Janette's need to feel emotionally connected in a reliable way as well as her need to feel she can trust Will and her father.

It is also helpful to ask the client why. In this case, why might Janette feel as she does? This will contribute to insight—insight as proposed by the client rather than the therapist—and help her to connect to the power of her unmet relational need to be able to trust in her important relationships [*loyalty* of her father and her partner as well as their emotional *reliability*].

- Emotions drive behaviors: Janette focused solely on her children to deal with the fear that she will be alone again with Will in the same way she felt with her father when she was growing up.
- Presenting, less useful emotions tend to drive problematic behaviors: the fear of being abandoned made it difficult for Janette to discuss her relational needs with Will, causing her to withdraw into the role of motherhood.
- More useful emotions tend to validate the client's experience and offer more appropriate options for satisfying unmet needs: if she had acknowledged her fear of being alone initially, Will and Janette may have been able to negotiate a more productive solution for Janette's relational concerns.
- Problem solving through collaborative work encourages more options for functional approaches to getting needs met: they could have agreed to set aside some "couple time" as well as "family time" together.
- When needs are met appropriately, problematic behaviors are extinguished: with Janette feeling more secure and emotionally connected to Will she could more readily include him in the various aspects of her life. Uncomfortable emotions will always exist, but problematic ways of coping with unmet needs will gradually be discontinued. When Janette becomes worried about trust and reliability in their relationship, she will be able to indicate more directly when she needs more assurance rather than isolate in what seems to have been a passive-aggressive statement to Will.

There are several advantages to interpreting the emotional possibilities along with client relational need by means of the universal needs-based themes present in the client's narrative. Because the narrative content is seldom universal but the process theme usually is, an effective emotion-focused intervention touches on situations that all members can relate to. Because those who enter a therapeutic setting are often anxious about being confronted, exposed, or punished, connecting with the client in a meaningful, reassuring way can be a delicate procedure. In the previous case, focusing on universally experienced relational needs and the embedded felt emotions makes it possible for Janette, Will, and the therapist to connect in a way that just would not have been possible if they had remained focused on the specifics of Janette's story. The true issue at hand was not that Janette's father had stood her up or even that Janette is finding it hard to control her drinking but that her drinking has developed as a result of her anger at finding herself in a situation where she does not feel supported or, indeed, connected. If Janette can learn how to use her anger more productively, rather than trying to hide it, she will no longer experience the need to drink to excess. Effective theme-based statements illuminate a theme within the narrative that can easily be related to. Who would not feel encouraged by statements that support, include, and reassure?

In the practice of therapy, the real and most meaningful challenge we therapists face is not being able to understand our craft academically (although that is certainly important), to discuss it in a scholarly fashion, or even to express our thoughts succinctly and clearly; instead, the challenge is to help our clients find their own voice, make their own emotional connections with their personal emotional archeology, and make healthy their relationships with themselves and others by taking real, concrete steps toward achieving their relational goals. This is how true, long-lasting behavioral change is carried out.

While one of the purposes of this book is to argue the case for using the Needs ABC model, which combines aspects of various models that have already been tried and tested, more important than any theoretical basis for therapy is the understanding that the end goal of therapy is to change the behaviors clients have been displaying that have been making them unhappy. To reach this goal, we as therapists need to enable ourselves to create a safe environment within which our clients know they can freely discuss themselves, their problems, their behavior, and their weaknesses. Only by doing so will they learn that, paradoxically, exposing our weakness to the ones we care most about can strengthen our relationship with them and our ability to overcome the feelings of impotence these weaknesses can cause.

While a therapist may develop certain theories or hypotheses about how and why clients are feeling and behaving the way they are, a true therapeutic intervention is reached only when clients are able to identify and vocalize these issues on their own and to make their own way toward developing a new set of behaviors related to the feelings that have been causing them problems in their relationship thus far. This simple fact is true regardless of the therapeutic model that is used, and this is the reason quite widely divergent models can all be useful in helping people to heal their own behavioral problems and, indeed, their personal relationships.

Prevailing Models and Trends in Couples and Family Therapy

In recent years, the tendency in psychotherapy generally has been away from the rigid "all or nothing" models that characterized the discipline in its earlier days and toward integrative approaches that permit therapists to use their judgment in devising a therapeutic approach best suited to their needs as well as to their theoretical and ideological background.

In drawing influence from a wide range of therapeutic models, the Needs ABC approach is consistent with the general trend toward the integration that has increasingly characterized the field in recent years. I agree with Stricker and Gold (1996, p. 52): "Insistence on a unidirectional model of change suggests, erroneously, that psychological life and psychotherapeutic effect are straightforward and simple." Furthermore, I believe that the client should always be at the heart of therapy as an active instigator of change rather than as a template on which therapists' theories of psychoanalytic practice are wrought. As Bohart (2000) says:

In most models of therapy the hero is the therapist. Clients are often portrayed as so pathological and dysfunctional that if it were not for the heroic efforts of the therapist the client would never leave his or her defensive, self-deluded, dysfunctionally thinking, and malconditioned state. (p. 129)

Of course, all therapists work toward the goal of their clients' well-being. However, it can be too easy to overlook that the secret to success of this goal lies with the clients themselves—that the role of therapist is enabler rather than someone who can fix and repair unilaterally. Ultimately, individuals must reach insight and a willingness to change by their own efforts and must put into practice the new behaviors that will effect this change. Again, to quote Bohart (2000):

There is considerable evidence consistent with the idea that therapy is a process primarily in which human beings, with active self-healing capacities, use the therapy relationship to solve their problems. Clients who are involved are more likely to benefit. A key component of why the therapy relationship is important has to do with its capacity for fostering client involvement. (p. 137)

As we will explore, the Needs ABC model bases its effectiveness on two strong predictors of positive client outcome: (1) the engagement of the client in the problem-solving process (taking responsibility); and (2) forming a positive therapeutic alliance (Orlinsky, Grave, & Parks, 1994, pp. 257–310; Orlinsky & Howard, 1986, pp. 283–300). Lambert and Barley (2001, pp. 357–361) and Teyber (Teyber & McClure, 2000, pp. 62–87) do an excellent job summarizing the research on the therapeutic alliance and components affecting outcome. They state that the therapeutic alliance has a broader definition than the facilitative conditions, including clients' contributions to the relationship. The therapeutic alliance is often conceptualized as having three components: (1) tasks; (2) bonds; and (3) goals. Tasks are the behaviors and processes within the therapy session that constitute the actual work of therapy. The goals of therapy are the objectives of therapy that both client and therapist endorse. Bonds include the positive interpersonal attachment between therapist and client of mutual trust, confidence, and acceptance.

A number of therapeutic models have been particularly influential, to varying extents, in the development and integration of the Needs ABC approach.

Family Systems Theory

Traditionally, Family Systems Theory has been, and continues to be, the foundation on which all marriage and family therapy has been based. To become qualified as a Marriage and Family Therapist (MFT) in North America, therapists must be specifically trained and show proficiency in this type of psychotherapy. Family systems theory derives originally from the work by Bowen (1966), whose theory of behavior envisioned the family as a discrete emotional unit and used the term *systems thinking* to describe the many complex interactions that occur within the unit. Families—and couples— are so deeply affected by what their various members do, say, and feel that they can seem to function as if they were a whole rather than the sum of their parts. When one member of the unit changes his or her behavior in some way, the other members will shift their stances accordingly, generally without a very high degree of conscious awareness of what is happening or why. Thus, one member of the family could become, for example, the one who assumes most of the burden of stress facing the unit, giving the other members carte blanche, as it were, to avoid responsibility or to place heavy expectations on him or her. The Needs ABC model recognizes the interconnectedness of couples and families and, further, explores how the individual components of these units seek to have their needs met within these relationships. By using the Needs ABC model, the development of the family or couple "system" is demystified, and it is easier to explain why and how to interrupt negative behavioral patterns.

The concept of complementarity can be considered a corollary to Family Systems Theory. Originally devised by Paul Watzlawick, Janet Beavin, and Donald Jackson (1967), it proposes that each couple has a personality "fit" of which they are largely unaware on a conscious level but that fills certain relational needs for them both. For example, the man who needed his relationship to demonstrate loyalty and reliability would likely seek a woman who sought competency and respect. A man who had supreme trust in his own levels of competency and a corresponding tendency to distrust others' might be inclined to seize charge of situations, challenging his partner's personal sense of competency and creating a scenario whereby she may become angry and frustrated by what she perceives to be a lack of respect for her ability to get things done. She may then respond by marginalizing her partner and by demeaning or "running down" his competency or problem-solving abilities, causing him to confide in others who seem not to want to criticize him and thus becoming less available to his partner while laying himself open to the suggestion that he is, on some level, betraying her.

The nature of a couple is that it is, or strives to be, complementary. One individual's weaknesses can be balanced by the other's strengths, and vice versa. In practical terms, household chores and responsibilities are often divided between the couple frequently—but not invariably—along gender lines. Therapists should also remember that complementarity applies in terms of behavioral patterns (Nichols & Schwartz, 2006):

> Family therapists should think of complementarity whenever they hear one person complaining about another. Take, for example, a husband who says that his wife nags. "She's always after me about something; she's always complaining." From the perspective of complementarity, a family therapist would assume that the wife's complaining is only half of a pattern of mutual influence. Whenever a person is perceived as nagging, it probably means that she hasn't received a fair hearing for her concerns. Not being listened to makes her feel angry and unsupported. No wonder she comes across as nagging. (p. 101)

Systems Theory considers that clients are attracted by their ability to acquire their relational needs as are their partners. In other words, when one member of a couple or a family group behaves in a dominant fashion, he or she elicits submission, and vice versa. Because complementarity often eventually predicts a lack of balance in the relationship, the Needs ABC model can illuminate, explain, and address the resulting ineffective behaviors that develop in the couple system used in the dominant member's attempts to have his or her relational needs met in a more balanced way.

Like the Systems Theory, the Needs ABC model considers that clients are attracted by their ability to acquire their relational needs as are their partners. If competency is important for the male partner, his female counterpart's validation of this need is one of the many important attracting features for him, or vice versa. She (this also applies to same-sex couples) may feel it necessary to be able to trust him [loyalty]. If he seems to be trustworthy (transparent, or whatever) then she will be more attracted to him. What I often find interesting in my work with couples is that, when four "primary" relational needs are agreed upon, one couple member usually has two and the partner the remaining two. For example, if one has the need to feel competent [competency] and respected [respect] then the other has the need to feel he or she can trust [loyalty] the other and that he or she is in a reliable or unconditional [reliability] relationship. In other words, what keeps them engaged systemically is their ability to give their partner what they need (positive feedback loop; Nichols, 2007) relationally while receiving in kind. Clients enter treatment when they feel that their needs are no longer being met and have begun to cycle in a dysfunctional (negative feedback loop) manner with each other. We will be looking at this in more detail at a later stage.

Cognitive-Behavioral/Motivational Therapy

As most of us are aware, Cognitive-Behavioral Therapy (CBT) is a collaborative, time-limited, structured therapeutic approach dealing with here and now (what clients are presently concerned about). Among other things, it supports clients in learning new ways to think about and to deal with their problem. In this way the hope is that clients will take these new skills and perspectives outside of the therapy room and gradually use them without the support of the therapist—in a sense, "become their own therapist." One such approach for couples was pioneered by Neil Jacobsen, who did a great deal of work, including substantial research, with couples in general (Jacobson, 1984; Jacobson, Follette, Revenstorf, Baucom, Hahlweg, & Margolin, 2000) as well as those involved in, among other things, spousal abuse with a focus on the area of cognitive behavioral therapy or on how to help people to become enabled to form new behaviors. His couples work focused on what he calls *behavior exchange*—the replacement of negative couple exchanges with positive ones—followed by problem solving through effective communication. His Behavioral Marital Therapy (BMT; Jacobson & Margolin, 1979) first attempts to extinguish problematic interactions and then places its focus on communication skills that will enhance problem solving for couples (Jacobson; Jacobson & Margolin). Together with Christensen, Jacobson focused on the issue of accepting aspects of one's partner as key in effecting successful behavioral change (Christensen & Jacobson, 2000). With regard to domestic violence, one observation was that, among couples in which one or each partner perpetrates domestic violence, there is invariably a strong degree of reluctance to admit that the other person can have a valid point of view at all. If and when couple counseling is indicated, however, the Needs ABC model can be extremely effective in helping couple members accept their partner as a "package," with positive and negative aspects to their personality. As in CBT, Needs ABC is a collaborative approach promoting autonomy in problem solving—helping clients identify their relational needs outside of the therapy session, problem solve, and go on successfully as a couple, or family, without the therapist's help. As in CBT, Needs ABC uses the "here and now"—what clients bring into each session in their narratives—to illuminate relational needs. Then, Needs ABC encourages couples to understand that the other's relational needs are pivotal to a successful relationship and to accept the "challenge" of helping the partner to acquire same. In other words, as with Jacobson, insight into needs and the emotionally determined behaviors they produce is the first step; the second is the acquisition of effective communication skills that will produce more useful and productive behaviors in the long run. Miller and Rollnick (1991) developed the concept of motivational interviewing (MI; another cognitive behavioral approach) following their experience of treating clients with problems with substances such as nicotine or alcohol. Motivational interviewing uses an approach that strives at all times to avoid becoming either confrontational or judgmental while demonstrating empathy and insight and respecting client autonomy or "self-efficacy." In therapy, in order to support their potential for real and lasting change, clients are helped to understand the problems that arise from the way they are currently behaving and are assisted in imagining how things could be better in the future.

Miller and Rollnick (1991) describe motivational interviewing as "… a directive, client-centered counseling style for eliciting behavior change by helping clients to explore and resolve ambivalence" (p. 52). Motivational interviewing attempts to narrow in on clients' specific problems and facilitate the pursuit of the therapist's goals of supporting clients in the achievement of their therapeutic objectives—for example, "I know that my tendency to bully my co-workers is damaging us all, and I want to stop doing it." It is crucial that clients desire change and that they use this desire and the messages learned in therapy as a way to actually effect lasting change rather than having change imposed from external sources. Similarly, clients need to recognize and deal with any personal ambivalence. Although the therapist directs and fulfills a leadership role in the context of therapy, this is done in a relatively gentle manner, eliciting information rather than demanding it and viewing apparent "resistance" to change as an indicator that clients are not as ready to embrace change as the therapist might like. It is the therapist's role to listen, understand, reinforce clients' motivational statements, and affirm the fact that they are free to choose their own direction. Unlike MI, Needs ABC is not directive and minimizes clients' "resistance" by collaboratively identifying and allying with their relational needs. The Needs ABC approach espouses this client-centered collaboration by using their vocabulary and perspective to label their unmet relational needs. Direction is always the client's choice, especially with regard to needs-getting strategies and emotional currency. On the other hand, like MI, incentive, or "motivation," is usually created by the understanding that clients' relational needs, once clarified, can be met through a process of collaboration again defined by the clients (couples and families), thus supporting the system's self-efficacy (Miller & Rollnick, 1991). Different strategies may have to be used in different situations, always with a focus on the acquisition of each client's relational needs.

The "stages of change" approach to therapy (Prochaska & DiClemente, 1983) is often used as an adjunct to Motivational

It must be kept in mind that relational needs will not be met 100 percent of the time and that compromises may have to be made. As long as each member of the system recognizes another member's relational needs and makes some effort to accommodate them, the system can continue to work toward more productive solutions to needs-getting.

Interviewing by practitioners who see change as something that can be approached incrementally and that can be divided into a series of recognizable stages or phases along the trajectory from point A, where the client is at the stage of presenting for therapy, to point B, where the client is when therapy has been successfully concluded. Patients are considered to move gradually from "precontemplation," when they are not even considering change, to "contemplation," when they begin to think about what change might mean to them, and then on to the various steps and phases involved in change. As clients become accustomed to the changes that are being created in their life, they need support and help to maintain momentum and prevent relapse. Intrinsic to the Needs ABC approach is the concept of *client-paced* work and *supportive challenging*. Needs ABC therapists understand that they must work collaboratively with clients to determine the tempo of the treatment. Within this framework, challenges are made respectfully and empathically. Examples of this can be seen in Alan Jenkins's (1990) book, *Invitations to Responsibility*, which also appears to integrate a motivational approach within the narrative school of therapy. Take, for example, this excerpt from Jenkins's book of a therapeutic dialogue between a man, whose wife has left him because of his violence toward her, and his therapist. Toward the end of this discourse the therapist says (portions omitted):

Therapist: It sounds like you have tried everything you can think of to get her back … and you're getting pretty desperate ….
Client: (nods tearfully)
Therapist: I know you want to see if you can get back together with Jill. There are two things I need you to help me understand so I'm properly in the picture. The first thing I need to understand

is what kind of a marriage you want to have with Jill? The second thing is what kind of marriage you have had in the past? (p. 70)

In this excerpt, the motivational factor is the "invitation" for the client to take responsibility for getting what he wants if he can have a second chance with his wife. Needs ABC would make a similar invitation by highlighting the client's unmet needs previous to his separation while enquiring how he thinks he can get his needs met more productively in the future—if there is one.

Narrative Therapy

Michael White is the creator of *narrative therapy*, which rests on the premise that people's lives become organized in an almost organic manner by the way they narrate them. In other words, the stories they tell about their lives and themselves create their selves and the way their lives unfurl rather than simply reflecting them. When clients' "stories" are unhelpful to developing or maintaining a healthy dynamic in their personal relationships, they can learn to move on by becoming more adept at externalizing their problems, challenging fixed negative versions of the things that have happened, and becoming able to create more positive stories.

For example, if Sean's personal narrative is, "I was born unlucky, and unlucky things happen to me," he is likely to recall events and relate them to himself and others through an "unlucky" lens. Thus, when Sean misses a bus, feels that he has lost out on a promotion he deserved, or burns his shirt when he is ironing it, this event will become woven into the story that he tells about his own life, on an ongoing basis, and will seem to confirm his rather negative view of his own experience and way of being. A narrative therapist will see it as her task to help Sean tell a different sort of story about himself through the use of "curious" questioning, helping to reframe the things that happen to him in a different context and perhaps to focus more on the times when things go right, using these to confirm Sean's new view that he is someone on whom fortune generally smiles. This will enable Sean to deal with problems when they arise, not as confirmations of the ill luck that seems to dog him wherever he goes but as normal dilemmas that could have presented themselves to anybody and to which he can find a solution. In other words, Sean then learns how to weave a new narrative about himself.

Needs ABC is very dependent on clients' stories, or "narratives," in determining what is missing for them in their relationships. For example, a Needs ABC therapist would help Sean focus on situations in which Sean felt "unlucky" to clarify his unmet relational needs. Why does Sean tend to feel unlucky? Could it be that his relationship does not meet his need for reliability? The Needs ABC model also maintains a sharp focus on how Sean's "negative" lens came to be created in the first place—in other words, which of his needs have been consistently unmet in his important relationships and thus led to his pessimistic worldview, which in turn led to the set of emotions he displays and to his less than functional strategies for solving the problems he faces.

Solution-Focused Therapy

Steve de Shazer and Insoo Kim Berg are best known for their application of solution-focused brief therapy (SFBT), especially the notion of the "miracle question" (de Shazer et al., 1986). De Shazer (1991, p. 58) postulated that all therapy is a form of specialized conversation and that, in their therapeutic process, the conversation is directed toward developing and achieving clients' vision of solutions:

> Problems are seen to maintain themselves simply because they maintain themselves and because clients depict the problem as always happening. Therefore, times when the complaint is absent are dismissed as trivial by the client or even remain completely unseen, hidden from the client's view. Nothing is actually hidden, but although these exceptions are open to view, they are not seen by the clients as differences that make a difference. For the client, the problem is seen as a primary (and the exceptions, if they are seen at all, are seen as secondary), while for the therapists the exceptions are seen as primary; interventions are

meant to help clients make a similar inversion, which will lead to the development of a solution.

The questions asked by solution-focused therapists are usually focused on what is working or has worked in the past with respect to the presenting problem. This reflects the basic belief that problems are best solved by focusing on what is already working and how a client would like their life to be in the *future* rather than on the past and the origin of problems. For example, they may ask, "What do you think will be different tomorrow if you have started to resolve the problem you came in with?" As well, they do not generally discuss clients' backgrounds in any great detail. They assume that clients are committed to change and that they already have the ability to change. By talking about solutions rather than problems, clients are taking positive steps in the right direction. De Shazer, in particular, emphasizes the power of words in effecting change and the importance of asking what things would be like if they were better so that clients can verbalize the situation they are working toward in therapy. In contrast, the Needs ABC's focus on unmet relational needs would examine clients' "always happening" problem as indicative of a "needs deficit," the "exceptions" as representative of potential areas for needs acquisition, and the problematic emotion as an impediment to problem solving. Where Needs ABC and SFBT come together is with the therapeutic principles espoused by each. De Shazer et al. (1986) state:

> Most complaints develop and are maintained in the context of human interaction. Individuals bring with them unique attributes, resources, limits, beliefs, values, experiences, and sometimes difficulties and they continually learn and develop different ways of interacting with each other. Solutions lie in changing interactions in the context of the unique constraints of the situation. (p. 2)

By addressing relational needs in the context of the couple or the family interactions are changed accordingly. "Brief therapy" is a solution-focused approach to clients' needs (de Shazer, 1982), and the therapists who use this approach look for practical solutions to presenting issues. Because of the relatively narrow focus of this therapeutic method, it is particularly apt in the case of specific behavioral problems that may occur in the context of the couple, such as drug or alcohol abuse or violence. However, it is also applied in the case of couples who present with issues such as jealousy and withdrawal. In these instances, therapists help couples explore what they are doing and what the consequences are without giving particular concern to why they are engaging in the behaviors that are causing the problem. Because the Needs ABC model focuses on "the problem"—client relational needs—once these needs are ascertained and illuminated it then becomes evident how to "solve" the problem through effective treatment planning. Therefore, Needs ABC therapies are relatively "brief" since relational needs are usually ascertained quickly, often in the first two to three sessions, using the following sessions to practice need-getting and -giving strategies.

Emotionally Focused Therapy

Perhaps the greatest influence on the Needs ABC model was the emotion-focused work done by Greenberg and Johnson (1988) in their book *Emotionally Focused Therapy for Couples*. This approach, originally developed by Leslie S. Greenberg (Greenberg & Safran, 1987), focuses on understanding the emotions that lie behind behaviors. This can help clients modify the same behaviors until a better place vis-à-vis their life partner has been reached. Greenberg and Johnson's approach combines the perspectives of attachment and structural systems theory, focusing on the internal organization, expression, and communication of emotional experience. They assume that all humans innately need connection with others, especially when they are having a hard time, and that in both childhood and adulthood this connection provides security and comfort. When relational needs are not met, people often react by becoming bullies or by sulking or otherwise engaging in less than helpful behaviors.

The most difficult behaviors of all emerge when people doubt that they will receive the security, comfort, or attention they feel they need. Needless to say, these behaviors only make things worse, far from obtaining for the individual the security they so deeply crave, with the result that the situation deteriorates yet further.

The Needs ABC model takes Greenberg and Johnson's (1988) model to another level by helping couple members gain objectivity with regard to their own and their partners' behavior. As in Greenberg's work with Johnson and others (Greenberg & Johnson, 1988; Greenberg, Rice, & Elliott, 1993; Johnson, 2004), emotionally Needs ABC works toward helping the client understand that, even though all emotions are valid, some emotions are less productive than others. In effect, as with Emotionally Focused Therapy (EFT), Needs ABC increases emotional awareness in clients, encourages them to regulate and examine their feelings, and helps them consider more useful emotional strategies in their relational interactions. This increase in objectivity is promoted since, in addition to broadening their emotional vocabulary, Needs ABC couples and families will be able to understand that their relational needs are important not only with regard to their relationship with their partner but with their other relationships as well, including their own relationship with themselves. Also, the understanding they will gain about how these needs and behaviors came to be will help them to plan better relational strategies with regard to what will make them feel emotionally safe and what will give them the kind of attention that they need to feel more comfortable in the couple dyad and in the wider world.

Edward Teyber—A Relational Approach

Edward Teyber's (1989, 1997, 2000, 2006) work supports the Needs ABC model in many ways. As with Needs ABC, Teyber's process-oriented work rests on the observation that most clients of therapy have experienced conflict in the context of their close personal relationships. He believes that "one useful way to conceptualize many of these interpersonal problems is along a continuum of separateness and relatedness" (1997, p. 13). Teyber's work concurs with the Needs ABC model in stressing how personalities and needs are formed in childhood in the context of the family and how these needs are brought into the adult individuals' interpersonal relationships. Like Needs ABC, Teyber also places importance on a therapeutic approach that provides the counselor with a structure while remaining flexible enough to respect the diverse needs of the client population; he points out, "Each client has been genetically endowed with a unique set of features, and each has been raised differently in his or her family." For example, Teyber states that "socialization is different for women and men; members of different cultures have different experiences; and economic class shapes opportunity and expectations" (1997, p. 22).

Teyber believes that as adults individuals tend to adopt responses toward themselves similar to those displayed to them as children. In other words, if a child's need for approval was met with scorn, the child will feel scornful toward his or her need for approval as an adult. Needs ABC, on the other hand, would see a lack of approval as an unmet relational need and examine strategies that might help clients acquire approval. Using Teyber's frame, clients' contempt for approval might create a behavioral pattern making it difficult for them to gain approval and would work toward relational interactions that would gain support from others. Teyber feels that, during the courtship phase of a relationship, people tend, erroneously, to perceive their new partner as someone who can meet all their unmet needs, a reaction Teyber refers to as "transference" (1989, p. 148). Inevitably, no one person can meet *all* of anyone's unmet needs, and problems can emerge as the relationship matures. In couples therapy, it is crucial to align with the unmet needs of *both* partners, and Needs ABC agrees.

As with the Needs ABC approach, to achieve a good outcome in therapy Teyber believes that therapists need to establish a good

I make it a point to describe to the couple what I feel are both partners' unmet needs and suggest, or ask them to suggest, a needs-getting strategy that might be appropriate based on what they are saying. Where possible, with some insight into their developmental history, I also suggest why the need is important to each of them because of this developmental history and how the power of the emotion related to their unmet relational need might cause them to use a behavior predicated on a less useful emotion.

interpersonal "working" relationship with their clients and to be able to respect with sensitivity and effectiveness to clients' interpersonal needs and to the pain they may experience. At the same time, they also need to be able to stand back and "conceptualize the client's personality and problems and to formulate what experiences in therapy the client needs in order to change" (Teyber, 1997, p. 28). Also, therapists need to remain firmly committed throughout the healing process to their client, their needs, and the goal of therapy, which is to achieve a healthier way of being.

John Gottman—Improving Positive Affect

A researcher at the University of Washington, John Gottman's focus in couples therapy remains consistently on the couple as the basic unit rather than on the individual people who comprise it (Gottman, 2002). When problems emerge in the relationship, his approach is to see how the relationship can be adapted rather than looking at how to alter its individual components.

In his work identifying which couples are likely to stay together, Gottman determined that increasing the positive feelings and interactions in a couple's relationship will support their ability to solve problems on their own—that conflict resolution in the therapeutic setting will become unnecessary (Gottman & Silver, 1999, p. 46). In essence, his thesis is that by reducing negative affect and improving positive affect in conflict resolution a greater feeling of connection will be established and that disagreements can promote intimacy through collaborative problem solving (Gottman, 1999). Couples who avoided conflict could have long-term relationships but tended to describe this form of "avoidant" relationship as "lonely" since they did not acquire the same degree of intimacy as couples who engaged in (healthy) conflict.

In using the Needs ABC model, "avoidant" and other less functional reactions can be diffused by helping couples understand what is actually going on in their relationship. That is, when each member of the couple honestly and appropriately discloses what he or she needs from the other and understands that the reaction to the other might not be, at base, a personal one but one relating to generally unmet relational needs, the closer the two can become. In fact, these needs deficits were most probably initiated in the initial stages of their relationship and have become at best elusive by the time they come for help. When clients begin to understand that their often conflictive strategies, or emotionally driven behaviors, have been used in an attempt to rekindle the earlier, more positive stages of their relationship without resolution and the etiology of their relational need formation, affect will improve, and negotiation and strategizing can begin around needs acquisition. These behaviors are what have brought the couple into therapy and have served only to help them disengage. Now, an understanding of what they want will help them reengage to collaboratively problem solve.

Introducing Couples Therapy in Practice

Before we apply ourselves to the details of how to use the Needs ABC model in professional practice as a couples therapist, and later in work with families, let's look at some generalities of the nature of couples therapy and some of the practical issues around this crucial and important therapeutic option; understanding the basic hows and whys of couples therapy is enormously important. A full discussion of the Needs ABC model in the context of couples therapy will follow and will form the major element of this volume.

2
COUPLES THERAPY

To the world you may be one person, but to one person you may
be the world.

Heather Cortez

The Nuclear Family

A couple is usually understood as implying a married or otherwise
"permanent" pairing of a woman and a man, and a majority of couples
are "permanent"—at least in terms of their original aspirations for
their relationship—if not actually formally married, although many
are as well. The couple is a building block of a majority of societies in
the world today.

Couples are often also the joint parents or guardians of a child or
children, which means that there can be a substantial degree of over-
lap between couples and family therapy or indeed between couples
and adolescent or even child therapy (although the Needs Acquisition
and Behavior Change [ABC] model requires some modification and
some creativity to make it more age appropriate to use it with very
young children). And, as we will see, the Needs ABC model is ideal
for helping adolescents deal with issues that arise in their personal
lives as they begin to embrace adulthood and couplehood in their turn
or in the context of their families of origin—the original couple that is
their parents. But, of course, couples can also be the same sex or even
two people who are not necessarily sexually or romantically involved
with each other but who, for one reason or another, have decided to
join their fates. It is worth stressing that there are no significant differences whatsoever when it comes to the interpersonal dynamics of

Figure 2.1   An example of a nuclear family.

same-sex couples or in the application of the methods promoted by the Needs ABC model in terms of providing such couples with help. Couples presenting for therapy do not have to have a family, intend to have one, or even have the biological equipment to create a family. They may have had families with other people; their children might even be fully grown; they can be adoptive or foster parents or have no interest at all in having children at any stage of their lives.

This chapter explores examples of all of these and shows that, despite the differences between these various types of relationship, they all have much more in common than one might think. We all have difficulties at times reconciling our personal views, aspirations, and goals with the united aspirations and goals of ourselves and the person whom we consider or at one time considered to be our life mate, and we all have issues with unmet or not fully met childhood needs that continue to impact our emotions and, often, our behavior, right into adulthood.

In any of the aforementioned situations, the relationship between the two people presenting for therapy is uniquely intimate and particularly difficult for a third party to penetrate and understand for reasons including the intricate codification of language and other forms of communication that occurs between couples. These are people whose aspiration it is—or has been—to share their lives, probably until one or both of them die. These are people who, in many if not most respects, think they know each other better than anybody else. This is a belief that is usually not misplaced. While they can never know *everything* their partner thinks or believes, they have often acquired a deep understanding of many aspects of their partner's personality and background, on a level that is conscious to varying degrees. For these reasons, when communication breaks down, is inadequate, or is responded to in a dysfunctional manner, the fallout can be dramatic and very damaging to all concerned. When one considers that couples also frequently share the parenting of children, attending to these problems, ideally before they escalate, is essential. It is well known that problems in one's family of origin can lead to emotional and other difficulties percolating through the generations. Seeking help as a couple, when and as problems arise, is an investment in the future happiness not just of the couple in question but also of their children and, potentially, their children's children.

Couples therapy can be seen as a division of family therapy, a discipline that "was born in the 1950s, grew up in the 1960s, and came of age in the 1970s" (Nichols & Schwartz, 2006, p. 7). At the time of writing, it has evolved from a situation in which therapists tended to adhere to a specific more or less rigid dogmatic approach to couples and family therapy to a situation whereby flexibility is now the norm. Effective therapists are able to tailor their approach to the specific needs of the couple in question, in the context of the relationship between both parties of the couple and of their relationships with any children they may have, to their own parents and family members and their friends and colleagues, always remembering that "the family is the context of human problems" (Nichols, p. 44).

The Family of Origin

It is in our own families of origin that we learn, for good or ill, how and who to be in relation to the important human beings in our lives. As children, we learn the emotional vocabularies and behaviors to which we will resort as adults. Typically, children copy the behavior modeled by their same-sex parent and often, in so doing, replicate as adults problematic situations and behaviors that have remained unresolved since childhood, not infrequently even reproducing to a considerable extent the very *same* problems that bedeviled the lives of their same-sex parent earlier. Such is the extent to which behavioral patterns can be inherited from one's family of origin. In therapy, the needs and feelings behind these behaviors can emerge and be addressed, and new ways of being and behaving can be created.

The Needs ABC model for couples therapy rests on a small number of relatively simple premises: (1) understanding that the unmet needs experienced by each member of a couple lie behind the behaviors that are contributing to the difficulties the couple is experiencing as a dyad; (2) realizing that the emotions produced by these unmet needs have more and less productive (useful) components; (3) acknowledging that an understanding of the origin of these needs will often lead to addressing them more easily; and (4) focusing in therapy on more productive ways of meeting the aforementioned needs. Understanding the etiology of unmet needs is not absolutely necessary, although it can be very useful and illuminating. Understanding the more useful emotion behind behaviors is, however, a prerequisite to the successful application of the Needs ABC approach. Understanding where emotions come from in terms of a client's life history is a way for therapists to "double-check" their assumptions of what needs are missing. However, the clients' narrative is often accurate and can be sufficient to help them understand "the missing piece."

The Couples and Family Therapist

Couples and family therapists can come from a relatively broad range of therapeutic backgrounds. Their initial training may have been in social work, psychology, counseling, or a related field. What all should have in common is a well-defined sense of empathy, a sound knowledge of the theoretical and practical bases of therapy, and the willingness and openness to help couples challenge their own presuppositions. We might bear in mind the insightful remark by Ralph Waldo Emerson: "Shall I tell you the secret of a true scholar? It is this: every man I meet is my master in some point, and in that I learn from him" (Emerson, 1904, p. 313). Therapists should always remain prepared to learn and, if necessary, to set aside their own presuppositions about the individual qualities people ideally bring to an intimate relationship; couples can interact respectfully and healthily in many ways.

The Needs ABC model makes the aforementioned tasks easier for therapists by providing a clear but flexible framework incorporating methodologies that help them to maintain their clinical objectivity while demonstrating a genuine empathetic understanding of what clients are searching for. As Kitchen (2005) says, "When therapists ask and listen for what their clients believe to be the cause of their problems and how they believe they will get better, the direction can tailor therapy to the individual client" (p. 17).

While using this model, individual therapists can also continue to create and evolve their own personal approach to therapy. At the same time, it provides couples with a vocabulary with which they can discuss their own situations, individually and as a couple, and with a safe environment in which to do so.

When Couples Therapy Is Not Appropriate

There are times when couples therapy is not appropriate or, at least, not appropriate "right now," even if it may well be a good idea at a later point. For example, in the case of serious spousal abuse, disruptive substance abuse on the part of one or both partners, severe mental illness, or a significant practical dilemma that is currently dominating the scene, couples may not be in the right "space" to deal with therapy; quite simply, their minds will be too exercised with the practical issue to concentrate on the intricacies of feeling. It may first be necessary to suggest some practical temporary changes to their living environment, such as the removal of a violent spouse from the family home or the appropriate psychotherapeutic or behavioral drug intervention to deal with psychosis or other psychiatric disorders. Effective therapy cannot take place when one member of the couple feels endangered by the other or when rational thought is inhibited by drug or alcohol abuse or active mental illness. At times, urgent practical matters may need to be attended to before couples therapy is likely to be effective, such as the provision of housing or social welfare payments or even the placing of dependent children in care, at least until the parents' situation has been resolved and they are in a better situation for caring for their family.

However, while respecting that not every couple will be ready in every situation to deal with therapy, it is also important to understand that therapy may be helpful at a later stage and to communicate this to couples in question or to the individuals in the couple who have requested therapy, should this happen. Knowing that therapy will be an option at a later point opens a door to the potential for a better future. It is also important to remember that individuals and couples without any problems whatsoever relating to their social position, drug use status, or financial well-being can still benefit enormously from therapy. Emotional problems, the associated difficult behaviors, and the profound unhappiness that can ensue are certainly not the exclusive domain of any particular social class or demographic.

What Makes the Needs ABC Approach Particularly Appropriate for Couples?

The Needs ABC model is distinguished in particular by its emphasis on the relational needs behind maladaptive behaviors rather than on the behaviors themselves and by its flexibility in terms of application to clients in a range of personal and therapeutic settings. In the context of providing therapy for couples, it offers a unique approach that helps clients to understand the origins of their behavior individually and in the context of their dyad and to formulate more constructive ways to react to stressors than those they have been using to date. Having originally been formulated in a group setting, the Needs ABC approach also provides a safe, structured format that respects the need to be heard from all—or in the case of couples in particular, both—of the individuals presenting for therapy.

Indeed, with respect to the relevance of a model originally created in the context of a group format, I would assert that it is more apt to consider a couple in therapy as a very small group than as two individuals, because couples therapy is, or should be, precisely *not* one-on-

one therapy, with both members of the couple in the room, but rather a form of communication, expression, and explanation that speaks to both elements of the couple *as a unit*, using a vocabulary that each can access and permitting each to provide insight and his or her own analyses of the things the other is saying. The same can be said of therapy involving parents and their child or children.

In the context of couples therapy, the Needs ABC approach maintains its focus at all times on a discrete number of issues. It explores the issues of *what* the individual members of a couple need from their relationship, *why* they need these specific things, *how* they have been trying to obtain them up to the present, and how and why their attempts to get them are not bearing fruit but, usually, serving only to drive a wedge yet deeper between both members of the couple with damaging results for them and for any children they might have.

Generally, dysfunctional approaches intended to obtain sought-after needs result in the thwarting of any forward momentum at all, often resulting in anger, blame, and recrimination. As this situation continues to prevail, the emotional landscape typically deteriorates, with each new frustrated attempt to obtain desired relational needs creating yet further stress and resentment. Ultimately, this sort of situation can end only poorly and, often, in the possibly unnecessary termination of the relationship, almost certainly with damaging levels of bitterness and recrimination, a great deal of which could probably have been avoided.

Understanding personal relational needs—their origins, the forms they take, and the way the individuals have been trying to have them met in the context of their personal relationship—enables couples to reach beyond their presenting problems and to work actively toward a solution that will enable them to communicate properly with each other and to move from the current plateau on which they find themselves to a situation in which they are able to grow, both separately and as a unit and ideally toward a healthier, more respectful, happier interpersonal relationship. Individuals need to understand the nature and origin of their relational needs to begin to practice new behaviors; equally, however, it is important for their partners to be aware of these factors. For example, the adult individuals whose parents were always distant and disapproving may seek approval and attention in their personal relationships, possibly by attention seeking in the form of a throwing a tantrum or shouting or even by resorting to physical violence or other forms of destructive behavior, which may be focused on others or even on themselves. While this will, in the short-term, obtain the attention they seek—albeit not necessarily the right *sort* of attention—it is not a good long-term strategy for securing the longed for approving attention that is so important to developing and maintaining a feeling of well-being. In fact, as usual, seeking the desired needs in such a dysfunctional way will prove only to "push" their loved one farther away.

Encouraging Positive Outcomes: The Involuntary Client

We generally use the term *involuntary client* to refer to clients who enter therapy because of some form of mandate (e.g., legal, vocational) rather than as a conscious choice they have made. As the term suggests, since these are people who have not chosen to attend therapy, they may enter the therapist's office reluctantly or even angrily, stating, "I didn't ask to be here!" or "'They' are making me do something I do not want to do." In couples or family therapy, the involuntary client can also be a spouse or child who reluctantly enters the treatment setting motivated by some form of ultimatum from a partner or parent: "I'm only coming because he/she said we were through if I didn't," or, "I'm here because my parents made me come."

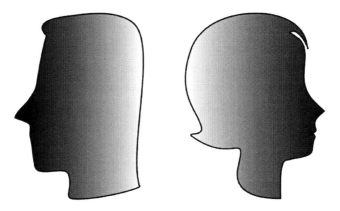

Figure 2.2   Involuntary clients.

However, despite what might appear to be a rather unpromising start, there is in fact no fundamental difference between these clients and people who have chosen to come to therapy by themselves, and the Needs ABC model of therapy can be equally effective in these apparently more challenging cases. We recognize that, in a very real way, *everyone who comes to therapy, in response to whatever initial stimulus, is an involuntary client.* People do not want to be unhappy in their personal relationships. They are not pleased to realize their behavior is causing them problems. They don't like to admit they can't seem to solve their problems alone. Therefore, in asking how we can help the involuntary client, we are really asking, "How can we help?"

Clients who have come to understand on their own that they need help are simply a little further along the trajectory of their therapy. However, they are also involuntary clients insofar as none of them would have consciously chosen to be unhappy, and they are also people whose difficult behaviors have arisen because their emotional needs are not currently being met in the context of their relationship or relationships. As therapists, our hope is that, regardless of how or why therapy is initiated, clients will eventually say, "I can't do this without help." As Needs ABC therapists, our role is to help clients understand the nature and origin of their unmet needs so that they can devise new behaviors to be met. Even clients who are forced to come to therapy will benefit from being offered a safe, secure therapeutic environment within which they can confront their demons and start to work productively on changing the damaging behaviors they have developed in an attempt to find a way of meeting their relational needs. In particular, Orlinsky (1994, cited in Gordon, 1999, p. 6) says:

> … Poor treatment outcomes are likely when patients experience the therapeutic relationship as hostile or oppressive; when therapists use intervention without skill, or use only weak intervention such as giving advice; when patients are not genuinely engaged in therapeutic tasks or are highly defensive, and when patients routinely experience insecurity, distress or confusion in sessions rather than support, relief or insight.

Conversely, when a safe environment is offered, even those who have been required to attend therapy are more likely to become able to disclose personal information and to engage with the therapeutic process. The therapeutic task is to minimize the potential for each member of the couple or family to become defended or untrusting of the therapeutic experience, to assure each of them that they will be heard, and to help them to identify their emotional needs and the behaviors that have already been involved in an attempt to get these met.

Various commentators in the field of psychotherapy (e.g., Asay & Lambert, 1999) have reported on the extratherapeutic factors that seem to be the greatest predictors of client outcome. For example, Asay and Lambert proposed the following influences, and their respective proportions, as highly indicative of a positive outcome to therapy:

- Client and extratherapeutic factors (e.g., strength of ego and social support), 40%
- Therapeutic relationship (e.g., empathy and warmth), 30%
- Expectancy and the result of therapy as "placebo," 15%
- Techniques unique to specific therapeutic models, 15%

In addition, in a careful examination of more than 2,000 process-outcome studies carried out since 1950, Orlinsky, Grave, and Parks (1994) identified several therapist variables and behaviors consistently shown to have a positive impact on treatment outcome. Some of the factors found to be predictive of successful treatment outcome included therapist credibility and skill, empathic understanding, the ability to join with and to engage the client, client support, and the ability to help the client to focus on their problem and the accompanying affective experience. According to Asay and Lambert (1999), Orlinsky et al., and others, therefore, most improvement that occurs in therapy is in fact independent of the specific model, mode, theoretical orientation, frequency, number of sessions, or specialization being used by the therapist (Hubble, Duncan, & Miller, 1999). While this might be a humbling blow to proponents of rigid psychotherapeutic models, the Needs ABC model strongly emphasizes supporting these very extratherapeutic factors that seem to be tremendously important in predicting client outcome and enabling clients, regardless of how their initial contact with the therapist came about, to foster and develop the important healthy external relationships. For example, by focusing on, and identifying, clients' relational needs, they will feel

Clients who have a sense of being in control of the therapeutic process are more likely to feel that their therapist is an ally. This can be achieved by, for example, asking them for their opinions and suggestions or brainstorming, in addition to supporting and rallying with them around their unmet relational needs. A feeling of alliance results in a less defensive posture when nonproductive behaviors are eventually challenged.

supported and understood rather than criticized and marginalized. When clients are encouraged to brainstorm strategies they feel might help acquire these needs rather than are given advice, they take more responsibility for the problem solving. This in turn supports this ability and builds ego strength and resource building.

Therefore, the Needs ABC model concurs with Reeve et al.'s (1993, p. 112) statement:

> We assume that clients are the experts of their experience and that interpreting their experience for them changes the nature of that experience and deprives the client of the important opportunity to interpret it for themselves.

Furthermore, when therapy helps a couple or family members identify how they are able to obtain certain emotional or relational needs from the important people in their environment, behaviors fostering this scenario are encouraged. Conversely, of course, when people are feeling vulnerable and weak, they will "tune in" to environmental cues that seem to confirm their feelings of weakness. This in turn will inevitably prompt the emergence of counterproductive scenarios, and the couple or family members probably will find themselves resorting to problem-solving strategies that have been used before, in other circumstances in which there seemed to be "no way out" (Jacobson & Margolin, 1979, pp. 24–25).

However, none of this means that the therapeutic model is not important, because of course it is. Clearly, while extratherapeutic factors and people's ability to interpret their own experience are hugely important, 15%—in the case of the Needs ABC approach, a model providing couples and families with the vocabulary and structure they need to verbalize, own, and repair their own behaviors—can make all the difference, regardless of why they initially started therapy.

Dealing With Defensiveness

The human brain is programmed from birth to strive for the survival of its owner. This means that, instinctively, we are all programmed to become defensive when we feel like we are under attack or to resort to tactics such as self-isolation, the seeking of revenge, or even denial that there is anything wrong at all (Jansen, Nguyen, Karpitskiy, Mettenleiter, & Loewy, 1995). Conversely, human beings are also innately strongly social with a basic need to connect to others, to be forgiven when they transgress, to receive and give affection, and to be involved in their family, community, and wider circle (Cacioppo & Patrick, 2008). These basic needs evolve, over time, to become more complex, more personal, and more specific to our own emotional backgrounds and landscapes. We go to great lengths in our attempts to have our needs met in the context of our important relationships. In childhood, when we feel ourselves or our place in the world to be under threat, we tend to act out our feelings. For this reason, therapies such as Art Therapy or Play Therapy are very effective in dealing with the needs of small children (Packman & Bratton, 2003). Adult individuals, however, should be able to express their feelings, wants, and needs verbally. "Acting out" in an adult is an inappropriate needs-getting response and is often the very reason clients come or are sent to therapy in the first place: their response to thwarted needs is an immature one that often has the opposite effect to that sought after. Helping these people to cease acting out and begin to verbalize their feelings and needs is the central focus of therapy. The Needs ABC approach focuses closely on identifying and understanding people's unmet relational needs and on helping them to construct healthier needs-getting behaviors than those they have been using so unsuccessfully thus far. By helping couples and families to become able to verbalize their relational needs, they are also enabled to assume responsibility for the problems that their

By taking note of the specific words used by clients and using the same words in observations and retelling of narratives, therapists can help to create a feeling of "being on the same team." So, rather than using the word *competency* from the relational needs list (given in Chapter 3), the therapist might use *adequacy* or feeling *good enough* if that is what the client used to describe the unmet need.

behavior has been causing: to "own" their behavior. Dependent on this occurring is the way they view their therapist and the extent to which they have been able to "join" with their therapist—come to like them, to put it prosaically. In other words, when clients like their therapists and when they contribute actively to therapy rather than sitting back and hoping to be "fixed," they are more likely to do well in therapy (Henry & Strupp, 1994, pp. 51–84; Johnson, 2004; Nichols, 1987, pp. 272–276).

Needs ABC helps to foster a situation in which clients join with their therapist by focusing on needs rather than behaviors, which makes the therapist an ally of each couple or family member rather than "one of them"—one of the people persistently critical of the client's behavior. While it is clear that the unproductive behavior cannot continue, the focus is also on understanding the "whys" behind it so that the person in question can move on by creating new behaviors with a better understanding of the importance of separating and individuating from "the ghosts of Christmas past." By focusing on what each partner or child needs to do to obtain his or her relational needs rather than on what others could or should be doing, the client is encouraged to take charge of the situation, to assume responsibility for his or her own actions, and to work positively toward the acquisition of useful alternative strategies for needs acquisition. In this way the therapist also becomes an ally of the couple and the family itself. Throughout therapy, it is essential to focus on each step—on the process of reaching a healthy relational situation rather than focusing exclusively or largely on the end goal. As Thomas Sexton remarks (Sexton, Ridley, & Kleiner, 2004):

When viewed as a process, the therapeutic relationship represented by the interactions between therapist and client(s) can become a process through which change can be promoted rather than merely a factor in change.... The qualities of the relationship and the dynamics that transpire between these participants have an important bearing on therapeutic change, because they serve as the forum in which and through which the professional expertise of the therapist and the personal experience of the client(s) interact. (p. 145)

Furthermore, as Kitchen (2005) points out, positive change is most likely to occur when the therapist's approach closely approximates the client's own ideas about how best to effect change: "When therapists ask and listen for what their clients believe to be the cause of their problems and how they believe they will get better, the direction can tailor therapy to the individual client. Not only will the techniques be tailor-made, but the other factors affecting outcome will also be enhanced" (p. 17).

In couples, family, and other therapies, therapists often follow a specific structure incorporating an understanding of treatment phases and client progress. The Needs ABC approach, in particular, respects the integrity of clients and provides a clear but flexible framework for each session, within which couples, families, and their therapist can work together toward achieving objective insight into the presenting problem and can collaborate to find new ways to address the behaviors that have been preventing them from making progress in their quest for mutual fulfillment in the context of their personal relationship. This is as important in the screening interview or first session as in the sessions to follow, even though the focus of this first meeting is on garnering all relevant situational, medical, and psychological data as well as a precursory assessment of their relational needs. The therapist's initial meeting with the couple or family will also set the stage for what is to follow. Thereafter, as we have discussed, the therapy should focus on helping the couple arrive at a deeper understanding of the origins of their behaviors and should start working toward forging new ones.

Process Versus Content

Yalom (2005, p. 15) refers to process as "the nature of the relationship between two interacting individuals," and Teyber (1997) and Sexton et al. (2004) would agree. As we have already stated, the Needs ABC model identifies couples therapy as, effectively, therapy offered to a very small group rather than as an extension of individual therapy, which indicates that couples therapy is effectively a subset of group therapy and that similar assumptions, practices, and theoretical standpoints all apply. This means that, in the context of couples therapy, *process* refers to the way the members of the couple interact both with each other and with their therapist and to how all three interact with each other as a group, or what I like to refer to as a *therapeutic unit*. It refers to the words they use and the things they say but also to the covert meanings of their statements and to other forms of communication, including body language, gesture, and, at times, the absence of communication, such as a failure to respond to a question or another invitation to speak.

The concept of process from the viewpoint of the Needs ABC practitioner refers to all of these. It also maintains, at all times and in all ways, a specific focus on the client's relational needs, because these exist within their presentation for help. While maintaining this focus, the Needs ABC's inclusive approach also incorporates other "meta" messages from client, couple, and therapist interaction, keeping in mind that below the surface of their communication lies a request for what they want from the other person in their dyad. The illumination, through discussion and insight, of what is implied within this process of communication is critical to problem resolution, behavior change, and a healthier and more fulfilling relationship for both members of the couple.

When a couple presents for therapy, and the two begin to discuss their problems and their origins in a new way, they are demonstrating that a change or "movement" has taken place in their relationship with each other and, separately, in their ability to understand and discuss their relational etiology.

Structure

Uncertainty about what to expect can be an aggravating factor for any anxiety or distress the couple may be facing. Conversely, providing couples with some information about what to expect and following the same basic structure each week is reassuring and fosters the growth of confidence in the therapist and in the usefulness of therapy in general. A simple structure that offers flexibility with the reassurance of routine is ideal. For example, couples might be encouraged to start every session by discussing if and how they have been able to implement suggestions from the previous session and end each session by unwinding and summarizing what has been talked about. However, I would like to caution by reminding that couples' progress is rarely, if ever, uniform and linear, and it would be inadvisable in the extreme to attempt to impose a schedule over the course of couples' intervention. While structure is important in the context of each meeting, providing clients with an understandable, predictable format that will help them feel at ease and that will facilitate the disclosures they make, suggesting to a couple that, "As we've been talking about your problems for 2 months now, we should have reached X stage," will be deeply counterproductive. If such a "stage" has, in fact, not been reached, couples may begin to feel that they are inadequate or that they do not measure up to other couples the therapist may have treated. The last place clients need to feel performance anxiety is in a therapist's office.

Treatment Phases

Following the intake session (which has similar elements for each couple), therapy sessions generally follow a certain model or plan that, while remaining flexible, provides considerable structure to meetings. In the Needs ABC model, the phases include a "sign-in" wherein clients are asked to begin to take responsibility for their treatment by talking about why they came to therapy or what, if anything, has changed with respect to their "issues" since their last session. Since the Needs ABC focus is on relational needs and emotions, the therapist uses reflective interventions that are needs based and are focused on the more relationally productive emotions expressed. For example, a client might say something like, "Since last week, I've been trying to think harder about what all my late nights at the office are doing to my family and discussing with my supervisor ways I could organize my time more effectively so that I don't keep getting home after the kids are already in bed." Comments of this nature show that the client has been applying himself to the task of exploring how his behavior impacts on his partner and provide the couple and their therapist with useful avenues to explore as well as indicating to the therapist how the couple is progressing. In this case, the therapist might say, "I guess you are feeling less frightened of criticism [competency] now that you are demonstrably showing your family more loyalty?"

Again, to elicit opening feedback from clients without asking questions that are excessively "leading," it is often useful to open sessions by inviting couples presenting for therapy to share "any thoughts" about the previous session, possibly in the course of mentioning or summarizing some of the issues discussed during the previous meeting. For example, the therapist might say, "Last week, we all talked quite a bit about how Molly's decision to attend night school to upgrade her qualifications—and the fact that she's away 3 nights a week—has impacted your life as a couple. Does either of you have any thoughts about the way we dealt with this topic last week?"

Following this, the therapist encourages both couple members to discuss the problem at hand and any developments with respect to how they are dealing with their problems. In this "working phase," those present are encouraged to dialogue around relational needs and the emotions they predict, problem solving, and other pertinent issues. In the case of Molly and her husband, their therapist may encourage them to explore ways they could set more aside more time to spend together on nights when Molly is not busy and how this has affected their relational needs-getting and the corresponding emotional well-being.

Toward the end of the session, in a "didactic phase," therapists can present their impression of how the session has gone and can highlight what new conclusions couples have come to and where a potential challenge still exists. As well, counselors can underline any potential solutions and strategies that were uncovered as well as examples of possibilities to ameliorate the clients' situation and avenues that they can explore in their quest to problem solve on a collaborative basis. For example, a therapist might say, "You know, John, I'm wondering if you are still feeling that Molly doesn't completely understand how much you miss her and how sad and lonely you feel when she's not around [abandonment]. Perhaps these feelings are preventing you from supporting her [respect] as much as she would like. At the same time, Molly, I suspect that you feel that John doesn't fully appreciate that what you're doing, what you're doing for both of you, [loyalty/competency], and feeling unacknowledged must be very frustrating. We still have quite a bit to discuss in this area, don't we?" Finally, as a "sign-out," clients are encouraged to share their experience in the session while using needs-based emotion-focused interventions, as required, to supportively challenge less productive strategies, to help them "fine-tune" their potential for problem solving.

As therapy progresses, therapists' and couples' understanding of the couples' challenges should gradually become more detailed, sophisticated, and focused. For example, a third or fourth session might go something like this:

> The therapist says, "Angela, you and Robert have been coming to therapy for about a month now. We've talked about the various ways Robert's alcoholism has made it difficult for you to trust him [loyalty] and how lonely you felt on those nights when he either was not there because he was out with his buddies or had fallen asleep or was ignoring you because he was out of it [abandonment]. We also discussed his need to feel adequate [competency] and valued [respect] in the relationship. Do you feel that you have made some progress?"
>
> "Well, the Twelve Steps is definitely helping," says Angela, referring to the self-help group that Robert has joined, "because he's not coming home drunk anymore. But I am also trying to do what we have been discussing. When Robert talks about the support he needs from me, that he was trying to get from his friends in the pub, I just bite my tongue when I want to say something sharp and work on being more positive. Over the years, we've had more good times than bad times, and focusing on being supportive rather than critical does help to emphasize that."
>
> "Yes," says Robert. "Angela is really making a big effort, and that makes me feel stronger when I'm struggling with my drinking problem. I tend to drink when I feel unimportant and useless, and knowing that she does notice and appreciate the things that I do for us as a couple, even if she doesn't always comment on them directly, does help me to find the strength I need. As for me, I've been thinking a lot about why I start to feel

anxious and edgy so easily in given situations, and I do think I'm making some progress in that department, too. My dad was always hypercritical of me when I was growing up—nothing was ever good enough for him—so when Angela yells, it just pushes all my buttons, and I just want to get out of the house and get away from the whole thing."

Angela's and Robert's beginning remarks have given several "ins" to a more detailed discussion about the problems they have been facing and their attempts to improve the situation, and the therapist focuses on helping them have a useful discussion around these topics. We can also see how by focusing on their relational needs—his need to feel adequate and respected despite his job loss and her need to feel reliably connected and emotionally safe rather than on the unpleasant specifics of his drunkenness and her criticisms—Angela and Robert have both been able to acquire a considerable degree of objectivity with respect to each other's needs and to work positively toward creating new behavioral habits.

Toward the end of this session, in the Needs ABC "didactic" component, the therapist's suggested task would be to summarize how he has reacted to what the couple has been discussing, what needs he detected that have emerged, and which client concerns surfaced during the working phase. This also affords the therapist an opportunity to share facts and problems about the presenting problem such as concrete information, acceptable proactive strategies, and other pertinent information.

In the case of Angela and Robert, the therapist might say:

"Angela, I guess it feels good that Robert is there for you more by not drinking and going to his meetings, and I'm sure Robert is pleased that by not overreacting when he does something that is less than perfect and by validating his competencies even when you become frustrated he feels less defective and more respected. And Robert, I am really impressed by your insight about how Angela sometimes reminds you of the criticism you suffered in your childhood and that you are able to separate yourself from the past and continue to pursue your relational goals."

For Angela and Robert to reach the goals they have set, it will be necessary for Robert to continue to understand his relational needs and to work at finding new, healthier ways to meet them. The therapist may also suggest to Angela that, even while helping Robert understand how he can continue to rebuild the trust between them that has been broken, she should continue to support Robert with positive reinforcement for what he does well and also should show her pleasure when he makes a big effort to work on the issues that have been troubling them. Finally, the therapist can ask them each to "sign out" with an invitation to share what they have gleaned from the session and to provide their feedback on what has been helpful and what has not as well as their insights as to interventions or approaches that might be more useful than those they have tried to date.

Since all clients develop at their own rates, literature acknowledges that the individual client passes through various stages during the therapeutic process, albeit at a personal, rather than a uniform, rate. The Needs ABC model subscribes to the recognition of stages that the individual client will pass through. These therapeutic developmental plateaus are labeled *safety, social, inclusion, collaboration,* and *continuity.*

Client Stages

Safety

The Needs ABC "safety stage" is the initial stage when a couple, or family, first comes for help. In some cases, one member of the unit will be there less than willingly and possibly even because they have been obliged (i.e., for legal reasons) to attend therapy. Even if both are active participants in seeking therapy, however, it is normal and usual for them to be apprehensive about what lies in store for them; after all, they have come to explore aspects of their own behavior that they already know or have been firmly told are less than ideal, and they will have to delve into subjects and areas that they personally find very challenging and uncomfortable or even traumatic.

At this point, it is usually difficult for clients to trust the process, even if they have been in therapy with the same therapist before and even if the screening experience has been generally a positive one. For all of these reasons, it is essential that an atmosphere of safety is established as early as possible in the course of treatment.

Figure 2.3 The safety stage.

Helping the client feel safe in this environment is the operative task for the therapist (Greenberg, Rice, & Elliott, 1993), and this can be promoted with empathy and patience or by modeling appropriate self-disclosure when it is appropriate to do so and by encouraging clients to do the same. Focusing on each client's relational needs rather than on the behaviors themselves promotes a feeling of safety insofar as the therapist is established as an ally rather than as a "critical" adversary. Of course, this is not to say that inappropriate behavior should be accepted, either within or beyond the therapeutic setting. While the Needs ABC model stresses the importance of allying with needs, challenging inappropriate behavior is always important. However, our premise is that such a challenge is more successful *after* an allegiance has been formed with clients. Those who feel that their point of view is understood will invariably be much more amenable to exploring how certain behaviors are inappropriate and how these can be changed.

Ensuring safety in the therapeutic environment (Johnson, 2004, pp. 42–43) is also, of course, important in the case where one half of the couple dyad, or one family member, may have exceptionally dramatic and destructive or otherwise unhelpful behavior, such as violence, substance abuse, or affairs. Here, we still refer primarily to the safety of knowing that one can discuss difficult emotions and needs without fear of recrimination while understanding that violence or other dramatic behavior of any kind is never an option, within or outside the therapist's office. Let's look at an example.

Marco, who was 38, had suffered with depression "on and off" since his late teens. Before presenting for couples therapy, Marco had engaged in anger management therapy for domestic violence and, by his longtime girlfriend Sasha's account, had been doing "excellently" in managing his anger. Marco, as well, stated that he had been taking antidepressant medications that, he said, "took the edge off things," although they had not prevented him from periodically lashing out to the extent that Sasha had felt compelled to call the police and have him ejected from the house because "she would not tolerate his hurtful language."

At the point of attending couples therapy together, Sasha stated that even though she was not presently concerned about her physical safety because it seemed that Marco had learned a lot from his treatment experience, but she still felt at times that she was "walking on eggshells." Despite these bouts of depression and the attendant violence, both Marco and Sasha agreed that when things were good they were very good and that they loved each other very much.

"Unless I can find a way of showing her that I have gotten things under control," said Marco, "Sasha will leave me, and I can't say I blame her. I know I've hurt her badly. It's not me; it's the depression, but still ..."

Although Marco is still unable to own his unpleasant and demeaning behavior, he has become able to acknowledge his own culpability to some extent, and the couple's therapist, Martin, sees this as a positive indication that he will be willing and able to explore the triggers to his violence and to work toward finding a solution.

"What makes matters more complicated," Sasha explained, "is that I'm wheelchair bound. It doesn't stop me from working—I'm a bookkeeper and can actually do most of my work from home—but getting out and about would be hard for me if we split up. It puts me in a very dependent situation and complicates the issues we are already dealing with a great deal. You know what this city is like; it's old and not especially wheelchair friendly. Even getting to the supermarket would be difficult for me on my own. I'd have to order everything online. And then again, when he does get violent, what can I do? I can't run away; I'm really very vulnerable. I have to call the cops every time, even when maybe he's not really as mad as all that, just to be on the safe side. That means that, even when we're not in a really bad situation, things can just snowball and get out of hand, with other people getting involved even when it is not strictly necessary. We really need to sort this out, because otherwise we'll just have to end it. I'm beginning not to be able to see another way."

Although the problems facing Marco and Sasha are considerable, Martin believes that a good outcome is achievable. First, they have made a positive step together in choosing to attend couples therapy following Marco's anger management treatment. Second, he feels confident that, when they realize that they can feel free to discuss anything in therapy, they will be able to access and begin to understand their underlying relational needs. Although Sasha seems to be apologizing for resorting quickly to calling the police when Marco becomes abusive, she is actually sending him a clear message that she is not willing to put up with his intimidation, that she does not accept his depression as an excuse, and that, despite her physical disability, she is refusing to allow herself to be cast in the role of dependent victim. As for Marco, he explains that, while his psychiatrist has diagnosed him as suffering from depression, he has also made it clear to him that it is not acceptable to use the illness as an excuse for dangerous behavior.

In discussion, Martin begins to suspect that Marco may have suffered from abusive behavior as a child but that he finds this difficult to admit to.

"Sometimes," Martin says, generalizing, "people who react violently when they are stressed are reacting to behaviors that they experienced 'on the other side' as children. It's quite common for children who have suffered physical abuse to grow up to be violent."

Marco blushes and starts to fiddle with his wallet, suggesting to Martin that a raw nerve has been struck.

"I've never really talked about it with anyone," he begins hesitantly, "but my dad used to think that I was stupid. When he got drunk, he got mad, and when he got mad, he would lash out. He even kept a special belt for the purpose and said it had my name on it. He kept it hanging on the back of the kitchen door so that I'd never forget that he had his eye on me, even when he was at work. The only time I ever tried to stand up to him was when he was hitting my mother, and even she told me to go away and mind my own business."

Martin comments that it is very courageous to recount such unpleasant memories and inquires, "Now that it's on the table, what would you say was the lesson you learned about violence in relationships?"

Marco sadly replies, "Any time I've been … like that … toward Sasha I've just hated myself afterward. I hated it when I saw it as a child, and I hate it now. I mean, a big part of me was glad she called the cops on me, because I know that what I did was unacceptable…. That damned depression."

"I think we can all agree that, when you've been violent, your behavior has been unacceptable," says Martin. "But I know that Sasha certainly doesn't think that *you* are unacceptable as a person, or she wouldn't have come to therapy with you. Despite everything, she is confident that you have the power to make the changes you need to make and knows that you both have what to takes to heal your relationship."

Sasha interjects, "I really don't understand why he can't figure it out ... that it's what *he does,* not what *he is,* that turns me off. Even when I've been so scared that I called the cops, I didn't stop loving him. Otherwise, I'd have left ages ago."

Martin continues, "Now, the first step is to reintroduce you to the anger log and to refresh your memory about the 'time-out' you learned about in your domestic violence treatment. The second step is to find out why you react so strongly to certain situations and to learn how to react in another way, even when you are depressed."

In further discussion with Sasha and Marco, Martin develops the hypothesis that, while his less useful emotion is clearly anger, the underlying emotion is a fear of being inadequate and that the emotional abandonment he feels will inevitably result if and when he fails to measure up. This probably resulted from the need, developed in childhood, for the reassurance that he was capable and loved unconditionally by his parents—reassurance he never received. His father had modeled violence as a problem-solving strategy and his mother's apparent emotional absence, despite the fact that her energy was largely occupied in preventing her husband from hurting her children or herself, or at least minimizing the damage he caused, had made him acutely sensitive to potential feelings of abandonment. Martin also suggests that for Sasha to get the respect she feels she deserves and to help her to begin to trust him he must consider ways of making the responsibility for his anger "all his."

In the previous example, Martin supportively challenged Marco while gently guiding him toward understanding his responsibility in their relational predicament. He was able, through his intervention, to show Sasha that he understood her point of view and suggested to Marco that he still had value despite his behavior and that there was hope for the relationship as long as they felt safe enough in their sessions to discuss "the ghosts of Christmas past" no matter how painful these memories were.

Social

The second stage of the clinical process, the social stage, involves the establishment of an appropriate relational base (Jacobson & Margolin,

Figure 2.4 The social stage.

1979, pp. 107–108) between the individuals in therapy and the therapist but most of all between the members of the couple or family that has come for help. People who attend therapy often fear that they will not be understood and worry that they are lacking sufficient social skills to clarify their problem or that they are skewed or defective in their perception of reality. They may even feel that, rather than their counselor helping them, he or she may criticize them on a personal level and make them feel even worse than they already do. Through the development of a safe environment, helping the client to "socialize" more readily within the context of the session, to dialogue rather than engage in a "struggle for power," is the next therapeutic challenge (Gottman, 1999, p. 235). The Needs ABC model is especially adept at helping clients achieve this goal since it avoids the potential for "finger-pointing" of some other behavioral models by allying with each member of the system around his or her relational needs and not around the behaviors he or she finds unacceptable in the other.

Helping the members of the couple to interact with each other is a way to encourage socialization. Chit-chatting from time to time about nontherapeutic issues, such as the state of the economy or the weather (something I call the "schmooze," which will be explained in a subsequent chapter), is a way of "seeding" this process before moving on to more important matters. This can also allow time for you and the client to gain some objectivity to consider additional needs-getting strategies.

The Needs ABC model espouses a "listen and learn" attitude, respecting the fact that couples and families attending therapy are the real experts of their own problems, whether they are able to recognize this on their own. In working with couples and families it is important not to intervene until sufficient information has been garnered to make a proficient need-based emotion-focused statement, even in the context of a passionate power struggle. Interventions that can give support to reaching the situation whereby meaningful dialogue can occur include empathy, reflection, appropriate therapist self-disclosure, and encouragement (Nichols, 2006, pp. 326–328; Johnson, 2004). As well, any improvement in a client's ability to relate to others in the therapeutic milieu can enhance self-esteem and communication skills and can provide tools for better social relationships in the wider world. For example, after one therapist's observation, a female client, Rose, "jumped in," saying:

> "That's exactly my point. Julian never listens to me. Instead, he just runs away."
>
> Julian interjects, "You're right! I was wrong to avoid you, but I was also feeling like … an … [looking at the therapist] 'accessory.' I was also feeling very lonely…. I just wanted you back!"
>
> Rose adds thoughtfully, "And I guess when you did try to reach out, I was just so annoyed I didn't listen and just became even more remote."
>
> Here Julian and Rose have begun to dialogue more appropriately around their dilemma of how to get their relational needs met while managing to avoid becoming angry and upset and resorting to the unsuccessful techniques they have evolved in their personal lives in their attempts to reach out to each other.

Inclusion

As before, when clients begin to feel reasonably comfortable in the therapeutic setting, they begin to be able to reveal more about what they are really thinking and feeling and to more adequately describe relational needs (dreams, hopes, and fears) and the thoughts they have about their potential to solve problems (Greenberg et al., 1993, pp. 114–115). In a sense, they begin to feel more adequate and important in the therapeutic process—that their ideas are good ones and that therapy is not just advice being given by an "expert" but that they can be "experts" as well. Indeed, at this point, the members of the system should be starting to realize that they were *always* the "experts" in this situation; they just needed help in becoming able to unlock their expertise. This feeling of inclusion prepares them for the next stage,

Figure 2.5 The inclusion stage.

in which working together and brainstorming with those at hand is a curative requirement.

Let's look at an example. We'll explore some of the issues currently facing Sarah and William and the progress that they have been making in their efforts to deal with them in a positive, constructive way.

Sarah and William came to therapy when they found themselves "on the verge of splitting up," after their failure to conceive a child using in vitro fertilization (IVF). They have already been through three cycles of treatment and are contemplating going through a fourth; however, they will need to spend a year saving to be able to afford it, and Sarah is not looking forward to the process, which she found humiliating, uncomfortable, and, with the constant injections of hormones, leaving her vulnerable to distressing mood swings that threatened to impact negatively on both her performance at work (she is a notary public) and on her relationship with her spouse.

"It was so damn expensive," William had explained earlier in therapy. "And we tried it three times, to no avail. I started to feel like it was all my fault [competency], although you can't blame anyone for that sort of thing.

We've both been tested, and, in theory, there's no reason we shouldn't be able to have a child. 'Unexplained infertility,' they call it. Which makes it worse, you know? Like you're being blamed for something but you don't even know how you are screwing it up. I mean, a friend of mine had the same problem, and he found out that it was because he'd had mumps as a kid. He was still upset, of course, but at least he could start to get his head around the situation. I just sort of put my head down and got on with things, but Sarah was obsessed. It was all about the baby for her, or the lack of a baby to be precise. I began to wonder whether she wouldn't rather just ditch me and find some guy with more motile sperm."

In therapy, both Sarah and William discussed how they both came from happy families and how each had hoped to recreate this happiness in the context of their own new family. They had hoped to have at least three children. When things didn't work out as planned, this was deeply upsetting for them both, and the scene was set for anger and recrimination, as their very identities seemed to be challenged. With a lot of hard work, Sarah and William have now reached the point where they feel like they can stop blaming each other for things that haven't worked out, are less defensive when they are criticized, and are increasingly able to empathize with each other's point of view and needs. In a sense, they each have moved from "being the bad guy" to feeling that their opinion counts—in other words, they have managed to help each other feel "more included."

Sarah says, "I *did* find myself getting increasingly obsessed. I'd see William drinking coffee and yell, 'What the hell are you doing? Don't you know coffee is bad for your fertility levels? Don't you even *give* a damn?' [betrayal] It seemed like I couldn't think about anything else, and I lost sight of the fact that the whole process was really difficult for William, too, not just for me. It's not simply a woman thing. He wanted—wants—a family as much as I do. But I do respect more than ever that we're in this together and that he should have a say, baby or no baby, and that we'll have to work hard to make things work out between us."

Collaboration

Collaboration describes the process of the clients actively working together with the therapist to become enabled to function better in the wider world (Jacobson & Margolin, 1979, pp. 241–248; Johnson, 2004, p. 187). In individual therapy, clients are encouraged to survey potential effective strategies by asking others (e.g., a mentor, a trusted friend, a colleague) how things can be handled. In couples and family work, the therapist encourages collaborative problem solving between the partners or family members by using "observations" or "invitations" for problem solving to seed the discussions. Collaboration can

Figure 2.6 The collaboration stage.

begin by working toward a sense of connection between the therapist and the clients and between the clients. We might usefully describe this as being a sense of, "We're all in this together." If a disconnected or, worse yet, adversarial position is established, this can be very damaging to therapists' prospect of really helping the couple or family that has come to them for help in making substantive progress. For example, the therapist might say, after elucidating each partner's relational needs as they have been agreed upon in their work:

> Inasmuch as you are beginning to succeed at the challenge of meeting each other's relational needs, it seems to me that you both still are feeling somewhat frustrated at not being acknowledged, at times, by the other.

In this way, "finger-pointing" is avoided, all members of the couple or family are applauded for the achievements they have accomplished to date, and tasks that are as yet unfinished are highlighted. This will encourage more dialogue around situations that may still prove frustrating or problematic despite the progress they have made. Once this is accomplished, they can begin the process of problem solving as a "team" by offering more concrete solutions to these specific situations: a "collaborative fine-tuning" of how to meet their relational needs. Let's look at an example.

Isaac and Esther first attended couples counseling about 3 years after their marriage and 2 years after the birth of their son, Moshe. Both are successful professionals. Esther is an attorney, and Isaac is an orthodontist. Money has never been a problem for this affluent family, but it has not prevented them from facing some real dilemmas in their relationship with each other. They both agree that they have decided to attend therapy because of Isaac's tendency to withdraw and isolate—he would "disappear" to his basement home office—when they would begin to disagree or argue. They stated concern first that because of this they never seemed to be able to resolve their issues and felt like they were beginning to avoid each other and second that this will have a negative impact on Moshe, who is increasingly aware of the relationships between the people around him.

Esther and Isaac report that they "still love each other" but argue a great deal, especially about what Esther feels is Isaac's obsession with work at the expense of family [loyalty]: "He'll miss any family occasion to put in a little overtime." Even when he is at home, Isaac is often going through the accounts from the office or is on the phone to colleagues or clients to discuss work matters. For his part, Isaac feels that the large salary he brings home is not respected as the valuable contribution to the family's welfare that it is [competence]. As well, he stated that "unless things happen the way *she* wants them it just isn't any good at all" [reliability].

"It's not that I don't appreciate all the hard work he does," says Esther in exasperation. "I really do. But it's that old cliché. When you're on your deathbed, do you look back and think, 'Gee, I really wish I'd spent more time at the office'? It's like he cares only about how fancy the food on the table and the clothes on our backs are—not about us as people or about where we are going as a couple and as a family. When I try to discuss this with him, even make a few suggestions, *whoosh*, he's gone to do more work on his computer. Even when he's at home, he's not with us."

Esther also makes it clear that she feels as if Isaac ignores her comments and suggestions [respect] and dismisses them as being unworthy of his attention.

Enrico, the therapist, begins by suggesting that inasmuch as Isaac doesn't feel valued for his work and that it's "her way or the highway," the way he reacts to Esther makes her feel betrayed and disrespected. As the couple seems to tentatively agree with this precursory hypothesis, Enrico begins gathering a little family detail about the pair's respective family backgrounds. Isaac describes his father as having held extremely high standards to the point where Isaac would lock himself in his room to study rather than meet his father's wrath. While all his children, now adults, had done well, he remained critical and even in recent years had often embarrassed Isaac by criticizing him vocally in front of other people and suggesting that, successful as Isaac is, he could have done so much more: "This guy could have been the president of the United States, but, no, he's happy to set up shop in his hometown." By contrast, Isaac's mother is described as a rather passive individual who "put up with everything" and lived for and through her offspring. Esther's father was always available to her in every way, while her mother, a decidedly independent woman, apparently cultivated her social life at the expense of her family and was both selfish and defensive.

Together with Enrico, the couple learned how to discuss the more and less useful emotions embedded in their testimony and experience, an approach that met with quite some success relatively quickly. With a greater understanding of the impact of their family backgrounds on their unmet needs, the two became able to understand how they had created a dysfunction cycle that served only to make their unmet needs feel more urgent. After a number of sessions, Esther agreed that she tended to make unilateral decisions about how Moshe should be raised, without involving Isaac. Isaac agreed that he tended not to listen properly or focus when Esther was talking about her needs or about how she felt they should deal with one situation or another involving Moshe and that it would be more useful to negotiate with her rather than argue or block her when she asked for more or other than what he felt was reasonable.

Esther and Isaac terminated therapy happily, feeling that they had made good progress and a solid foundation on which to grow. However, about 6 months later, Isaac contacted Enrico again and asked for an appointment during which he explained that he had been offered a partnership in a prestigious clinic and that he was suffering from panic attacks and couldn't understand why, as things were "just going great at home."

> "I can't seem to get rid of this lump in my throat," he explained miserably. "I went to the hospital last week because I felt I couldn't breathe. I took all sorts of tests, and everything seemed to check out.... The emergency room doctor advised me to seek counseling ... so here I am."

Isaac explained that his new position was quite high profile. In his old position he had worked under a friend he had known for years, but now he had to work with a larger organization, including one partner who he felt disliked him. In addition, he was traveling quite a bit, spending time away from his family. While Esther had been supportive, there was a concern that this would damage all the good work they had done toward improving their relationship. In an attempt to compensate, Isaac had cut back on the time he customarily spent with his friends. This did not detract from the fact that his need to be "the perfect husband and father" was being challenged by his new responsibilities; at the same time he was aware that his friends were hurt that he had suddenly stopped spending time with them, and he missed the "downtime" these periods had represented to him.

Working together, Enrico and Isaac put together a number of strategies, with the intention of reducing Isaac's panic. They agreed that he should do the following:

- Log high-anxiety situations and indicate how he felt he had dealt with them.
- Meet with Esther and decide exactly what each would be responsible for in the marriage for the time being, with a reevaluation when Isaac felt more settled and happy in his new position.
- Clarify with friends exactly what his limitations were regarding his potential to participate in sports with them and go to the gym, as much as possible, on his own schedule to help with his potential to become anxious.
- Meet with his local liaison to discuss his commitment to his new job and to address, as much as possible, his specific concerns with regard to his effectiveness in the new role.
- Meet with his new supervisor in a month or so to discuss how she perceives his abilities in this position.

Following a one-to-one meeting with Enrico, both members of the couple attended a session to discuss all the measures that had been decided on. Esther enthusiastically agreed that she would help Isaac however she could, reiterated her support for him in taking up his new position, and added that she would join him in the gym whenever possible. While Isaac and Esther still had things to work out, it was clear that they had

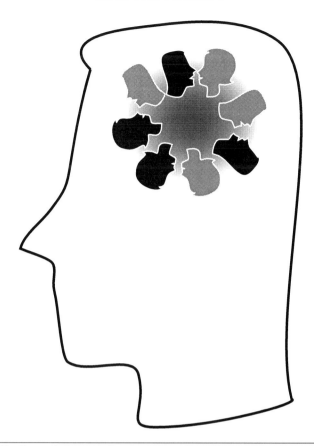

Figure 2.7   The continuity stage. Here, the best teachings of the group are incorporated into all aspects of the client's life.

acquired a considerable understanding of their unmet relational needs and the importance of partnership and collaboration in meeting them.

Continuity

As the therapy seems to be coming to an end, every clinician's hope is that clients will take their experience from the treatment setting and into the "real" world, if they have not already begun to do so (Jacobson & Margolin, 1979; Johnson, 2004, pp. 196–200). Ideally, by the time this stage has been reached, progress that has been made in the therapeutic context will have begun to translate to real, tangible improvements at home. Specifically, clients will be able to approach relationships with the same functional reciprocity that they have dis-covered works in therapy. Clients will also be able to refer back to spe-cific learning situations, when familiar feelings of discomfort begin to resurface. Here the therapist can provide an injunction for each to highlight where they might run into problems in the future and how they will resolve them after treatment. The counselor might also say something like:

> So, now that you have decided to move forward and "go it on your own," why don't we discuss what you have learned about your buttons and how you will do your part in supporting your partner?

At this point, the therapist can also make it clear that returning to therapy at a future point is always a possibility and that doing so would in no way represent a failure on the part of the couple. At the same time, it is also important to give a strong, positive message. A comment such as the following might be made:

> You have made enormous progress as a couple, and I am confident that the positive changes you have made and that you continue to make will reap real benefits for you. At the same time, I am hopeful that you will also continue to be prepared to request outside help in the future if you need to and to remain vigilant around emotions that might indicate that your needs are not being met.

Facilitation and Pacing: Following Their Lead

The caveat, "Facilitate, do not lead," holds true in couples and other forms of psychotherapy (discussed in more detail in Caplan, 2008a). The optimal approach is one that helps clients to lead themselves, assisting them in "staying on track" and helping them, as individu-als and as a microcosm of society, to find their own voice (Miller & Rollnick, 1991, pp. 58–60; Teyber, 2006, pp. 83–92). Metaphorically, the clinician does not take the reins but finds a way to hand the reins over to the people about whom the therapy should be. With this in mind, a good clinician must learn to set aside ego, to listen, to prompt rather than command, to suggest rather than forcibly challenge, and to empathize with and identify the clients' motives for the maladaptive behaviors with which they present. Note the emphasis on the reasons behind the behaviors rather than the behaviors themselves, as this is a crucial element of the Needs ABC approach that should never be overlooked.

When one couple member states his frustration at the way problem solving has been done in the past I might encourage the other to suggest a solution that could be mutually acceptable using an emotion-focused relational needs approach. For example, I might say, "Jan, you seem frustrated about being marginalized in the way this incident was handled. I wonder if Lorna might have a suggestion as to what might work better for both of you with regard to meeting your relational needs in this situation."

It is unlikely that all clients will arrive for help at the same level of preparedness or "stage" simultaneously. In other words, some people will be able to begin constructively exploring their own behaviors and emotions and implement new strategies in their daily relational interactions before others. So it is with each couple member. While this absence of synchronicity can seem challenging, it is not a problem, since the one couple member who is ready to explore his or her behaviors and emotions earlier can positively model a constructive engagement in therapy for the other.

However, the fact that client movement does not occur at uniform rates means that therapists must evaluate each participant's progress before planning their interventions. Let's explore an example.

Justin and Sylvie have been involved in a discussion about their anger at and fear of not being able to trust family members. Sylvie, who had previously disclosed feelings of disconnection from her family, has not yet entered the discussion. Having noticed this, the counselor waits for an appropriate break in the discussion, turns to Sylvie, and says, "It seems to me that you and Justin seem somewhat alike in how you saw your family when you were growing up."

During the brief silence that follows, Sylvie appears to carefully consider what has been said and then cautiously says, "Yes, I suppose Justin and I come from pretty similar family backgrounds. But he seems to be able to talk more freely about how he feels this has impacted our relationship. I get so angry that I just can't talk…. I'm afraid I'll self-destruct or something."

"Believe me, I still feel that way sometimes," Justin comments. "But I feel it is important to talk about things here. I need to get this stuff off my chest since I think that my anger sometimes gets transferred to you."

"That's it," exclaims Sylvie. "I'm afraid that if I cross a line here I will do the same at home. Our relationship isn't so great right now, and I certainly don't want to make it worse."

Now that Sylvie has self-disclosed in the therapeutic environment, both Justin and Sylvie, with help from the therapist, can proceed to examine the issues that impinge on their relationship in a more balanced way and hopefully progress toward real change for the better.

Pacing a session simply refers to the concept of doing work at clients' rather than therapists' pace to help clients better assimilate problem-solving strategies and more readily meet their treatment goals. People do not all progress at the same pace. Progress does not necessarily occur along an even trajectory, and this is not a prerequisite. Some clients will appear to make little or no progress over a period of time, only to suddenly register a demonstrable, significant improvement in their ability to relate to their partner following a breakthrough in their level of understanding of the reasons behind the behaviors they have adopted. The Needs ABC approach subscribes to the promotion of participant statements in setting the course of collaborative discussion through the illumination of the needs that emerge during the session, in the context of needs-based emotion focused statements.

For example, when a client says, "I know that there are two sides to a story, but I would like to talk about what *she* does before we talk about me for a change," the therapist can acknowledge the client's apparent fear of being singled out or marginalized as "the problem" by saying, "I guess it's scary to think that your side of the story might fall on deaf ears—that she might be doing stuff that's wrong as well." In this way, the client can take time to acknowledge his concern that he is the only "defective" partner and encourage a dialogue around his need to feel competent; then he might be more inclined to examine his responsibility for meeting her needs in the relationship.

While it is clearly the therapist's role to control the situation and gently lead the direction that therapy takes, it is essential to remember that the real "experts" are both elements of the couple and to respect their opinions and insights. If the clinician is overly directive, client competency might be compromised, and opportunities to validate clients in their participation may be lost. In effect, this is a way of pacing the client by putting them in the role of expert and "hearing" what the client, and not the therapist, deems important.

In effective clinical work, clinicians are encouraged to take a "frugal" approach to their interventions. As well, it is important to remain aware of the internal emotional responses that might arise during the session for both themselves and for their clients. So it is with all other therapy formats where direct and indirect cues suggesting where clients "are at" must be tended to with a certain degree of objectivity. The therapist must listen, watch, and learn. Being able to do so means becoming able to set aside many of our own prejudices and opinions and learning how to see the world through the eyes of other people, regardless of how different they seem to be to us.

In couples therapy, as in other therapeutic modalities, clients' words must be considered in the context of the information they have already shared and in conjunction with body language, posture, and changes in tone and voice modulation. Effective clinicians subscribe to the notion that the most important text embedded in the words clients choose to use is often the least obvious one. For example, Johanna, who seemed to deny she had any issue with competency and had a very successful career in the field of architecture, described her parents as having been extremely overprotective. I asked whether she had ever been assertive with them as she seemed to be able to do in her career, and she stated, "Every time I told them I wanted to do something my way they said, 'Later, dear, when you're older.... Now it's better to do it our way.'" On further reflection, she concurred that her parents were quite critical and that she often doubted herself in her relationships outside of her business milieu.

Staying on Track

It is a given that one expectation for any practitioner is the ability to keep on track in terms of maintaining focus on the specific topics under discussion, the explicit or implicit emotional components extant in the client's narrative, and the relevant process issues that arise in the session (Greenberg et al., 1993, p. 94; Johnson, 2004, pp. 91–94). Staying on track also calls for the ability to supervise and to take back control from the couple when it is evident that the current range of avenues under exploration is less than useful. Conversely, when the couple *is* on track, the therapist should know when to "keep out of it" and to gently help both parties in their explorations rather than intervening with suggestions that might remove their focus from the all-important discussion at hand. In addition, a seasoned clinician will store information and perspectives gleaned from individual clients with regard to problem resolution, to be used later for optimal effectiveness. In my clinical experience, knowing when "to keep out of it" makes it easier to take charge of the session when necessary and makes it easier to integrate observations about the individuals presenting for therapy and about their relationship as a couple. As well, sitting back and observing what is transpiring while gathering information to be used at optimal moments in the session allows for better designed interventions focusing on client issues rather than interventions that make clinicians feel as though they are "putting out fires." How many marriage and family therapists cringe at the thought of a returning couple who, in their last session, created chaos with their persistent arguing, leaving the therapist exhausted from being the "referee" and feeling helpless and hopeless about doing effective work?

For example, Pauline and Gerald came to counseling because she felt that he always disregarded her suggestions and, to make matters worse, seemed to marginalize her in social situations.

Almost from the moment they entered the therapy office, Pauline and Gerald began to bicker and argue. Pauline hurled allegations that she had "told him 20 times to wait until she returned home from shopping before preparing dinner." For his part, Gerald retorted that "she was a control freak" and said that preparing to make dinner wasn't such a "big deal" and that it "wasn't like he started to eat without her." Harry, the couples counselor, sat back and listened to epithets being hurled back and forth as they yelled at each other about how he never let her speak when they were at parties and how she never left the parties when she said she would—that from the time she said they were leaving it took a good half hour to 45 minutes to leave because she had to say goodbye to "absolutely everyone" even though half of them were "in the bag."

After listing carefully to the lively bickering, Harry surmised that it actually represented, initially, Pauline's need to feel important [respect] and Gerald's need to feel that he might have some good ideas [competency] or suggestions about how they led their lives. As the couple's arguments seemed not to be leading to any useful breakthroughs, Harry finally interjected by saying, "Pauline, I guess you often feel unacknowledged in your relationship, and it appears to me that Gerald seems to feel that you don't give him much credit for his suggestions. How does each of you feel about this possibility?" With this, the couple were able to move from a power struggle as to who was right and who was wrong to a discussion about both of their unmet relational needs—Gerald's need to feel he could contribute to and her need to feel important in the relationship.

How to Intervene Supportively

Roselle Kurland (2004) suggested that the best intervention is made by the therapist as observer, with the intervention made as an "observation" rather than a fact or an "invitation" to problem solve—a suggestion I emphatically agree with. The ability to gather information about client perspectives and functioning and presenting these findings as observations at the right time and in an economical way allows clients to take responsibility for their treatment (Greenberg & Johnson, 1988, pp. 154–155; Jacobson & Gurman, 1986, pp. 161–162). Observations and invitations are less threatening to clients and are seen as engaging rather than coercive. Examples of each follow.

Observation

- What I see is …
- From my perspective …
- It seems to me …
- I've heard the two of you talking about …
- What I hear you saying to each other …
- I get the sense that John seems to be having some difficulty understanding his responsibility. Is this accurate …

Invitation

- Does either of you have some ideas about …
- Here's a thought I'd like to throw out …

- Help me understand this better …
- How does this help either of you get closer to …
- Has either of you had similar experiences …
- Lois, I wonder if you can explain what John meant by his last statement …

Regardless of whether it is called psychotherapy, counseling, treatment, coaching, or something else, the purpose of such interventions is to help clients resist the unproductive reflexive behaviors they tend to use in uncomfortable situations by giving them the support they need to endure the anxiety they experience in replacing old behaviors with new ones. Research has shown that the most effective forms of treatment are those in which clients are encouraged to take charge of the therapeutic process by taking responsibility for what is needed to meet the therapeutic goals and to problem solve effectively (Orlinsky et al., 1986, pp. 283–330; Orlinsky & Howard, 1994, pp. 257–310; Lambert & Barley, 2001, pp. 357–361).

In addition to this, following a structure with an understandable and identifiable "beginning," "middle," and "end" will promote emotional safety, regardless of the therapeutic focus, as it removes a substantial element of the unknown from each interaction between therapist and clients and provides a clear, recognizable framework within which dialoguing can take place. Understanding that clients must "crawl before they can walk" and pacing clients as well as the therapeutic interventions accordingly should prove more effective in all clinical work than following a preconceived timeline or agenda. Helping individuals and couples to challenge themselves and each other in a supportive way while promoting appropriate and respectful dialogue becomes more powerful and effective than, as a clinician, taking on most of the responsibility for clients' treatment.

Couple Process

The term *couples process* refers to the way both members of the couple interact with each other and with their therapist, as they continue their exploration of their relationship and how to heal it (Nichols & Schwartz, 2006). An acute awareness of the development and

The usefulness of this model in working with couples and families is made evident in the introduction to my book on group work (Caplan, 2008a), as follows. The Needs ABC model is dedicated to the exploration of these (client) issues in a safe, client-centered environment that allows [those seeking psychological services] to reach their own analyses of why they have sought help and how they can start making things right. It is about wise leadership [intervention strategies] but, much more than that, it is about facilitating individuals in their striving to take the reins of their own lives and emotions. Crucially, it is a model that is relevant to all individuals, regardless of gender, age, social class, ethnicity, and level of education. Everyone's problems are unique, but emotions are universal and tend to be expressed in a limited range of ways, referred to throughout this book as the "universal themes" [theme-based needs].

evolution of process is essential for the therapist and the couple, and an explanation of this evolution with an explanation of the resulting counterproductive cycle that the couple brings in is often extremely helpful to all concerned, especially when described in the context of relational needs and the useful versus less useful emotional component. In particular, the therapist must be aware that not everything that passes between the two members of the couple will be expressed in words or in explicit statements; an understanding of needs embedded in statements and of subtle ways of interaction is very important. By observing the couple's process and occasionally intervening with an observation about relational needs to deflect tension, or an invitation to problem solve, the therapist can help the couple to become enabled to learn or relearn a better way of communicating with each other and of finding ways to meet both partners' relational needs in the context of their personal relationship. At the same time, each individual client will be going through the process of expressing relational needs in a new way and will be requesting for them to be met without resorting to less than useful language and behavior.

For example, when Mary and Fred come into couples therapy, they begin by arguing that each has marginalized the other—that the other is selfish and inattentive to the other. During this "he said, she said" interaction, Fred stated that Mary had been oblivious to his needs while he had the flu—that she had been too busy to even make him a meal because she was "occupied" with the children and her friends. As well, he stated that when he did cook for himself she always criticized that "he left the kitchen a mess." On the other hand, Mary rebutted that "he never cleans up any of his messes and always leaves them for me to take care of—you would think he is a child, and I have two others to take care of." Mary went on to say that she felt he was the critical one and that she was always walking on egg-shells in case he didn't like the way she cooked his dinner. "At some point I thought, 'To heck with him; let him cook his own food.'" Here the couple counselor intervened by explaining that it appeared to her that Fred was feeling that Mary's loyalty was elsewhere and that he could never live up to her expectations. She suggested that what Mary thought of as his placing of conditions in the relationship was just a reaction to his perception of her criticisms of him. The problem was that by doing what he was doing Mary experienced his emotional abandonment and felt that she did not matter to him. Her response was, then, to gravitate to where she felt an allegiance and assume that he didn't even want to try to meet her needs.

Additional Practice Concepts

Linking and Inclusion Techniques

It is very important to avoid, as much as possible, finding oneself effectively performing one-on-one therapy with each of the individuals in the room rather than addressing them as a unit. Even if one member of a couple, or family, seems to be resisting the therapeutic intervention or is less adept at expressing needs and emotion, the person can be "drawn in" with patience and skill. One should always avoid engaging with the "easier" partner in the couple excessively, inadvertently giving the impression that the other's views, needs, and problems are somehow less valid or interesting. Using linking and inclusion techniques can be very useful in this context and, as described in the previous section on inclusion, can make them feel important to the therapeutic process. Let's look at an example.

Patricia and Austin have been coming to therapy for a couple of months. Consistently, Austin has been more forthcoming about the things that make him feel dissatisfied, about why he thinks he feels the way he does, and about what he feels he needs from Patricia. While Patricia has generally been able to engage at least somewhat in the treatment process, today she has remained quiet or has given minimal answers. As well, she resists "catching the eye" of the therapist and tends to spend rather a lot of time gazing out the window or even scrolling through the list of contacts on her cellular phone, apparently not even listening to the discussion at hand. Both had agreed that "she gets like this sometimes" and that nothing unusual had occurred since their past session. Austin, perhaps feeling the obligation to fill the "quiet spaces," has been even more verbal than normal. "I think that one of the reasons I argue so readily," Austin muses during their eighth session, "is because I grew up in a big family with lots of sisters and brothers. We all had to struggle to negotiate our space."

The therapist responds to Austin that Patricia, coming from a "small" family (having only one younger brother), didn't seem to have to fight in the same way.

With this Patricia seemed to awaken and angrily interjects, "Are you kidding? I fought for *years* trying to get some attention from my father. As soon as my brother—a boy—was born, it was like I didn't even exist—not now that the sacred male heir had been born. My mother gave me some of her time but would always do what my father wanted, so I didn't get much from her either. I finally gave up. No … nothing serious happened since last session, but I still feel that Austin doesn't listen to what I need in the relationship.… I guess I've given up on him as well."

In this case, by linking the couple together through a discussion of family size and remembering that Patricia had described herself as sometimes feeling invisible in her family of origin, the therapist was able to touch on two important relational needs for Patricia: feeling marginalized [respect] and feeling impotent [power], something she was still struggling with in her relationship with Austin.

In couples therapy, as in other therapeutic modalities, recognizing clients' personal expertise helps them to acquire a sense of being in charge of their own treatment. No couple is the same, and, within couples, no individual is the same. Therapists need to learn how to recognize that couples will have to progress at their own pace through the various stages of treatment and that progress will not necessarily be uniform but may occur in "fits and starts" on their journey toward meeting the goals that have brought them into therapy.

In the previous example, for instance, the therapist didn't press Patricia to engage; he only used an "observation" about the innocuous general topic of family size to seed the discussion so that his clients could pursue various avenues of thought, hopefully productively. Patricia seemed to feel misunderstood enough by the therapist to correct what she felt was his misperception of her need to "fight" for recognition in her family. The counselor could now "invite" the couple to dialogue around how they could "fight" for the couple as a couple so that each could feel acknowledged and visible in the relationship.

Within the structured format of the meeting, flexibility, receptiveness, and understanding are all crucial. Also, we can bear in mind a number of key issues that will facilitate the effective use of the Needs ABC model throughout any given couple's period in therapy. In the chapter that follows, we explore ways the uncovered needs deficit can be used to elicit further cognitional breakthroughs and in creating strategies for the creation of ways these unmet needs can be answered.

3

INTRODUCING THE NEEDS ABC RELATIONAL NEEDS AND EMOTION-FOCUSED COMPONENTS

The Fundamentals of the Needs ABC Approach: Maintaining Focus on Needs

The Needs Acquisition and Behavior Change (ABC) model rests on the premise that most emotional experience is built on a foundation of a finite number of basic relational needs, primary or secondary, that are usually formed in the individual during childhood (Aylmer, 1986, pp. 107–148; Nichols & Schwartz, 2006, p. 36; Teyber, 2006, pp. 5–15). (Of course, these needs may be altered or modified later in life by a traumatic event or exceptional circumstance.) The task of the Needs ABC therapist, keeping in mind how and where the client is situated socially and environmentally (Greenberg & Johnson, 1988, pp. 32–35; Nichols & Schwartz, 2006, pp. 7, 10, 378–379; Teyber, p. 14), is to listen to clients' narratives to identify the themes that describe the needs they are seeking that are couched in what they are saying—what they are describing in the therapy session. These narrative themes are client specific and therefore express client-specific relational needs. These needs-based themes seem to express the way clients see the world in general (their worldview; Orlinsky & Howard, 1986) and automatically take into consideration clients' culture, ethnicity, and religious beliefs, all of which normally contribute to their perspective (McGoldrick, 1996) and, by association, the formation of their relational needs. Differentiating between the content of a client's narrative and the theme-based need embedded therein (Nichols &

Schwartz, 2006, pp. 125, 134; Teyber, 1989, pp. 22–23; Teyber, 2006, pp. 70–78) is critical to this model. These narrative embedded needs will help define what is lacking with regard to clients' relational needs (needs deficit)—what they have been trying to get unsuccessfully. Clinicians and clients alike can relate to these needs, whether they are part of clients' presenting issue. Because of the universal quality of these needs—the ease with which they can be understood and identified with—clients can collaboratively problem solve or help each other to examine more productive problem-solving strategies and more productive emotions that will result in improved problem solving.

While the list of relational theme-based needs provided in this chapter should not be assumed to be exclusive, it is a good starting point. It is important to understand that the labels used to describe the relational needs are not monolithic or mutually exclusive of other identifiers; they should be used only as a template from which to work. The best choices are those most consistent with clients' experience. It is important to understand that the issue that brings people to therapy is not that of their emotional needs but the way and extent to which they react to them. If I feel competent in the world in general ("competency" not being at the top of my personal needs list) and my competency is challenged, then my reaction to this challenge should be more functional. For example, if Mark is told that he is a poor farmer (though all the evidence to the contrary makes him feel competent in this regard) he will definitely react to that statement, but his reaction might be more of one of surprise or sadness that the other person feels that way. He would probably react by saying something like, "I'm sorry you feel that way" or might think, "This is not about my ability to farm well but about something going on with the other person" and try to resolve the issue productively. If, on the other hand, Mark is personally concerned about his ability to farm well, then he will probably react

A mark of the relational need's importance is the degree to which the client reacts (or remains objective) when challenged in the session, especially when confronted by the partner.

by becoming defensive or by attacking. Certainly, his response will be one that is less productive. Thus, it will reinforce his fear of not reaching an acceptable level of competence.

Fear/Themes/Needs Paradigms

The Needs ABC relational needs paradigms were gradually developed over a period of time alongside the evolution of the Needs ABC model. The list provided in this section was created as a way of helping therapy interns learn the model's concepts, especially with regard to the identification of relational needs extant in clients' narratives. The first incarnation was a list of *global* or *universal* themes and consisted of the following (Caplan & Thomas, 2004, pp. 53–73):

- Marginalization
- Lack of respect
- Avoidance of responsibility
- Incompetence
- Abandonment
- Intimacy
- Betrayal
- Grief
- Powerlessness

These themes appeared to be most often extant in the narrative of clients' "story" as it emerged in the context of therapy and with which listeners could easily identify even if they were not currently experiencing the same needs and feelings. With the realization that these themes actually represented client needs—what they were looking for in their relationships—they were reconfigured to represent needs rather than themes. For example, "incompetence" represented a need for competency, "betrayal" a need for loyalty, "intimacy" a need for closeness or distance, and "avoidance of responsibility" responsibility taking. It also became evident that the need for closeness or distance ("intimacy") could depend on how much or how little trust had been established in the relationship or how reliable the emotional connection was. In addition, "marginalization" indicated a "lack of respect" or a need for respect.

To clarify these relational needs paradigms, consider a client who describes a dinner conversation in which he is in the process of relating an anecdote pertinent to the discussion at hand. No sooner had he begun than one of the people at his table jumped in with a totally different topic. If you were the one being cut off it might be fair to say that you would view the interloper as disrespectful; you might feel fearful that you were not important enough to be heard; you might feel sad that your participation was not being acknowledged or that what you had to say had no real value to the others. Similarly, you might feel concerned that you were not adequate to hold everyone's attention.

The relational needs list evolved over time by examining the previously provided universal themes to see how many could be listed as "unique" or exclusive of the others in the list. It was co-created, over the years, with my colleagues and with clinical interns whom I supervised in various clinical settings. While others such as Maslow (1998), Gottman (2002), and Greenberg and Johnson (1988) have described similar interpersonal requirements in their writings, none seem to have identified client-specific relational needs as succinctly as the Needs ABC model.

The following list is, therefore, the result of the distillation of evident client needs-based themes into two groups: (1) primary needs, representing basic relational requirements (i.e., what people need from the "important" people in their lives; and (2) secondary needs, which are a corollary to primary needs, adding another dimension. Following the needs are suggestions for the concerns clients feel in their relationships (i.e., "FEAR"), the dominant need being expressed (i.e., "THEME"), and what they are attempting to acquire in the relationship (i.e., "NEED").

Primary

- Reliability (Availability)
  - FEAR: abandonment
  - THEME: conditional relationship
- NEED: emotional connection, constancy (consistency), and predictability

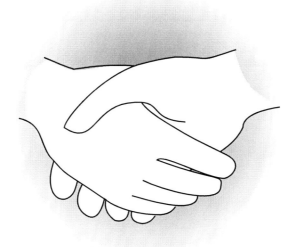

Figure 3.1   The relational need for a reliable relationship.

- Loyalty (Trust)
    - FEAR: being taken advantage of
    - THEME: betrayal
- NEED: trust, allegiance
- Respect (Self-Worth)
    - FEAR: being irrelevant or marginalized
    - THEME: invisible, unimportant, objectified
- NEED: acknowledgement, value
- Competence (Self-Efficacy)
    - FEAR: not being good enough, of failing
    - THEME: inadequacy, incapable
- NEED: adequacy, proficiency

Secondary

- Intimacy (Closeness/Distance/Trust)
    - FEAR: too much or too little emotional/physical space
    - THEME: suffocated, disconnected
- NEED: closeness or distance

Figure 3.2   The relational need for trust.

Figure 3.3   The relational need to be respected.

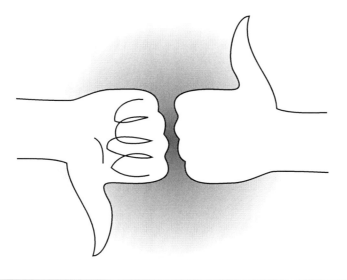

Figure 3.4   The need to feel competent.

Figure 3.5   A secondary need for more or less intimacy.

Figure 3.6   The secondary relational need for power.

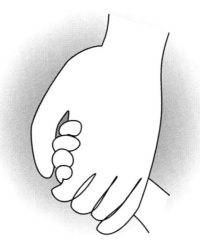

Figure 3.7   The secondary need to take more or less responsibility.

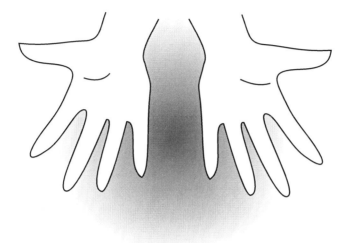

Figure 3.8   The secondary need for a time-out.

Figure 3.9   Less productive emotions. Presenting less useful emotions tends to drive problematic behaviors.

- Power (to Get Needs Met)
  - FEAR: loss of control, powerlessness
  - THEME: helpless, hopeless
- NEED: control of one's environment
- Responsibility (for the Problem)
  - FEAR: blame, culpability
  - THEME: environmental control
- NEED: safety, security
- Grief/Loss (a "Time-Out")
  - FEAR: change, acknowledgment
  - THEME: paralyzed, stuck
- NEED: acceptance, recognition

Most people consider the concepts of *grief* or *loss* as referring to feelings about those who have left them "forever" through death or circumstance. Inasmuch as this is often true, in the psychotherapy room this can also refer to a loss of confidence or identity. For example, if someone has to leave his profession because of age, infirmity, or a situation beyond his control, he may be unable to move forward and recreate an alternative "self" until he has adequately processed and emotionally dealt with his present situation. It is important to support the client's right to grieve and "stay put" until he is able to move on with his life. Here, the Needs ABC therapist will help to co-create transitional strategies that are productive but respectful to the client's state of mind.

Primary Versus Secondary Needs

Throughout this book I highlight clients' relational need by placing its name in square brackets. While most of the case examples focus on the primary need, I have also included some references to the secondary need implied in clients' narrative. Again, it is important to understand that the primary need is what clients are trying to attain through their behavior in their relationship. The secondary need can be regarded as a corollary to the primary one. For example, a man who has "competency" as a primary relational need may distance himself from his partner if he feels that by getting close he will be criticized or punished for what he does. This could establish a need for more "intimacy" on the part of the partner and less "intimacy" on the part of the man in question. The partner's feelings of "powerlessness" to get him to come closer may be another secondary need for both partners since, try as they may, nothing they do seems to be effective in getting their needs met. To determine how powerful, or important, this secondary need may be for each client, a brief developmental history can be taken. In taking such a history, the clinician must determine whether the present context is similar to or removed from what the clients remember from their childhood. If the present situation appears to be a metaphor for what I like to describe as "the ghosts of Christmas past" (borrowing from Charles Dickens), then the secondary need will be important for that client. A brief clinical example follows.

George and Lara came to see me with regard to what Lara described as George's depression: "George is just not himself anymore." Both had been married before and, until about 1 year before, felt that "things just couldn't get any better." After two sessions where I learned that George had failed in his last business venture and that Lara had always worked with George as his bookkeeper and financial expert, I decided to meet them individually to see what else I could glean with regard to their relationship and their past.

George informed me, becoming very tearful, that he thought Lara was having an affair [loyalty]. He feared that, because he was no longer the major breadwinner, she had lost her regard for him [competency]. He stated that "they didn't even hold hands anymore" [intimacy]. His developmental history corroborated his need for affection since he described his mother as being quite cold [intimacy], though dutiful, and his father as often absent, but very critical [competency] of all his children (he was the eldest of two brothers and one sister). He remembered often being promised a treat or a reward only to have his mother "forget" [loyalty].

Lara, who had been quite tight-lipped in both of the previous couple sessions, did not understand why he was so cold and withdrawn [reliability]. She told me that she felt extremely disconnected and almost invisible at times [respect]. She went on to tell me that there was nothing more that she could do and that he was the problem; in essence, Lara was not taking any responsibility for the relationship.

In this example, George's need is to be able to trust his wife [loyalty] and to be validated for his successes in their relationship [competency] since they, nonetheless, were able to continue to live a comfortable lifestyle despite his last failure. All he wanted "was a hug" [intimacy]. Lara, on the other hand, felt she no longer felt valued by George [respect] and felt it was his fault that she no longer able to prove her worth because "he sunk the business" [reliability]. It seemed, in that session, that she refused to examine any possibility that she could also make a positive difference in their relationship [responsibility].

Overall, treatment planning could include how to encourage George to pay more attention to Lara, who seemed to need it badly to begin to consider taking some responsibility for the potential success of the couple relationship.

It should be remembered that, even though we all have similar relational needs in general, what matters is not whether the need is experienced but how powerfully (viscerally) we react to it. For example, if I come from a background where I understood that trust was earned over time and that betrayal was a possibility that had to be considered, then if I am not paid back the twenty dollars owed to me by a colleague I will feel disappointed or sad but would chalk it up to experience and never lend money to that person again. I would understand that it was my choice to lend the money and that there was a chance I would not get it back. On the other hand, if I was extremely trustworthy and assumed others would be just like me then not being repaid would cause me to react quite strongly emotionally and I might even try to "get even" in some way (a visceral response).

So why have two sets of needs? And what do we mean by defining one set as primary and the other as secondary? The primary set succinctly describes specific client-centered needs that are important for them to acquire in all their relationships. Needless to say, the emotional currency becomes greater as the importance of the relationship becomes greater. In other words, husbands, wives, and intimate partners provoke stronger reactions than colleagues at work or mere social acquaintances. The secondary set can be compared to what an adjective is to a noun, or as a relational need corollary. For example, if "loyalty" is described as a relational need, one of the artifacts of this need could be a fear of trusting others enough to get closer—a fear of "intimacy." Alternately, if clients perceive their relationship as conditional ("reliability"), then the possibility of taking on too much "responsibility" to avoid abandonment may emerge, causing them to need to cede some of this responsibility for the relationship to the other. Let's look at an example.

Kristina, a 34-year-old receptionist for a large department store, was the eldest of four children by 3 years. Both of her parents worked long hours and overtime throughout her childhood and adolescence, which necessitated her caring for her younger siblings until at least one parent came home, from when she was aged just 9 or 10. She was responsible for heating up the meals left by her mother the night before and making the lunch sandwiches. She would even be asked to stay home from school at times if one of her siblings took ill and could not go to school. As a result of all the extra responsibilities she bore and the missed school days, she barely made it through high school and went to work at the age of 17, the day after her graduation. Kristina always felt that she could have done much better at school had she been given a chance.

Kristina met Ron a month after she turned 18 and had had three children with him by the time she reached 23. She began working as a receptionist after her second child was born. Ron made a reasonably good living, and she was able to work part-time, or take time off, when necessary.

When they presented for couples work, Kristina complained that Ron was spending more and more time away from home, having joined two soccer leagues and having a once-weekly "boys' night out." She felt like he wasn't pulling his weight with the children and that she never had any time to do anything for herself. Ron complained that she was always reminding him what to do—"Did you do this; don't forget that"—from the moment he stepped into the house after work. "It's just that I needed a break from all that pestering."

As the therapy progressed it became clear to all concerned that Ron wanted only for Kristina to trust him [loyalty] and to give him credit for his ability to follow through on his responsibilities [competency]. Kristina admitted that, because she had not been able to accomplish as much as she would have liked in her life, she tended to care for others, including her female friends. She stated she was always unconditionally there for all the people in her life and felt that they respected her for that. She did, however, feel that Ron was not always there when she needed him [reliability] and that he didn't pay attention to her [respect] the way her friends did. Because of the dysfunctional strategies used to get these needs met, Ron felt he needed to distance himself [intimacy] from Kristina's tendency to take too much *responsibility* for their relationship by "controlling him as if he was a child."

How Does Focusing on Need Enable Understanding?

The relational needs as listed are easy for both therapists and clients to relate to in the context of therapy, even when a discussion of needs presents in the personal narrative of only one member of the pair. While not everyone will experience the *same* set of needs and the associated emotions, the easily understood and accessible vocabulary used to discuss these commonly felt needs helps in reaching a mature discussion of issues that hitherto have been broached only in highly personalized, often hurtful ways serving to push one's partner's buttons and ignite arguments, litigation, and distress to both parties. Focusing on needs, as opposed to the behaviors that have created the need for therapy in the first place, helps to define what is lacking with respect to clients' relationships and what they have been trying unsuccessfully to get. Focusing on these relational needs versus the behaviors they have used in trying to acquire them encourages clients to take responsibility for what they want in the relationship and in their therapy instead of asking others to "do it for them." Focusing on need also minimizes the potential for clients to adopt a shame-based defensive posture and makes it possible for them to focus on the development of new strategies to generate more positive modes of behavior in the future. For the Needs ABC model, this means that therapy can help clients not only stop behaving in certain ways now but also create new behavioral patterns that will work for them in the future and that can help them to form a stronger, healthier, more respectful and durable relationship.

But how can the therapist help the couple that has come to him for help isolate unmet needs and discuss them rationally? How can he help both partners work toward a viable solution or set of solutions to the behavioral situation that has been causing problems in their relationship? Although often, if not usually, unmet needs are not specifically vocalized, they are likely to emerge as recurrent elements in clients' narratives—for example, when the same client says, "I get angry when my wife stands me up to go to lunch with her mother," and, later, "Fred agreed to discuss the project with me first but went ahead without my input. This isn't the first time he's done it, either." In each case, the client is expressing his frustration at what he experiences as his own marginalization, as his unmet needs are relevant to his emotional experience, regardless of whether they emerge as issues in the context of his personal or other relationships.

By focusing on needs, rather than on specific grievances or on given reactions to particular situations, it is possible for the therapist and the couple undergoing therapy to neatly side-step issues of blame and control and to concentrate instead on both the root cause of the problem and on ways of eliminating it, both now and in the future.

The role of development in relationships in forming the adult person is often very apparent when individuals model behaviors they saw enacted by same-sex parents. Of course, as children we learn from our parents and other caregivers how to behave in a relationship and how to be an adult. When the acquired behaviors are problematic (e.g., domestic violence, substance abuse, infidelity, rough "macho" behavior) or were appropriate in a parent's culture of origin but are less so in the context of the new family, they will generally continue to be problematic when they are recreated in the new couple. At the same time, as we have mentioned, opposite-sex parents are usually very formative in terms of the definition of individuals' relational needs as these emerge from childhood and continue into adulthood. Siblings can also play a role in determining how individuals' character develops, and exploring clients' relationships with siblings, particularly in childhood, can be a valuable source of information about the etiology and nature of relational needs.

It will be important to ask clients to describe their experiences during their earlier, preadolescent, developmental phase. Ideally, one will avoid leading questions or assumptions by asking questions like the following:

- How did you view your mom when you were in elementary school? What kind of person was she?
- How did you view your dad when you were in elementary school? What kind of relationship did you have with him?
- Do you feel that your parents have a favorite child? Who was it? Why do you say that?
- Are you more like your mother or your father? In what way?

- How did you get along with your sisters, brothers, and other important family members when you were growing up?

Spending a little time explaining why and how clients' developmental history is important is helpful in terms of understanding the nature of their relational needs today and will provide useful insight into their current situation. Knowing that the same developmental issues are also applicable to others with regard to their evolutionary background in the creation of relational needs and emotional patterns in adulthood will make clients' explorations of their past less personal and easier to approach from an objective point of view.

It is important to remember that unmet needs are often referenced obliquely, perhaps because the topic is too painful to confront head on, because clients lack or are not comfortable with an adequate vocabulary for discussing this painful subject. Some examples are as follows:

- "My wife is always saying, 'That's fine, but what have you done for me today?'" [competency]
- "I'm really not interested in what you have to say right now." [respect]
- "One day my wife says she wouldn't know what to do without me; the next she says, 'I need my space.'" [reliability/intimacy]
- "Why is he always confiding in his secretary and not in me?" [loyalty]
- "He insists that he loves me very much but has to play hockey or go out with the boys at least three nights a week." [intimacy/reliability]
- "No matter what I do, it doesn't work. I just want to give up trying." [power/competency]
- "I just can't seem to get off my behind. I never made this kind of mistake before. I just don't seem to want to do anything right now." [grief/loss]

In addition, the emotions described in clients' narrative are often those that are less productive but more socially acceptable.

By focusing on needs rather than behaviors, the Needs ABC approach makes it infinitely easier for the practitioner of therapy to arrive at the whys and wherefores of a couple's relational needs and why and how both partners have been failing to achieve them in the context of their relationship. Exploring the origins of these behaviors is also important, as it allows individuals to get to the root of the issue, to understand it, and to use this understanding in the creation of new, more useful behavioral patterns.

The Importance of a Client's Developmental History

Inasmuch as clients' relational needs can come from almost any stage in their development, in my experience focusing on the elementary school years of childhood is particularly fruitful in helping people understand why they feel the way they do in certain given situations and how their behavioral patterns developed in response to these feelings. While I am certainly not suggesting that the impact of events that occurred in infancy and toddlerhood is negligible, the imperfect recall or even complete absence of conscious, coherent memory of these years means that discussing them is not as likely to yield any interesting results that will assist clients in understanding themselves and their own behaviors better (Aylmer, 1986, 110–112; Greenberg & Johnson, 1988, pp. 77–78; Nichols, 2007, pp. 89–91). Instead, clients generally can remember the events that happened to them during the early years of childhood, from the age of 5 or so, or at least events that were particularly striking and impactful for them, and are able to discuss the strategies they used to deal with their relational needs in that early stage of development.

One technique I sometimes use while taking clients' developmental history is to ask them to "free associate" (Freud, 1960) about situations they remember during this period of time. With this exercise their relational needs may be further clarified since, in all probability, what they remember will relate directly to their current situation.

Later developmental stages, such as adolescence, can also be important. Of course, it is essential to explore any events that clients experienced as exceptional or traumatic, regardless of when they actually occurred. As well, a notable lack of memory of events that occurred during a specific time period might also signal an exceptionally difficult period for the client and might also indicate the witnessing or experiencing of abuse or trauma. However, especially in the earlier phases of therapy, when the therapist will, of necessity, play a stronger "leadership" role than later, when client confidence grows, focusing on the experiences of this phase of childhood can prove enormously valuable in understanding how the personalities, needs, and behaviors of adult individuals have been formed.

But Why Focus on Childhood?

Childhood is when we become ourselves—when our personalities, characters, and family histories merge to form who we are. Childhood is when both body and mind of individuals are formed. Anything that happens in childhood continues to reverberate throughout each person's experience of adulthood—particularly through their relationship with others, most notably their partner, which is usually, if not always, the most important relationship they have and the one that has the greatest impact on their sense of well-being. As children, we are firsthand observers of our parents', or parent figures', relationship with each other and with others, and from our parents we learn how to be in relation to our partner and others. The lessons we learn as children are very difficult to unlearn, because they represent "just the way things are" to us. When these lessons include the development of certain behavioral patterns—for example, tantrum throwing or social withdrawal—that continue into adulthood, often in a modified form, they can have a crippling effect on our emotional landscape and our relationship with the people around us, including those we hold most dear (Horvath & Greenberg, 1994, pp. 22–23; Jacobson & Margolin, 1979, pp. 59–64).

While in childhood those who parent us are the crux and focus of our relational attachments and most personal selves, in adulthood this role is overtaken by our life partners. This means that everything they do and everything they say to us can have great resonance. It also means that we will try to have our relational needs met not only in our relationships in general but, most importantly, also in the context of our intimate relationships. If this does not occur, often because our own attempts to acquire these needs are not functional, we are likely to react strongly and negatively.

Bonding with other human beings in significant relationships of various types is fundamental to the human condition. The instinct that babies and children have to bond with their own parents and family members is as strong as their drive to eat, except in the case of children with disabilities such as serious autism or with difficulties relating to very severe emotional deprivation in childhood. We are aware that, in some cases, children who have suffered a lack of human contact in their very early months and years—such as children in overstaffed orphanages or infants who have had to spend a great deal of time in hospital—are very likely to develop emotional problems as they grow up and in fact often "fail to thrive" physically, even when they are receiving adequate nutrition and exercise, which shows just how crucial warm human contact is to the healthy emotional and physical development of the human individual.

As we have already discussed, throughout childhood our most important relationships are with our parents and family members, and it is from them that we learn to be members of society, members of our family, and, indeed, full-fledged members of the human species. It cannot be too strongly stated that the relational dynamics in one's family of origin are crucial in forming the adult self. Easily identifiable coping strategies that emerge during childhood (because of the absence of autonomy in babies and infants, they cannot emerge until then) can become the basis of the dysfunctional behaviors that clients bring to treatment. Parents teach their children, implicitly as well as overtly, how they should behave in relation to others, "appropriate" gender behavior, how adults relate to each other in the context of a marriage or other significant relationship, and how to negotiate challenges such as work, the use or abuse of alcohol and other substances, and more. Everything they do is observed and can be replicated in their children's own adult lives. Let's explore an example.

Stanislaus grew up in a small town near Krakow, the only child of a mother who was a minor bureaucrat in the local town hall and of a father who was a school teacher. During the 1970s and '80s, Poland was still part of the Soviet empire; although most people had enough to eat and were adequately housed and clothed, "extras" were hard to come by, and for most people life was a question of getting by as best they could with luxuries and treats few and far between. Stanislaus's father was "Polish through and through," but his mother was of Russian origin. She spoke Polish, but Russian remained her first language and the one in which she was most comfortable expressing herself. Stanislaus grew up bilingual and, to some extent, bicultural. Although it was not always expressed directly, Stanislaus gradually became aware of some serious grievances in his extended family, especially toward his mother, who was a member of a rather privileged group in Poland at the time. Although she was not actually in a position of great power in their community, there did seem to be the suspicion that, because of her ethnicity and her role in local government, she could "report on" members of the extended family [loyalty]. As a result, Stanislaus remembers that, as a child, he often felt excluded from the wider family circle, which disapproved of his mother and made this disapproval felt in myriad subtle and not so subtle ways. She in turn was both defiantly proud of her ethnic background and resentful of her exclusion, feeling—quite reasonably—that her ethnicity was not something that she should feel ashamed of or need to apologize for.

In the early 1990s, the whole family emigrated to London, where Stanislaus's father worked as a taxi driver and his mother as a cleaner. Although his parents actually earned far more than they did in Poland, they had underestimated the cost of living in London and still found themselves going without "extras" far more often than they had envisioned when they arrived more than 10 years prior. Also, cast into a foreign culture, they both tended to become rather morose and somewhat resentful that, in middle age, they were both working in relatively unskilled jobs.

At the time of therapy, Stanislaus was a recent graduate of the London School of Economics, one of the most prestigious universities in the United Kingdom. He was a very bright high school student and managed to get by with a scholarship and by working part-time in a fish-and-chip shop. A year prior to therapy, he married his classmate Anna, and now the couple is, rather unexpectedly, awaiting the arrival of their first child. Although both partners, newly emerged from university, are still very young, news of the pregnancy was greeted joyfully by both sets of grandparents. Anna has been welcomed into Stanislaus's family and he into hers. However, despite all the goodwill, Anna's pregnancy has heralded what she considers to be very unreasonable behavior on Stan's (as he now prefers to be called) part. Both Anna and Stan report that their previously blissful marriage has become characterized by bickering, hurt overreaction, and a general sense that all is not well.

"I don't see what the big crisis is," Anna says, during one of their early therapy sessions. "OK, so we're quite young, but I have a trust fund, and my parents bought us a flat when we got married. We won't be stinking rich, but we'll have a lot more than most parents our age. No rent, think of that! And we're graduates; we're intelligent people. Everything is going to work out. But ever since Stan found out about the baby, he's become a *control freak.* He asked me to start keeping a note of every single thing I buy—even take-away coffee—so that he knows how much we're spending. It's crazy!"

To stress the seminal importance of the family of origin is not to say that one cannot move away from teachings received in childhood but simply that one should never underestimate the significance of upbringing on the adult person or attempt to dismiss problems originating in childhood with a statement such as, "It's time to move on from that now," or "But that was a long time ago and has nothing to do with where you are right now." Here, as well as reverting to the then necessary penny-pinching of his childhood, when Poland was still an element of the Soviet Union and times were tough, Stanislaus has begun to question whether he can trust Anna: will she be loyal, or could she betray him as, it seems to him, his family betrayed his mother? After all, just like his own parents, he and Anna are from different cultural backgrounds—a difference further compounded by the gulf between his and her families' economic status.

As mentioned earlier, people often come to therapy to deal with maladaptive behaviors that typically have their origin in childhood and that have evolved while they were actively seeking, as young children, to learn how to negotiate the maze of relationships that is our world. They are, in a sense, survival skills. For example, consider the man whose father abandoned the family when he was 6 years old and whose mother had to work two jobs to support the family, becoming less available to her child, because she was rarely physically present and, when she was, was too tired to engage actively with her family. If, in adulthood, his partner appears to be less connected to him than he would like, he will connect his present situation to his past and react accordingly, often with behavior that is seriously dysfunctional and damaging to himself and others.

It should be stressed that, while people who grew up in abusive or seriously dysfunctional families often need therapy in later life, even those of us who grew up in generally happy, reasonably affluent circumstances can reach adulthood with unmet needs that continue to impact our behavior in a less than helpful way. It is hardly surprising that the person in our life likely to be affected most by our words and actions is the one who is most intimately involved with us (Rowe, Gomez, & Little, 2007, p. 312; Sager, 1986, p. 328).

In tandem, feelings and emotion-driven behavior learned in the past and situations in the present can combine to create a painfully difficult emotional landscape, disabling the adult individual from being able to take an objective stance with regard to problem solving and frequently resulting in immature, maladaptive responses that aggravate the situation further and that can also render the unmet needs of the individual's life partner more difficult to deal with.

Clients' relationships in childhood and adolescence are key determinants in creating their relational needs when, as adults, they enter into a partnership. Clients who strongly express their hatred of "feeling ignored" will generally state that, as children, they were either "the center of attention" or "felt invisible." Similarly, clients whose parents had "a place for everything and everything in its place" may present as either perfectionist or disorganized, depending on how they saw each parent.

It is almost a cliché to state that the opposite-sex parent often defines important relational needs. This is certainly frequently but not always the case, and although this scenario should always be explored, the therapist should also remain open to other relational possibilities. Similarly, it is typical but not invariable for individuals to emulate same-sex parents in terms of obtaining control over their circumstances. However, it is safe to say that our experiences as children will affect how we behave in relation to others; this is one generalization that can always be made. Those who are excessively controlled as children may seek, as adults, to control the others in their lives, and those who experienced themselves as competent as children will wish to continue proving their competency in adulthood, even to the detriment of their partners. A common realization of individuals undergoing therapy as part of a couple is stated as follows, "Oh my God! I sound just like my mother/father."

Finally, at times it can be difficult to determine clients' relational needs, especially when working with an individual, because he or she presents information that can be construed in different ways or has difficulty remembering helpful details, or the therapist perceives several needs but none that appear significant. Carrying out an examination of clients' perception of their relationships with their parents (or parental figures) in their earlier development can clarify what is most important for them to get in their adult relationships.

More and Less Useful Emotions

The Needs ABC model considers that, while the explicitly expressed emotion is generally valid, there is an underlying emotion, more deeply embedded in clients' narrative, that is more useful to explore, often being more deeply felt and thus more difficult to verbalize. While Greenberg and Johnson (1988, pp. 4–9) classify primary, or the "here and now" (Greenberg, Rice, & Elliott, 1993, pp. 75–76) emotions, and "secondary emotions, or those that "often obscure the primary generating process" (Greenberg et al., p. 75), we use the terms *more useful* and *more productive* and *less useful* and *less productive* in the discussion of emotion in reference to the fact that, as in Emotionally Focused Therapy (EFT), the feelings underlying behavior can be multifaceted and that clients often find it relatively easy to vocalize their feelings relating to one of the emotions they are feeling rather than to the others.

However, in my experience, generally the emotions that seem to prove too difficult to speak about are frequently more useful to access in therapeutic terms. In other words, by enabling clients to access these deeply felt, difficult emotions, they often become able to understand the origins of their behaviors, to find the words they need to discuss their emotions and feelings, and to work constructively toward a new way of interacting with their partner. More simply put, emotions can be divided into two categories: (1) emotions that "call" people to action (active emotions); and (2) emotions that "dismiss" people from taking action (less active or more passive emotions). When active behaviors are problematic, such as violence or impulsivity, it would be better to encourage clients to access a less active emotion, one that might offer them some time to choose an alternative strategy. If passivity, inactivity, or compliance proves ineffective for needs acquisition, a more active or "energized" emotion could help with relationship problem resolution. Take the example of a woman who is the victim of spousal abuse. She may enter a shelter not knowing what to do next while presenting herself as frightened and helpless because of her partner's power. If this woman can also access the anger she has about being treated in this manner, she may then be able to consider alternatives to living this way, such as setting limits, accessing additional resources, or even leaving her partner altogether. To further illustrate, using the previous examples:

- "My wife is always saying, 'That's fine, but what have you done for me today?'" Here, the husband might react angrily (a less useful emotion) rather than acknowledge his fear (a more useful emotion) that he will never live up to his partner's expectations.
- "I'm really not interested in what you have to say right now." Here, the expression of sadness at being shut out might prove more productive than being irate at being "brushed off."
- "One day my wife says she wouldn't know what to do without me; the other she says, 'I need my space.'" Again, here we see sadness at feeling lonely when he feels disconnected or distanced from his wife could work better than hurling epithets about her lack of reliability.
- "Why is he always confiding in his secretary and not in me?" Even though this woman seems fearful of what else this situation might mean, if she were able to assert her position about her need to trust her partner, perhaps by getting in touch with her anger, she would be able to set limits more effectively.
- "He insists that he loves me very much but has to play hockey or go out with the boys at least three nights a week." Again, being more forceful with regard to her need for her partner to choose her over her friends would be more helpful than a barrage of tears.
- "No matter what I do, it doesn't work. I just want to give up trying." A more energized emotion like annoyance or anger might be more motivating for success than the apparent depressive state in this quote.
- "I just can't seem to get off my behind. I never made this kind of mistake before. I just can't seem to want to do anything

right now." When this client is ready—since he might have to take a brief time-out—harnessing an emotion, like fury, that pushes him out of his despair would be more useful.

Crucially, we need to understand that the useful paradigm refers to the emotion that will be more or less productive in problem solving *at the time of the situation in question*. Depending on the circumstances that arise, different emotions may need to be accessed.

Applying Needs ABC Paradigms to Therapy With Couples

Common Client Expectations Versus Client-Driven Treatment Goals

Clients may present for therapy with diverse expectations of what the intervention can do for them, and expectations may vary within couples, too. While some will think, "The therapist will tell us what we have been doing wrong and fix this situation for us," others may think, "This relationship is basically over already. I just need confirmation that we've really screwed everything up badly so that I can walk away and try to start over with a clean slate." Yet again, another person might think, "I'm not the problem here. The therapist will explain to my partner that his/her behavior has been causing us all these problems, and as soon as my partner understands this, we'll be able to get on with our lives."

It is the counselor's job to listen to what both partners in the couple are really saying, often in ways that are not immediately obvious, and to assess what their genuine needs and emotions are so that they can be helped to set their own, real goals and to work productively toward them. In the course of therapy, and preferably in the early stages, it needs to be communicated to the couple that no one individual can "fix" the relationship. While therapists can facilitate this journey, they cannot simply tell couples what to do and provide them with a tidy solution to all their problems. Helping couples find their own way toward viable solutions to the practical and emotional problems that have been besetting them is the core role of the therapist.

Behaviors Often Seen in Presenting Couples

Because the decision to attend therapy is often made in a highly stressful situation, it is far from untypical for couples attending therapy
to present with aggressive, passive, or otherwise difficult behaviors.
While these behaviors can present a challenge to therapists, they
can also provide very useful insight into the internal dynamics of the
relationship. For example, if one member of the couple talks, inter-
rupts the other, or dominates dialogue in an aggressive or threatening
manner, he or she is also sending a significant message that power
and control are important issues for that individual. Similarly, if one
member of the couple tends to get angry quickly, it may well be that
another, more useful, emotion is locked behind the angry façade.

Many marriage and family therapists have told me that their worst
nightmare is when couples begin to argue with one another, raising
their voices and "losing control." Many therapists are taught that, in
these situations, they must take charge of the session immediately by
directing clients to "take turns" (some even employ a "talking stick" to
hold when it is their turn) or to not look at each other and to address
their remarks only to the counselor. But there is a wealth of information in what clients are saying, especially when their emotions are at
their peak. When clients begin to bicker, argue, or fight (verbally;
potential physical danger must be addressed immediately), I sit back
and listen until I am able to glean the unmet relational needs they
seem to be expressing. Then, I will intervene with an emotion-focused,
needs-based statement describing the dynamic being acted out.

For example, when Nat and Fredrika came into my office, Nat
explained that Fredrika had planned on canceling the session but that
he had stopped her just in time. He went on to explain that she never
tells the truth and that she often hangs up on him when he calls her.
Fredrika reacted immediately in a moderately loud voice that what he
was saying wasn't true. Nat responded, equally loudly, that she has a
short memory and remembers only what she wants to. At that point
they began yelling at each other, and I was grateful that I had spent
money on good soundproofing and a good sound screen.

As the argument progressed, Nat made some scathing statements
about Fredrika's "history of sexual promiscuity." Fredrika responded

with the comment that he would not let her get a word in edgewise and that she was tired of constantly being interrupted and demeaned—especially if she did not comply with his wishes. After about what seemed to be forever to me but was probably 1 or 2 minutes I interrupted them by saying:

> Can I just jump in here for a minute? It seems to me that Nat has a lot of trouble trusting anyone [loyalty] and is very sensitive to being criticized [competency], while Fredrika feels that she is being pushed around [power, respect] and that she needs to always acquiesce to Nat's wishes [reliability].

Both remained silent for a moment, and then Nat started again to describe his concern about his partner's loyalty, though this time with a bit of a smile and with much less volume. I continued to support each of their relational needs as they continued to "joust," and each time they seemed to decrease the drama in their dialogue. By the end of the session they were prepared to examine both needs acquisition and needs provision and seemed more optimistic about the future of their relationship.

I call a smile "the recognition reflex." This means that both you and the client have a degree of understanding about what is actually going on; the client knows that you know.

Some Ways of Addressing Unmet Needs

Emerging Need and Emotional Components

Since one of the basic premises of the Needs ABC model for couples therapy is that some emotions are more useful than others, exploring these emotions, their origin, and their relationship with the subject's behavior will be useful in devising a way forward. Frequently, as we have discussed, more useful emotions are masked behind less useful, often more socially acceptable feelings. Socially acceptable feelings are generally emotions that are felt by the wider culture to be appropriate to individuals on the basis of their gender, social class, and ethnicity. Try as we might, few if any of us are able to achieve complete freedom from the way society feels we should behave, and this factor influences us all. For example, in many societies anger is considered a more acceptable emotion in a man than fear or sorrow, which are supposed to be weaker, more feminine sentiments. As a result, many men will feel able to verbally express and discuss angry sentiments and will find it difficult to expose what they see as their more vulnerable side. Conversely, many women will find it difficult to express anger, considered in many cultures to be unwomanly in its aggressiveness, so it may be masked behind apparent sorrow, fear, or anxiety. Helping clients to recognize and embrace the more useful emotions that lie behind their needs and the related behaviors is crucial. Let's look at an example.

> Joe explains that he and Sarah have come to therapy because of Sarah's drug and drinking habit, which caused her to display increasingly erratic behavior and to lose her job. In addition, Social Services has visited their house on several occasions during Joe's work trips away because she had been drinking and the children had been left playing in the garden on a cold winter's night on many consecutive evenings. The neighbors were all aware of Sarah's problems and were disturbed and upset by her neglect of her two young children. Although they hadn't wanted to interfere on the many occasions when they had seen her apparently drunk or on drugs, the general consensus on the street was that "enough was enough" when it looked as though the children might be harmed as a result of her negligence.
>
> "It just makes me so mad," said Joe, "to think of the bright, fresh young woman I married and what Sarah seems to be letting herself become. You know she has a master's degree in art history? She used to care about things. That's why I was attracted to her in the first place; she was so smart and articulate. I thought, 'Now here's a girl I can really respect.' Now she's drunk or sniffing coke half the times I come home, while the kids are just playing on the carpet in their dirty diapers. And that's on a good day. You heard what happened with the neighbors. I have to tell you, I just don't even recognize her anymore. I don't know who she is. I don't think that I can even trust her on her own with the children. Well, I guess I *know* I can't trust her, at this point. What if something terrible happened to the kids when she was supposed to be in charge? With her out for the count, it's not exactly unimaginable, and with her not working anymore, I have to take all the overtime I can get just to keep the whole ship afloat, knowing that she'll just take half the housekeeping money and spend it on drugs. Sometimes I just want to … I don't know … punch her or something."
>
> In fact, Joe *has* punched Sarah, on several occasions, although most frequently he just yells until both she and the children are in tears.

Reba, the couple's social worker, has already spent several sessions with Sarah and Joe. She knows that the couple had several very happy years and that, while Sarah had always "been inclined to have a few too many" and had always seen herself as "something of a party girl," she had started drinking seriously and also taking cocaine after a bout of postnatal depression following the birth of Jack, her second child. Reba learned from Sarah that she had difficulty in school, apparently from an undiagnosed learning disability. She also understood from some individual sessions with Sarah that her parents "loved her only if she got good grades" and felt they must have hated her for "rarely getting any more than a pass." Overall, it seems that Sarah felt that she never had any reliable relationship, one that she could count on unconditionally. Reba also suspects that Joe, in fact, may be terrified that she will never recognize his concerns about what is happening and is experiencing profound feelings of sorrow resulting from the effective loss of the woman he once married and her replacement with this apparent stranger whose behavior and habits seem to be destroying their family, along with all the hopes they both once held for their future together.

Needs and Emotion Versus Behavior

One of the primary elements of the Needs ABC approach is the emphasis on need and emotion rather than on behavior and the assumption that dealing with needs not currently being fully met in the context of individuals' personal relationships will facilitate the replacement of dysfunctional behaviors with functional ones. As therapy progresses, couples should be assisted in transferring the progress they are making in therapy to their everyday lives. As their understanding of themselves, their problems, and therapists' approach to them becomes increasingly mature and sophisticated, therapists can also become more explicit in their explanations of the concepts behind the Needs ABC model, especially the remark that when individuals behave in a dysfunctional way, they usually get exactly what they don't want.

When addressing clients, I often use an emotion that I consider more productive without explanation. In other words, if the client says, "I am angry at my wife for going to lunch with her mom instead of me," I might reply that "it must be scary to feel second best to her mother." The client can then decide whether that might also be an appropriate emotion to consider as more productive in problem resolution.

Focusing on needs puts responsibility on clients for getting needs appropriately rather than on others to meet them. Focusing on need minimizes shame—the shame of doing "shameful" things (to get needs met). For example, if the woman says to her partner, "You threw a tantrum when I had lunch with my mom instead of you" (or "when I forgot to call you back as I had promised"), it will be nonproductive to focus on the tantrum and more productive to focus on the need that is inherent in the comment [respect]. Once the need is illuminated, it is important for the partner to get his needs met productively by understanding that his "fear" of being unimportant is more productive than his "anger" at her forgetfulness and by communicating this need to her in a way she can listen. For example, the man in the previous scenario might respond by saying, "It's a bit scary when you stand me up for lunch or don't call me as you promised, since I feel that maybe I'm not important to you."

4

EXPECTATIONS FOR AN OPTIMAL THERAPEUTIC SETTING

The job of the therapist is to help couples make the best choice possible under the circumstances to improve their situation and to maintain their relationship in its new, "improved" state, not necessarily to keep them together. However, clients generally initially come to therapy with some hope of becoming able to stay together and of being able to find the joy and fulfillment their relationship used to bring them. Building strategies to enable themselves to maintain this status quo is frequently the happy outcome of therapy; certainly, it is the most satisfying one.

At times, however, enabling couples to separate amicably while causing the least possible distress to themselves and any children they may have can also be a good result. Therapy can help people in this situation to improve their skills of communication and co-parenting with respect to their spouse or partner subsequent to a split, and it can also make it easier for each member of the former couple to healthier new relationships in the future.

It is the therapist's role not to intervene actively in solution finding but rather to facilitate couples in understanding themselves better as individuals and as a dyad and in finding their own solutions. In fact, it has been my professional experience that the clients often come up with better problem-solving strategies than I can; after all, in most cases, because they have known each other for many years, they often can more readily discover what works best *for them*. However, to be enabled to devise these strategies, couples need a place away from their everyday lives, where they can focus on determining what they need, what they have been doing "wrong" thus far in trying to obtain their needs, and what else they can do to be successful in improving their relationship with each other. The role of the therapist is to enable this voyage of self-discovery, providing couples with a safe, nonthreatening environment in which to explore what are often very difficult and destructive emotions and with an emotional vocabulary they can use to help them access their partner.

En route to finding the way to that best possible choice, a few therapeutic premises will help the therapist to remain focused and on target, and these should be borne in mind in the context of any therapeutic interventions for couples. The Needs Acquisition and Behavior Change (ABC) model suggests the following:

- We tend to use whatever works at the time to solve problems in relationships, especially solutions that seemed to work earlier in our development, in particular during our childhood.
- When adults use behaviors that worked when they were children, these behaviors often prove to be problematic since as children we tend to act out, rather than verbally express, our needs.
- As adults we tend to want relationships that will give us what we had as children that felt good or that will give us what we were missing as children that will make us feel good.
- The Needs ABC Law of Relationships says, "Whenever we use a dysfunctional behavior to get what we want, we always get exactly what we do not want." Furthermore, exploring the etiology of the dysfunctional behavior can reveal a great deal about what it represents, as such behaviors usually represent the emotional needs that the client experiences as being unmet. For example, a person who feels that he is disrespected and experiences "respect" as a crucial relational need is likely to engage in "knee-jerk" responses and reactions of disrespect to emotional triggers.

These premises can also be communicated overtly to couples presenting for therapy, preferably in the context of their own self-discovery. For example, if Adam reveals that, as a child, he frequently resorted to tantrums to obtain attention from his apparently distant parents, he might be helped in making a link between this behavior in childhood and his tendency to "explode" whenever he feels that his wife, Natasha, is not awarding him the attention he deserves or is being dismissive of his feelings.

Getting to Know You: From the Telephone to the First Interview

A number of books on therapeutic intervention discuss the importance of the initial client contact, and most therapists would agree that this is a significant event, with the potential to set the scene for positive engagement with therapy (Johnson, 2004, p. 129; Nichols, 2007, pp. 35–58; Teyber, 2006, pp. 49–53). The first contact with clients (which often occurs over the telephone) can be just as important as the first session in motivating and encouraging them to take responsibility for their participation in the therapy or treatment as well as in helping them start to assume responsibility for the behavior or behaviors that have brought them to therapy in the first place. For example, in their research article on client engagement, Noel and Howard (1989, pp. 798–805) state:

> It is important to note that in this treatment setting it was expected that patients would proceed through the screening process before a decision was made about their acceptance for psychotherapy and subsequent assignment to a clinician. Patients were prepared for this process during the initial telephone interview and were unlikely to expect therapy to begin with the first visit to the Institute. Thus, some of the possible negative consequences of being transferred to a different clinician could have been moderated by the clear procedural expectations. In addition, a positive initial experience both with the telephone intake worker and the screening clinician, may enhance a patient's expectation of receiving help from the assigned therapist. It is possible that when patients feel they are likely to receive the help they want after the screening process, they begin to form a relationship to the institution, not just to the screening clinician.

Therefore, observing whether the individual calling to ask about the possibility of engaging in therapy as a couple identifies one or other member of the couple as the specific "problem" can begin the process of gaining insight into client relational needs. For example, when a client states something like, "We need therapy as a couple because we are having difficulties with my husband's obsessive working," or, "We are looking for therapy because my wife has been so unhappy since

> Even on the phone, clients need to feel like you understand what their needs are. Use emotion-focused, needs-based interventions whenever possible to set the scene for the first session. So, when the woman in the previous example states her concern about her husband's work habits, you might say something like, "It must make you angry to feel like your husband's work takes precedence over you" [loyalty].

our children left home to go to college," or, "My wife has just been acting crazy since she had a baby," the needs of intimacy, reliability, and power may be implicit. Of course, more information has to be gathered to make suggestions with a degree of certainty.

Clients can also make initial contact with therapists at the behest of social services, law enforcement authorities, or other official agencies. In these cases, as when a client rings autonomously, the same applies: listen carefully to what is being said, both overtly and between the lines.

Of course, the caller's identification of the presenting problem is unlikely in the extreme to be a full and complete analysis of the situation at hand (Nichols, 2007, pp. 35–38). However, it does give some insight into how the couple is dealing with—or, more saliently, failing to deal with—the more substantial underlying issues affecting each partner's relationship with the other or at least into how one element of the couple is attempting to understand things, and it provides a glimpse of the couple's current life situation and the practical issues that may be exacerbating their unmet relational needs at the current time.

Let's look at an example of how initial phone contact can go.

Sylvain called a therapist in great distress as, the night before, his partner of 10 years, Sophie, threatened to take their three children, leave home, and initiate divorce proceedings immediately. She also added that she would probably make it as difficult as she could for Sylvain to obtain joint custody and that she was, in fact, considering taking up residence in a distant city where he would rarely be able to see his children. In the course of a furious argument that lasted for several hours, she accused him of being emotionally distant and controlling.

"I don't understand what the problem is," Sylvain tells the therapist. "But this whole thing is freaking me out—I don't want to get divorced, that's for sure, and I absolutely cannot face the prospect of not seeing my kids—so I said the first thing that came into my mind, which was that I was prepared to go into therapy if Sophie felt that that might help. And she said, 'OK then, you arrange it.' And we stopped arguing, for the time being at least."

"It seems as though this has come as quite a surprise and you are feeling distanced [intimacy] and abandoned [reliability] by her. Many couples find therapy useful, and we can discuss in detail how we might be able to work with you and Sophie," says the therapist. "But perhaps, before we make an appointment, you can tell me why you think Sophie feels it's a good idea?"

"She just says we've grown apart, especially since we had our last child, and she's always accusing me of being cold and uninvolved. I don't know, I suppose this is our last attempt not to split up. I try to help out when I can, but she doesn't seem to feel I have done enough. No matter what I do, she says it's nothing. It's not that we don't love each other. I mean, she acts weirdly a lot of the time, often redoing what I have done, but I do love her and I think she cares about me, too."

"Well," says the therapist, "her sense of being unimportant [respect] in the relationship feels very real to her. I think that, despite your difficulties, it's very positive that you suggested therapy, since Sophie might feel that it's a step in the right direction toward the support she might feel you're not giving her. Perhaps she's feeling overwhelmed?"

"Yeah," says Sylvain. "Maybe. Three kids under 4 are a bit much, and Sophie is thinking of going back to work, which will make a lot of stuff even more difficult than it already is. We'll all be under more pressure then."

"Since Sophie agreed that it was a good idea to try therapy, I think that she is still prepared to give your marriage a chance for everyone's sake, so I'm looking forward to meeting you both.

Although Sylvain is clearly in distress and has also hinted at his own underlying long-term frustration and confusion, the phone call ends with his making an appointment with the therapist—a relatively optimistic note. Furthermore, in addition to placing therapy in a more positive light with regard to both partners' commitment to each other and to their children, the therapist has successfully managed to glean some indication of their individual unmet relational needs. From this conversation, it seems that Sophie is feeling marginalized and powerless (as was suggested to Sylvain) with regard to her role in the marriage, while Sylvain might feel abandoned and incompetent to "fix" the problem. It might also be useful to consider whether Sophie has lost her trust [loyalty] for Sylvain. In

It is sometimes a good idea to ally with callers by suggesting why they might be reacting the way they are. For example, the therapist could say, "Sylvain, perhaps your lack of support [respect] for Sophie is the result of your frustration at feeling criticized [competency] so often?"

the first session, therefore, the therapist could elicit some feedback on these possibilities.

Before he hangs up, Sylvain says:

Well, I'm glad I got in touch. You seem to understand the situation, and, hopefully, this will help us to work things out. I think Sophie will be relieved, too.

The First Interview

The importance of initial telephone contact notwithstanding, it is universally understood that all therapies require a screening interview, or assessment, to evaluate clients' status, state of mind, appropriateness for specific types of treatment, support, and so forth, as well as obtaining information about contraindications to immediate therapy, such as the presence of serious mental illness, domestic violence, or a substance abuse problem (Gottman, 1999; Jacobson & Margolin, 1979; Nichols, 1987). While couples in which such problems are present can benefit from therapy, it might be necessary to address these important underlying issues first. Meeting the couple together for the first time can also provide an interesting view into just how differently both people feel about the source of their problems (Gottman; Jacobson & Margolin; Nichols). Whereas a husband calling for the first time might say that his wife is unhappy because their children have left for college, the wife may tell the therapist in the screening interview that the problem is her husband, who is feeling threatened by her plans to return to full-time work after 15 years of working just part-time. They may both be right and wrong in equal proportions, but the underlying problem will invariably be the fact that each has certain relational needs that are not currently being met in the context of their relationship with each other. This is the root issue that will need to be explored in therapy, quite apart from any practical problems relating to their life and work situations and to specific circumstances they are currently undergoing.

The first interview with couples serves not just to obtain some basic information about them—although this is clearly very important—but also to start to build a rapport between couples and the therapist (Horvath & Greenberg, 1994, p. 7; Johnson, 2004), something that is crucial if couples are to feel like they are in a safe place where they can discuss their more intimate concerns and anxieties without risk of being blamed, ridiculed, or condemned for the things they do and feel (Gottman, 1999; Johnson). Even if the first contact is with just one member of the couple, the companion should be "present" insofar as the therapist broadens questions to include him or her in the course of the initial information gathering and keeps the focus wide, which might also include a suggestion of the other's relational needs—always important if couples therapy is to avoid sliding into a sort of one-on-one therapy session and is instead held in tandem, as it should be.

Because people are often angry and upset and even in a crisis situation at the point at which they contact a counselor, they may suggest that therapy is needed because something is wrong with the behavior or attitude of their partner while failing to recognize in any substantive way their own contribution toward the difficulties facing the couple. Their self-righteous anger can serve as a way for them to deflect their own attention from dealing with the difficult issue of what they may be doing wrong or how they may be contributing to an ongoing situation that is causing unhappiness to them personally and to their partner. By keeping the focus broad and inclusive and on their apparent relational needs "deficits," the therapist can help them not to fall into the blame game. The therapist can also work toward establishing a therapeutic environment that may be uncomfortable and challenging at times but within which the therapist is clearly identified as a bringer of stability and as a professional individual of insight.

The initial contact with couples may, in some cases, suggest to the therapist that some practical issues may mitigate against couples therapy for the time being or that other interventions might also be necessary concurrent with the therapy. If one or both members of a couple present with substance abuse problems, for example, or if one or both seem to be depressed, it will be necessary to formulate a strategy to help deal with these problems in addition to embarking on therapy or even before therapy begins. For example, in the case of substance abuse, a couple might be encouraged to attend a 12-step program as well as therapy, and in the case of a severe underlying psychiatric problem, the condition will certainly have to be stabilized and most probably treated with medication, possibly for the medium- to long-term. This is not to say that such issues are necessarily a counterindication to therapy per se but merely that the practical ramifications should be mitigated against first.

As well as working toward understanding the nature of couples presenting for therapy and obtaining information about their personal view about what has brought them there, initial contact is also the right forum for obtaining basic personal details including the point at which the presenting problem seemed to manifest itself, the level of education obtained by both members of each couple, the pertinent couple background information, the presence or absence of children in the family home, and their relationship with their children and the nature of other important relationships. All of these issues can be discussed in more detail as therapy proceeds.

Let's take a look at how an initial interview might take place.

When Sylvain and Sophie appear for their intake interview, they both behave relatively pleasantly toward each other, and both are courteous toward the therapist. The therapist notes, however, that while Sylvain is dressed rather smartly in formal pants and a sports jacket, Sophie is casually dressed to the point of being sloppy, with unbrushed hair and bitten fingernails that are not as clean as they should be. In fact, one of the first things Sophie says is, "I'm glad I have a good opinion of therapy, because it was so difficult getting organized to get here, what with the kids and everything. I was tempted to just stay home."

The therapist asks Sophie and Sylvain in turn to say a little about why they feel they need therapy.

"Well," Sophie says, "Everything was great until we had baby number two, and I stopped working. My salary covered only the child-care costs, and it just wasn't worth it anymore, between the stress and the pittance left over after dealing with the exorbitant fees the daycare place charges.

Then I got pregnant again—so much for the theory that breastfeeding is an effective contraceptive—and suddenly we had three kids under 4. All boys, too, and it's true what they say about them being more boisterous. It's a madhouse. All our wedding china has been broken. Of course, I love them all to pieces and I'm really glad that they're all here, but it's a lot of hard work as well. I have no time to get dressed up or really do anything but take care of the kids, and then Sylvain comes home in the evening after having had a beer with the boys and wants me to talk about politics or the latest winner of the Nobel prize for literature and have a nice meal ready, on the small housekeeping budget he seems to feel I should be able to manage with, and I'm there with baby spit on my shoulder, having spent the whole day singing the *Barney* theme song to keep them happy. It's all too much. There are times when I feel as if my brain is turning to sawdust, after a whole day of talking about *Bear in the Big Blue House* and playing with Play-Doh. That's not why I did a lengthy apprenticeship. This isn't the person I always thought I would end up being. Sometimes I just want to curl up and die or just take the kids and go somewhere I'm appreciated. I don't know—all I know is that I want everything to be different."

Sylvain says, "It's not really like she says. She decided to give up work, and I thought the decision made sense so I supported her decision and also accepted that I'd have to work plenty of overtime to pay for everything on my own. With more than one kid, the cost of daycare is too much to cope with on Sophie's salary anyway. Plus, Sophie's a cook, so she can always go back to work later on if she wants to. It's not like she doesn't get plenty of practice at home anyway. I'm in programming; even a year out of the business could have a really bad impact on my future career. But for now I'm the one earning the money, and, as it's difficult enough paying for everything, surely I should have a say in how it gets spent?"

The therapist says, "You've both given me some good insight into the practical issues that are facing you as a couple and as a family. I think that, as we explore your relational needs and how you are each trying to get them met in the context of your relationship, we will find that the solutions to these practical issues become easier to see. Initially [turning to Sylvain] it sounds like you feel connected to Sophie only when you do things on her terms—and even then it isn't good enough. I guess a cool beer after work seems like a refreshing option compared with coming home to someone who's ticked off with you even before you've put the key in the door. But Sophie seems to be feeling that your loyalty is elsewhere and that no matter how hard she tries to get your attention about this it seems to fall on deaf ears. Just so that I can get to know you both a little better and to learn a little more about where you are coming from, perhaps you can each tell me a little about your backgrounds—the families you grew up in."

What is important to consider at this point is the inevitable fact that just one member of a couple is involved in making the first

Clients' historical family information can be extremely effective in helping them to understand the evolution of their relational needs and their importance in the context of their present situation. The use of family background information will be described more thoroughly in Chapter 7.

telephone contact, even if the decision has been discussed and agreed upon at home. In doing so, that person becomes the spokesperson for the couple or for the problems the couple is experiencing. This may be because the person perceives the current situation as more stressful or because, in the dynamic of the person's personal relationship, he or she typically plays a more active role. However, it is necessary to establish early that the therapy is for *both* members of the couple—for the couple as a unit. Both members of the couple should be acutely aware that they are as respected and listened to as their partner. Even if one member of the couple is more expressive or interactive than the other, it is essential to avoid lapsing into a situation where it can appear that sides are consistently being taken with regard to uncovering their unmet relational needs.

How to Use the Needs ABC Model

The Needs ABC approach focuses on the relational needs that lie behind unhelpful behaviors and on the emotions that perpetuate these nonproductive strategies. It also places a clear emphasis on the acquisition of more useful behaviors in light of having achieved a better understanding of how these emotions work and why certain needs exist in the client. In consequence, the Needs ABC model can be applied literally, in terms of helping clients to define their relational needs and to recognize more productive emotional states to devise better strategies for finding them in the context of their personal relationship. Let's look at an example.

John is the adult child of two very successful academics. When he was little, his parents had to focus very strongly on their respective careers, but his mother did spend a few years working part-time to care for him and his

I sometimes tell clients that, unlike the lack of power to change a given relational situation that a child experiences, as an adult they can relay their needs to their partner and can negotiate around them. We would then collaborate on strategies for doing just that.

sister. As a consequence, her career path faltered somewhat, and she did not receive promotions at the same rate as her husband. Although things have gone well for her, she has never quite caught up, and for an ambitious, competitive person this has always been a source of some stress. While she has never overtly suggested that this was in any way the fault of her children, John sometimes felt guilty, as if he were to blame that she did not receive tenure until 10 years after her husband. Also, although John works in a highly skilled white-collar job, he suspects that his parents would have been much happier had he followed them into academia, as he was "supposed" to do; in fact, he abandoned a Ph.D. halfway through and spent a few years rather aimlessly deciding what to do with the rest of his professional life.

Because John has always suspected that some of his choices have been a little disappointing to his parents, he tends to be both defensive and to "show off" in conversation. His wife, Amy, often feels that it is difficult to "get a word in edgewise" and that he is trying to belittle her views and opinions to bolster his own.

In therapy, John arrives quite quickly at an understanding of the origins and nature of his relational needs. Together with his therapist, he works on finding a way to obtain feelings of worth and recognition within the context of his career and his relationship with his wife, without resorting to acting out the feelings that have lingered in him since childhood.

The Needs ABC model can also be invaluable when wielded as a tool to make interventions that help to join with the client. Consider the following example.

Alessia has struggled for years with feelings of inadequacy resulting from what she sees as the submissive role she was forced to play in her family as a result of being "not as pretty and not as smart" as her younger sister, Robin. As a child, she dealt with these perceived inadequacies by acting out, initially by misbehaving and then, as a teenager, by regularly getting drunk or high.

"It must have been horrible feeling that you had to go to such lengths just to get noticed," commented her therapist.

By consistently encouraging clients to come up with their own suggestions rather than being overly directive by offering advice, a metaphor of client empowerment is created.

"It did; I really felt as though I was invisible unless I made a big fuss about things. Only then did they seem to notice me."

"As an adult, can you think of any other ways that might be useful in making the people you care about realize that you need a little support?"

The Needs ABC model can be used as a way of listening to make interventions based on your own, or other therapy, model. By focusing on difficult behaviors and on the unmet needs behind them, the therapist and client can work together to understand the emotions involved.

Roger has had a long battle with alcoholism. He has been in Alcoholics Anonymous (AA) for years, and his drinking had remained under control until recently when his mother, now aged 60, told him that she was terminally ill with cancer. Since learning of this, Roger has been drinking again and has even started being verbally abusive to his wife, Stefanie. "I'm afraid that one day I'll want to hit her, and I won't be able to stop myself," he says.

An exploration of Roger's relationship with his mother reveals that, when he was 10, his parents divorced, and his father was awarded primary custody. Roger felt then that his mother had willfully abandoned him and his dad; in fact, divorce proceedings had started because of an affair she had had with a colleague. While he and his mother did establish a very good relationship during his teenage years that has persisted to the present, the knowledge that she is going to "leave"—because she is seriously ill with only a year or two to live—has awoken all the feelings and behaviors he experienced as a child in relation to his parents' divorce. The difference is that, now, the brunt of these difficult behaviors is being borne by Roger's wife, Stefanie.

Understanding the origins of Roger's behavior will facilitate his work with his counselor toward dealing with his relationship with alcohol and, by extension, with his wife and with his mother, as she faces her final illness.

It is difficult to remain abstinent just for abstinence's sake. If clients understand what needs they have sabotaged with their substance abuse and that they can be more productive in the acquisition of their relational needs in "sobriety," then they might be more motivated to remain abstinent to pursue their relational goals.

Maybe problems seem easier to cope with—more manageable—when they have been given a name. The Needs ABC approach uses an accessible vocabulary that provides clients with a means to discuss the issues that have brought them to therapy succinctly. Consider the following.

> George has had persistent difficulties controlling his temper throughout adulthood "and even before"; his bad temper has, on occasion, prompted him to engage in destructive activities such as smashing all the dinner plates in the house. Now that George has children—18-month-old twins—he is very aware of his short temper and is afraid that one day he will "lose it" and do something that he might regret, perhaps even hurt one of the children.
>
> The fact that George has been able to identify a potential behavioral problem in such a way indicates that he is already a good candidate for therapy. However, in the earlier sessions, he seemed completely baffled when he was asked to consider the reasons behind his behavior. Knowing a little about George's background, his therapist did have some hypotheses. Mooting one, he said, "It seems to me that you often feel powerless to get control of your environment and that to be in control is a big issue for you; it's scary for you if you feel that you can't handle any situation."
>
> "That's true," said George. "And there's more to it."
>
> By introducing concepts in ordinary language in this manner, the process of talking about feelings and behaviors becomes largely demystified and much more approachable.

With a focus on unmet needs and the less productive emotions that lie behind the behavior, the Needs ABC model enables people, as individuals and as couples, to understand why they are doing what they are doing that has been causing them problems personally and in their relationship. With this knowledge, they are better equipped to learn a new and more productive approach.

Working "behaviorally," especially in the initial stages of treatment, is often counterproductive to problem resolution in couples. Discussing the inappropriate behaviors will tend to activate defense mechanisms in each client by increasing the vulnerability each already feels in knowing right from wrong. Highlighting both partners' relational needs will make them feel understood by the therapist and their partner, paving the way to supportively challenging their less productive behavior later.

Keeping the Ball Rolling

Early in the development of therapists' relationships with their clients, it is also necessary to obtain certain basic information about where couples are "at" in terms of the evolution of their relationship. This will help therapists to arrive at a basic working hypothesis related to precisely what has brought them into therapy:

> The early phase of the treatment is devoted to refining the therapist's hypothesis into a formulation about what's maintaining the problem and to beginning to work on resolving it. Later, the strategy shifts from building an alliance to challenging actions and assumptions. Most therapists are able to figure out what needs to change; what sets good therapists apart is their willingness to push for those changes. (Nichols & Schwartz, 2006, p. 66)

Problems that were rarely expressed or that did not seem to be that big of a deal can suddenly come to the fore when a significant shift in couples' circumstances occurs. The possibilities are endless: a new baby, the loss of a job, a mother's (or, less frequently, father's) decision to give up work or go part-time to spend more time parenting, the loss of an elderly parent, the marriage of someone who shares parenting with one member of the presenting couple, an affair, grown children leaving for college—the list goes on and on.

We all define ourselves largely in relation to the people around us, and this is also true of couples. When something happens to the significant others in our lives, our personal identity and our identity as a couple are altered, and what once seemed like small differences can acquire new magnitude. Behaviors we previously found tolerable, acceptable, or even charming in our partner suddenly seem infuriating. Imagine the couple in which both parties have always worked, only for the mother to give up her job when twins are born. While the decision makes sense, at least for a few years while the children are small, she may resent the loss of social contact at work, may feel on some level that her status in the relationship has been diminished and that her dependence on her husband is belittling, and may on some level resent her spouse for enjoying the freedom and financial autonomy she feels are no longer hers. At the same time, as in the case of Sylvain, the man may feel like, now that he has the chief earning power in the household, he should get to decide how and when household money is spent or at least have greater input on this matter than his house-based spouse. To a certain degree, he may also feel that his wife's status in the relationship has been diminished, although he may find it difficult to admit this "politically incorrect" view, even to himself.

Then again, think of the middle-aged father whose only remaining parent suddenly and unexpectedly dies. While he is still relatively young, he is forced to accept that, in his family, he now represents the "older generation," and he is suddenly obliged to reassess his self-image while also dealing with the fear of mortality that is common to us all. These feelings, and a sudden surge of anxiety about aging, may prompt behaviors such as spending an excessive amount of time away from his family, in the company of friends who are supposed to help him "feel young." This could lead to a situation where he returns home late, often drunk, defensive, and upset, to an angry, tired wife who does not understand the reasons behind his behavior and who may, in turn, engage in behaviors intended to teach him a lesson but that serve only to exacerbate the situation.

These stressful situations more and more often prompt couples to explore the possibility of therapy for the first time because they feel like they may be nearing the breaking point or on the verge of splitting up or because they are both quite simply deeply unhappy in their relationship and think they need some outside help to make it better. When children are involved, there may also be feelings of duty toward the larger family unit, and people may say things like, "We don't want to split up for the children's sake; we really want to keep this family together."

In fact, couples therapy often helps parents to maintain the family unit or, at worst, to find a way of separating that is as easy as possible for the children, who are the shared responsibility of the couple in question. It should, at the very least, help couples make an informed decision about the future of their relationship rather than allowing them to be led by emotions and behaviors that are unhelpful in the extreme. The therapist might take advantage of the earlier encounters with a new couple presenting for therapy to assure both of them that experiencing discomfort or anxiety around major life changes is perfectly normal and that seeking help in these situations is a sign of strength rather than of weakness. Let's look at a case study.

Olivia and Sean arrive together for their first interview with their therapist. The appointment was made by Olivia, who said over the phone that their once happy marriage had become almost intolerable since Sean had taken early retirement from his job at the bottling plant. The plan was for him to start a new career; in his early 50s and in excellent health, he was certainly young enough to do so. Normally, a man of Sean's age would expect to work for another 15 years or so. As well, his early retirement package had included a substantial payout from the company, which was enough to open a small business. Before, Sean had often said that he would enjoy running an Italian deli. He had a passion for good food and really enjoyed preparing elaborate meals at home. He had even taken some courses on wine tasting and Italian cuisine and definitely had flair in that area. But instead, Sean had taken to "lurking" in the house. Olivia said that he seemed to be very unhappy and was taking it all out on her. As she works largely from home as a realtor, the constant brooding presence of an unhappy, self-doubting husband was both distracting and disturbing, and she felt that they never had any time away from each other at all. Her work was suffering, and their relationship with each other had taken a serious turn for the worse. "We seem to be almost incapable of having a respectful conversation with each other anymore."

During the first interview, the therapist turned to Sean and asked him why he felt they needed therapy.

Sean shrugged. "I don't feel that we do, frankly," he said. "Obviously, it's kind of because Olivia is feeling insecure. A woman thing, perhaps. The menopause, maybe? Then she went crazy when she saw me looking at a girly magazine. I'm just a normal guy, and I don't think it was such a big deal."

Olivia had not mentioned anything about "going crazy" or about being annoyed with Sean for looking at a "girly magazine."

The couples therapist can see that Olivia is getting angry, so he intervenes.

"I see that Olivia is quite upset about what is happening in your relationship," he says mildly. "All I know is that Olivia mentioned that you had both been having some difficulties in your marriage and that she felt that you could do with some outside help. Perhaps we can start by you, Sean, telling us a little about yourself and about how you see what is going on in your relationship."

Sean told the therapist that he had originally come from Boston but that he had grown up in Chicago, the member of a fairly large, blue-collar but reasonably "comfortably well off" family. He had married Olivia when they were both quite young, and they had raised a family together. Their first child had been born "9 months to the day" after their wedding. Both of them had always worked, although Olivia had gone part-time for a few years while their children, Ashley and Joe, had been little. Both children had now grown up and left home and had a good relationship with their parents although, as each lived in a different, distant city, they did not see them very often and remained in contact every few days by email, telephone, or instant messaging.

"I would describe myself as a pretty good provider," Sean said. "I had to start working young, when Olivia got pregnant with Ashley. Early on, it was just unskilled work on the assembly line, but I was good at it and was good at getting on with the bosses. I went up through the ranks until I was area supervisor. In the early years, Olivia was just doing 10 hours a week at a convenience store, so my paycheck was the main one. Then we got taken over by Coca-Cola, and they offered me a redundancy package. It was generous enough, and I don't see why I shouldn't take things easy for a while before I decide what to do. I've worked all my life; don't I deserve a little time off? Olivia is working—she never bloody shuts up about it, actually, and I have to watch TV with the headphones on in case I distract her from her oh-so-important work—and there's no pressure."

Next, it's Olivia's turn. Olivia describes how they have always been happy throughout their 33-year marriage, at least until Sean lost his job.

"Sean was always great," she says. "Early on, I just did a bit of waitressing and things, like the convenience store stuff, just to help out, and he was supporting the whole family while I did the Mom thing. Then he supported me for a while, while I was training to get into the realtor business and even for a few years while I was getting established. It wasn't really until I was in my early 30s that I started bringing home a good salary. And I've often told him how much I appreciate all his support. I always did; I still do. But ever since we heard that Coca-Cola was taking over the plant, he's been like a bear with a sore head. I've been tip-toeing around him trying not to set him off on one of his rants, and at the same time the housing market has been going crazy and I've been working really hard. The money's really been coming in, too. Last year, I took us both on a luxury cruise in the Caribbean for Christmas. It's true that we're fine for money and that there's no need for him to rush back to work, but it's like he never does *anything*. I come home, the house is a mess, the dog hasn't been taken for a walk—nothing—and then one day last week, it seemed like the last straw. I had been working late, and Sean had said that he would cook supper. I got home at 8. The house was dark, and although the heating had come on he had forgotten to close the windows and it was cold. In fact, I thought he'd gone out and just left everything like that. Well, I was pretty annoyed—and hungry, too. I started looking for one of those flyers the pizza people stick under the door so that I could ring for take-out when I heard a noise from upstairs. I found Sean in my study. He'd made a big mess of my desk, and, to top it all off, he was sitting there reading *Playboy*. Well, I don't really care about *Playboy*; at that moment, though, feeling cold and tired and hungry and pissed, it was like the last straw, and I really let him have it. Since then we've been down each other's throats the whole time."

Although very little has been said yet, both Olivia and Sean have given the therapist several "ins" to what may be the origins of their problem. In listening to the narrative, the therapist has had to focus on a number of things: not only the explicitly stated problems of Sean's boredom and loss of identity after leaving work and Olivia's feeling that she is not being supported and respected but also the deeper, underlying emotional component of the situation described and the needs embedded within. From what Sean says, it is clear that a crucial part of his identity was always the value of his role as a provider. He was supportive of Olivia when she was at home with their children, and he has been working since he was very young. In fact, Sean has spent 30 years of his life working at the same bottling plant, building up friendships and alliances and a sense of self that was intimately connected with the organization. When the company was taken over by a larger group, he was no longer needed. Suddenly, no longer is he "the provider" for his family; in addition, he has lost daily contact with the many people who have been, in their various ways, almost as close to him as his own family members. At the same time, Olivia has been blossoming as a person and as a professional. From being an almost full-time, largely financially dependent mother, she has become a successful realtor. As she points out, she is now in a position to support Sean, and she feels that if he is not working he should be doing more around the house, as she did back when Sean was the main breadwinner.

While early therapeutic sessions focus to a large extent on understanding what the problems are and on gaining some insight into their origins, it is also important to recognize what couples expect from therapy, to alleviate any anxieties they may have, and to determine why they have chosen this precise point in time to explore their relationship in a therapeutic context.

It seems clear, from the initial contact, that both Sean and Olivia are having trouble adjusting to Sean's new role in the family. Sean is proud of Olivia's success in her white-collar job, but he is also resentful of it and a little taken aback at finding himself reduced to a feeling of dependence by what he sees, on some level, as his wife's "superior" achievements. He had to go out to work when he was still very young and was so busy providing financially for his wife and children that he ended up spending three full decades in a bottling plant performing an endless series of rather monotonous tasks. While he has achieved a lot, it is also undeniably true that his job and his family responsibilities have prevented him from exploring other avenues he might otherwise have ventured down. When Sean's job was taken from him too, it felt like the last straw. Sean's feelings of loss—loss of his value and respect as a colleague at work, as a hard worker, as a competent provider, and as the one who was able to "take care of his family no matter what"—seems to be the key presenting issue for him. For Olivia, it seems to be her feeling that she has lost the emotional connection she once had with Sean and betrayal that he is no longer helping her "carry the ball" with regard to their family. The therapist suggests to Sean and Olivia that, before the next session, they both consider the accuracy and pertinence of the suggestions made as to what they seem to need from each other before considering ways they can meet their relational needs. In the first session, it is important to highlight for couples the "possible" unmet relational needs that have brought them to therapy in the first place. These can then be verified by examining their individual families of origin—in other words, their preadolescent relationships with their individual parents.

Client recollections from the "latency stage," or elementary school years, are taken both because this is a "verbal" stage and because clients in this period are usually unable to challenge their environment in a productive manner. As a result, they often bring these "survival strategies" into adulthood that are, more often than not, dysfunctional in adult relational problem solving. These recollections will help to confirm client relational needs and help them to understand why they react the way that they do.

While considerable information can be acquired from presenting couples in the early stages and hypotheses can be formed about the origins of the unhelpful behaviors that are damaging them, it is also important to remain flexible and alert to the new information that will invariably emerge. Understanding the nature and etiology of the unmet relational needs of clients is key to the Needs ABC approach to couples therapy.

5

USING THE NEEDS ABC MODEL IN COUPLES AND FAMILY THERAPY

At this point I would like to examine some commonly understood therapeutic principles in light of the Needs Acquisition and Behavior Change (ABC) model's approach to working with couples and their families. As we know, in all clinical modalities—including couples, family, individual, and group—it is important to have a clear understanding of what it takes to do good clinical work. Generally, these qualities can be divided into the following components: session phases; client stages; facilitation versus leadership; pacing; awareness of clinical process (self and other); and the ability to stay on track while storing information for future use. However, what it takes also transcends practical knowledge and know-how.

We would all agree that the primary qualification for couples and family therapists is the ability to tap into their reserves of empathy, a quality that must be worked on steadily throughout their professional career. Training, formal qualifications, and research are important, of course, but even more crucial is the ability to use one's instincts and sense of common humanity in any interaction with clients. Without empathy, therapists' ability to truly understand and provide insight into others' problems is severely limited. The Needs ABC model facilitates this process and reduces the possibility of building client–therapist contextual resistance.

Understanding Family Background

Practitioners are aware that we all receive our first lessons in how to be one half of a couple from our parents, or parental figures, starting with our earliest interactions with them and continuing through childhood and adolescence. This is as true of same-sex couples as it is of heterosexual pairings. Even when both members of a couple grew up in happy, functional families and had generally very good relationships with both parents, differences in the ways their parents related to each other and the views and behavioral patterns that the people attending for therapy acquired as a result can become problematic in the new dyad they have formed with their coming together. Citing the work of Murray Bowen, Nichols & Schwartz, (2006, p. 116) point out that there is "… no discontinuity between normal and disturbed families, but that all families vary along a continuum from emotional fusion to differentiation."

One Needs ABC strategy is for the therapist to help couples explore their family backgrounds, without judgment or suggesting that one way of being a pair is better than another, and to help them to understand how and why these have impacted how they behave in their own personal relationship with regard to their relational needs and the emotions they have predicted. We have already looked at the great importance of the family of original in the development of the individual. Helping people understand their own backgrounds is, of course, very important. Let's look at an example.

Kate is a guidance counselor, and Sam is an engineer. Both are 28 years old. They met at university as postgraduates and have been together ever since. While Sam earns substantially more than Kate, they are both doing very well in their chosen careers, and there is no reason to think that this situation is likely to change. Both are bright, mature, driven individuals. Their marriage is not in a crisis situation, they report, but they are becoming increasingly irritable with each other, bicker often, and feel that until this situation is resolved it would not be responsible to start a family, something that each longs to do.

"For me," says Kate, "the problem is that I feel that Sam doesn't respect my job on any level. He wants to use his money to pay the bills and the mortgage and suggested that I save my salary for pin money and vacations. Once he even proposed that I set some of it aside to 'spend on pretty shoes.' I can't even begin to tell you how insulting that is. I'm getting really upset and angry right now just thinking about it. I'm not earning as much as he is—not yet, anyway—but my job is not just a silly little hobby. It's something that took me 6 years to train for, and it's something I take very seriously indeed. And I like to think that it actually makes a difference to the world, beyond, oh, I don't know, building another damn highway bridge or something."

"Kate is just so damn touchy," Sam interjects. "I guess you see what I mean, right? That outburst? Of course I respect her job. It just seemed to make more sense for me to take care of the big bills, because I have more money coming in, and I probably always will. And I don't see what's wrong with being a good provider anyway. If we're going to become parents, won't that be a big part of my role? Maybe even the most important element of it."

Kate raises her voice. "This is just the sort of thing I'm talking about! This assumption that I'm going to be baking cookies with the kids on my own all the time while he's hanging with the guys at the office. I don't want to have a child with Sam unless he's going to pull his weight. So what if we have a little less money? Surely having a good life with one's family is more important than being able to own three cars? Who says that *I* have to be the one to give up a career I love while he gets off on being the mighty provider?"

After suggesting some relational need possibilities—respect (that Kate might feel that Sam doesn't value her contribution, that her contribution is irrelevant) and loyalty (that he would choose "the guys at the office" over her) for Kate and competency (that his suggestions for sharing couple responsibilities are inadequate) and reliability (that unless he does what she wants she will remain unhappy and emotionally disconnected) for Sam—the therapist asks Sam and Kate to stop discussing what they consider to be the presenting problem for now and to revisit their family backgrounds, which have already been discussed in some detail in the course of earlier sessions. While there is a practical dilemma at hand, it seems likely that it is the symptom, rather than the cause, of what is really troubling their relationship. He gathers the following information.

Sam and Kate both grew up in very happy families. Sam's father was a minister, and his mother, a stay-at-home wife who enjoyed taking care of her large family, was a very competent cook and housekeeper and was actively involved with a number of voluntary associations in her area. They enjoyed a good relationship, were overtly affectionate in front of their children, and, Sam feels, taught him much about how to have a happy marriage.

"Mom was at home," he says, "but that doesn't mean that Dad was the boss, ruling the roost and telling her what to do. They were each in charge of their own space, and, boy, did we kids know it."

Kate's parents were also happy. With two children, they both followed academic careers. Kate grew up in a small university town in the American Midwest—the sort of place where children could play outside unsupervised all afternoon. Like Sam's parents, her mother and father were clearly affectionate and fulfilled with each other and in their relationship. Kate's mother, a sociologist, was an avowed feminist, who raised her daughter to be fiercely independent.

"Not working was never an option for me," says Kate. "Mom taught me that women have to be able to stand on their own two feet, and that's a lesson I agree with. That's what I would want for my own daughters."

While both Sam and Kate rightly regard their parents as positive role models for a happy relationship, they have not quite understood how there are different ways to be happy, all of them perfectly valid, or that they need to find their own model for behavior as a couple rather than attempting to duplicate precisely the sort of families they experienced as children. Understanding how their family backgrounds created their perceptions of couplehood will be of great assistance in their quest and will be a good starting point for therapy, with ample opportunities for the therapist to help them to distance themselves from their own specific situation and to draw insight from their backgrounds.

The Importance of a Safe Working Environment

Inevitably, therapy is a place in which painfully difficult issues will be discussed, dissected, and explored; however, couples who have found the inner strength to seek help for their problems need to feel secure that their therapist's office is a safe place insofar as they will not be punished, regardless of the complexity and even, at times, downright nastiness of the sentiments that they might need to discuss. A detailed exploration of one's inner self and of one's limitations and even failings as a couple is always going to be difficult, and there will certainly be times when both members of the couple feel emotionally drained, upset, or strained and times when they must express feelings or beliefs that are flattering to neither party to the relationship. In these situations, an experienced therapist will know how and when to give couples "a break" from the painful topics under discussion so they can recharge their emotional batteries and return to the subject when everyone has had a little time to calm down. We will be discussing a few techniques pertinent to acquiring this ability in due course.

A technique I often use to help my clients "take the office home with them" in their problem-solving efforts is to mention my name as an introduction to a request for problem solving. For example, if I suggest that a couple meeting (which we will discuss in Chapter 7) be arranged after the children are in bed to resolve an issue, the individual requesting the meeting might say to his or her partner, "*Caplan* suggested that we meet when we have an issue to discuss with each other, so ..." In this way, it is possible to recreate the safety zone represented by my office in the domestic environment, at least for long enough to carry out a discussion of the issues at hand—specifically their unmet relational needs as formulated in the therapy session.

Speaking from my own experience, I can cite instances of how, in the safety of my office, I have asked couples how they each feel about a given situation and they have replied, after discussing it honestly and in some detail, that they have not spoken about the issue before this. The safety zone represented by my office provides a forum for mutual disclosure that is simply not available to them at home. They know that in my office their partner will not run away, that they will be listened to and heard, and that they will be provided with the opportunity to brainstorm or negotiate around the problem, regardless of how difficult or how unpleasant the process may be.

Shifting Focus

Initially, and as early as possible in the first session, the therapist's task is to shift the communication from the couples' views of the behaviors that have brought them into therapy to labeling the relational needs that have predicted these behaviors. Then, as the relationship between the therapist and the couple develops, the focus of therapy should facilitate an exploration of why and how these behaviors evolved, based on the clients' unmet relational needs, and how new, more productive ways of interacting with each other can be forged. If the therapist encourages and supports a relational needs discussion, couples will feel safer in their environment by examining what they want relationally rather than what they feel as though their partner has done *to* them. This strategy will also allow the therapist to gain some distance and give couples space to engage with each other more spontaneously in the safer environment of the therapist's office. Since, invariably, flawed communications have contributed in large part to couples' need for therapy, this approach will also provide an opportunity for them to relearn how to speak to each other in a meaningful way.

One of the tools I often find useful in the context of providing therapy is projective techniques or displacement (Nichols & Schwartz, 2006). One tactic is to describe another personal situation that may provide the presenting pair with some useful insights. Let's explore an example.

George and Sheila started attending therapy in the wake of problems arising from George's discovery that Sheila was having what he calls an "online affair" [George's feeling of betrayal] and what Sheila refers to as "just a bit of fun [her need for unconditional acceptance]—nothing serious." Apparently, Sheila had looked up and found an old flame from her high school days, and the pair had been enjoying a rather steamy email exchange, which George found one day when he was, as Sheila put it, "snooping around my private business without even asking." Sheila's online paramour is living in New Zealand, while Sheila and George live in Portland, Oregon. Her insistence that there was no plan to actually take her flirtation further seems more than likely. This is George and Sheila's third therapy session, and, for the third time, they have resorted to bickering and arguing, with very little productive work being done. Clearly, this is a cycle that will have to be broken very quickly in therapy, if the couple is to be enabled to learn and to take these lessons to the wider world.

Their therapist intervenes by saying, "I'm reminded of another couple I know—we'll call them Max and Emma. Emma found out that Max had bumped into his old girlfriend at a work conference and that they had been exchanging emails and meeting up for coffee for a few weeks. Now, Max hadn't actually done anything wrong, but I think Emma was badly hurt that he hadn't told her that he was meeting this woman [Emma's feeling of betrayal]. All three had gotten to know each other at their former workplace, and it would have been expected for Max to mention something. Emma wouldn't even have minded him meeting his ex for coffee. It wasn't so much that Emma thought that Max was likely to do anything wrong; it was the idea that he didn't seem to feel able to share with her the fact that he had been communicating with this other woman."

"That's very similar to the situation I'm in," George says, turning his attention from his wife to the therapist. I bet Emma thought, 'If she's keeping this from me, what else don't I know? Is she planning to have an affair? Has she had an affair before? How will I ever be able to trust her again?'"

"Or," Sheila interjected, "Max might be thinking to himself, 'Emma hasn't so much as looked at me for weeks without complaining about something. Sometimes it seems that I just exist to give George something to complain about [her feeling that George is happy with her only when she does what he wants—a lack of reliability and a feeling of incompetency]. He never even suggests that I might be attractive and interesting or that I might occasionally do something right. It's just nice to have someone pay me the occasional damn compliment for a change!'"

In this case, by removing the glare of attention from Sheila and George's specific point of conflict and exploring the circumstances of another couple, both are able to acquire some perspective and make appropriately self-disclosing comments without arguing. From the slight distance awarded them by the focus on the other couple, they are able to communicate some very important information to each other.

Being Aware

Keeping in mind that that couples, more than anybody else, can communicate with each other in myriad subtle ways that are not easy for the outsider to penetrate, being aware of what people are really saying to each other between the lines is extremely important. This means being acutely aware of what Bateson referred as "report and command," (Ruesch & Bateson, 2006, p. 180) or, as Nichols and Schwartz (2006, p. 19) summarize:

> All communications have two different levels or functions—report and command. Every message has a stated content, for instance, "Wash your hands. It's time for dinner"; but, in addition, the message carries how it is to be taken. In this case the second message is that the speaker is in charge. This second message—metacommunication—is covert and often goes unnoticed.

These second messages or metacommunications being an intrinsic part of the way human beings communicate with each other, especially in the context of their intimate personal relationships, is exceptionally important in using the Needs ABC model. Thus, by paying detailed attention to what is being conveyed between the lines, one can learn a great deal about needs, emotion, and the balance of power in any couple. Let's look at a case study.

Guy and Tricia present as a fairly traditional, blue-collar couple from a medium-sized industrial city in the Midwest. Tricia used to be employed as a hairdresser in a busy salon downtown, but she stopped working when she realized that she was expecting their second baby, in part because the cost of child care was almost as high as her modest salary but mostly because, like her mother and grandmother before her, she simply believes that a mother's place is in the home, taking care of her children.

Tricia is dressed in very "feminine" clothes, wearing a pink dress and small, delicate items of jewelry. With her very youthful face and her bobbed curls, she almost looks like a little girl playing dress-up with her mother's clothes.

Guy is making quite a good living working for a demolition company. He is a man of great affection but few words, who enjoys watching television with his wife and meeting up with his friends to talk about football, a simple pleasure he engages in less and less now that he is taking on so much overtime. The couple lives next door to Tricia's widowed mother, but Tricia explains that "she doesn't have a lot of time to help out, especially because her back is bad." They have decided to come to therapy because Tricia recently realized that, with her second baby just 6 months old, she is already expecting their third child. This situation is causing quite a bit of stress, especially for Guy, who feels that they are already barely making ends meet as it is and who had been under the impression that they had agreed not to have any more children until they could afford to buy their own place rather than renting.

"She told me she was on the pill," Guy says rather wearily. "I would have taken precautions otherwise. I don't understand why she let this happen; I trusted her, for heaven's sake. That's pretty stupid, huh? We can barely afford to pay for things as it is. I'm the only one working, and my salary goes only so far. How many times is she going to do this to me? Not one of our children was planned, and we're only 25. She could keep going for another 20 years. Am I supposed to pay for 20 kids?"

Tricia's response is to start to cry and cradle her as yet unswollen abdomen in a gesture of what seems like unnecessary drama.

"My mother always warned me against you," she says, addressing Guy but speaking loud enough for the therapist to hear. "She always said that you'd never amount to anything."

"I'm working all the hours that God sends," says Guy. "And it's all for you and the children. You have to know that I really love you all, and of course God knows I'll love the new one too. Work is going well, but maybe if you hadn't given up work to stay at home it would be a little easier or even if you hadn't gotten pregnant for a third time so soon after the last one. Sometimes I feel like I am carrying the world on my shoulders." Guy looks exhausted after what is an uncharacteristically lengthy speech for him.

"Oh," Tricia intervenes. "And who was going to help me take care of the kids? You, I suppose? Well, I'll believe when I see it, and not a moment before."

While, ostensibly, Guy is in a more powerful situation, being the only member of the couple to work and support the family and the only one to go out regularly and engage with the wider world, Tricia is, very effectively, sending him some serious signals about her own realm of power within the family. While she feels that she should be at home with the children, it seems far from unlikely that she may have used her own fertility to underline Guy's relative powerlessness over whether their family grows. Both Guy and Tricia report that the issue of birth control is "left up to her." She hints both obliquely and overtly that it is her belief that he is not "much of a man" if he feels overwhelmed at the prospect of supporting their rapidly growing family at the age of 25. This puts Guy in the painfully difficult situation of being effectively unable to speak when he feels the need to discuss areas where he may sometimes feel vulnerable and weak. Tricia has cast herself in a position of feminine frailty and, ironically, is using this supposed frailty as a very effective weapon in her arguments with her husband. Their counselor will have to remain acutely aware of the real issues of power that lie beneath the apparently straightforward division of labor along gender lines observed by this young couple. A Needs ABC therapist would automatically understand the power struggle extant in getting their relational needs met and take this into consideration when evaluating their possibilities for functional needs acquisition as the treatment progresses. Here the therapist might identify that a need for *loyalty*, or feeling betrayed, is something Guy is missing in light of the "surprise" second pregnancy. As well, Guy might feel that she is marginalizing his concerns and will not listen to reason. Tricia, on the other hand, might feel that she cannot do anything right in Guy's eyes and feels emotionally abandoned when she displeases him.

Being Objective

Complete objectivity is probably almost impossible for any human being to achieve, and therapists strive to be aware throughout the therapy of their own presuppositions and assumptions about appropriate behavior and sensible views for couples and individuals. However, before referring out to another helping professional, let's examine how the Needs ABC model can help couples and family therapists achieve as high a degree of objectivity as possible. Again, let's look at an example of how difficult it can be to maintain objectivity in the clinical environment.

> Levi, the therapist, is from a secular Jewish background with a mathematician father and doctor mother. His father, in particular, is an avowed atheist, and Levi grew up in an atmosphere where anything his parents considered excess faith or superstition was ridiculed in no uncertain terms. As an adult, Levi is broadly in agreement with his parents, but, as a therapist, he often has to work closely with people whose belief systems can be very different from his own. Usually, this doesn't present a problem, but Levi is about to realize the boundaries of his own objectivity.
>
> On this particular occasion, the couple attending therapy strongly identifies as New Age. They have a 3-year-old daughter and, in the course of therapy, have mentioned to Levi that whenever their child is ill they take her to a crystal therapist "before we let any doctor set eyes on her" and that, in any case, they have a strong preference for aromatherapy and similar treatments over conventional Western medical treatment, which they see as exploitive and "filling people up with chemicals they don't need."
>
> Levi is appalled by this information. Although the couple has been making very good progress with him, and he likes them personally, he finds this nugget of information to be gnawing at him until it is the first thing he thinks about every time he sees or even contemplates the couple. Soon, he finds himself dismissing far too easily their ways of expressing themselves and thinking uncharitable thoughts about their naïveté. After a few more sessions, the couple terminates therapy, saying that the vibe wasn't good anymore, which Levi accurately interprets by understanding that the couple had realized that he had become rather judgmental of certain choices of theirs. It is difficult for Levi to admit to himself that, this time, he has not given his clients the attention and respect they deserve, but on making the admission, he resolves not to allow his judgment to be similarly clouded in the future. Instead, he determines, he will remind himself that, even though he may disagree on some very fundamental levels with another's worldview, they are in no way a lesser being.
>
> If Levi were a Needs ABC therapist, the task of maintaining objectivity would be made easier by maintaining a focus on each client's relational

need—not on the behavior that, in this case, was about using nontraditional medicine and other treatment modalities. He could, in fact, inquire as to how each of them feels about this stance and why they are, or are not, in accord with each other on this issue. In addition, he could, upon recognizing his diminishing objectivity, examine his needs with these people and what historical data might cause them to be pushing his buttons—that is, causing him to move away from the concrete to the emotion-focused needs that might be clouding his judgment.

As it happens, the next week, a couple subscribing to a minority fundamentalist faith presents for therapy. As their faith is very central to their identity, as individuals and as a couple, it is mentioned several times in the course of the intake interview. To say that Levi's first, internal reaction is not charitable is understating it. Both partners also mention that they are raising their children within the faith and that they hope that they will grow up to become good members of the community. Privately, Levi winces. His personal views about literalist religious beliefs are anything but flattering, although he has no reason to have any specific problems with the polite couple sitting in his office. But he has learned from his shortcomings in this respect in the past, and he will not let them interfere with his role as therapist this time. Again, by focusing on their individual relational needs and examining more potentially constructive emotional responses, his objectivity will be enhanced, and his own needs with relation to the people presenting for therapy will be diminished.

It has been argued that there is no such thing as complete objectivity. However, things that can enhance our objectivity in all clinical settings include the understanding of cultural issues, gender awareness, and our own biases and prejudices. Staying focused on client relational needs within the context of the therapeutic relationship can diminish these one-sided interpretations. So, as the husband and wife began to explain to Levi what their presenting problem was, he was able to put his religious preconceptions aside by focusing on what was missing relationally in *their relationship*.

We understand that, overall, it is always important to treat the client with caring, empathy, and respect, regardless of the problem at hand. Regardless of, for example, clients' level of education, political views, intellect, or ethnicity, a deeply felt appreciation of their common humanity and essential worth is crucial. However, at times cultural or other differences will pose a challenge to communication. This can always happen. It does not need to be a problem or a barrier to the provision of effective therapy, though.

Couples today, more than ever, negotiate a potential minefield of confusion about who should do what and why, and changes in the way men and women approach work, child care, and the shared duties of

I usually ask couples directly if I have a query about a religious or cultural situation, hoping to engage both members in this discussion. This can provide another "in" to client relational needs as well as promoting insight and serious, honest, and useful discussion. A useful adage to observe is, "When in doubt, ask."

the home mean that it is no longer possible to consider simplistic or stereotypical notions of gender appropriateness. Because an understanding and acceptance of changes in gender roles and of the fluidity of gender-related behaviors is important, a Needs ABC approach will keep the therapist from being too subjective because of rigid gender stereotypes, be they traditional or feminist, and can minimize the potential damage caused when clients' realities are out of sync with how an ideological practitioner feels the world should be. A Needs ABC approach will help both men and women in therapy to feel free to broach and discuss emotions not stereotypically associated with their gender without fear of ridicule or criticism, especially from the therapist. For that matter, a relational needs approach can support them in expressing their feelings when these *are* stereotypically associated with their gender, even if they suspect that this is "politically incorrect." It will not matter what political, sexual, or racial standpoint clients embrace since the relational need will be theirs regardless of how they live.

Being Respectful

We would all agree that the issue of respect is closely bound to that of objectivity, since having respect for others, regardless of how different they may be from us, means being able to see other people's views and beliefs from their standpoint rather than our own. As we have seen already, we may not always agree with other people's life choices or religious or political views—inevitably, we will often find ourselves in violent opposition to them—but effective use of the Needs ABC approach will help us to serve our clients properly as therapists by respecting them as human beings as well as respecting their right to hold views utterly at odds with our own.

> When Natasha and Simon arrive for their first therapy session, Julia has a hard time reconciling her first impressions of the pair with the fact that they are a couple. Natasha is about 30 years younger than Simon and is a walking advertisement for all the latest plastic surgery interventions; she looks like a Barbie doll. Her pregnancy "bump" seems completely incongruous on her silicone-enhanced body. Simon is a well-preserved, well-to-do man in his 70s, who unashamedly refers to Natasha as a trophy wife and who also seems to have had recourse to the surgeon's knife. Julia is not sure whether Simon's comments about his wife are meant to be tongue-in-cheek. Either way, she is finding it difficult to respect the choices of this apparently very different pair, whose views on life seem to be completely at odds with her own.
>
> Natasha and Simon are expecting their first child; in fact, this situation, and the changes it has wrought in their relationships, is what has prompted them to attend therapy. For Natasha, this is her first baby, but Simon already has a family, grown and now in their 30s with offspring of their own. Natasha feels that Simon "isn't excited enough" about the impending arrival, whereas Simon, for his part, is afraid that he isn't going to know what to do with his new baby, because the last time he became a father was so very long ago and he feels that times have changed and that he will no longer know what he should be doing. "In those days," he says ruefully, "nobody expected the father to be there at the hospital when the baby was being born, let alone do anything like changing a diaper. That's the type of parenting I'm used to: hands-off. But they tell me it's all different nowadays, and Natasha says she won't let me get away with my old, lazy ways."

Julia is going to have to set aside her assumptions about this couple and learn how to respect them as individuals and as a pair. Their concerns are not just strongly felt but also very legitimate, and if they are to be able to share the parenting of their new baby well they will need her help. Remembering that what is important here is to focus on their needs as a couple—what is missing and what they want from each other—she takes a deep breath. Julia senses from the dialogue exchange that while Simon is afraid he will not live up to Natasha's "new world" expectations for parenting Natasha is fearful that she might just be a "trophy wife" after all. She says: Well, it's wonderful that you have found the strength to come to therapy because you're both going to be very tired after the baby is born, that's for sure.

As therapy progresses, Julia will examine Natasha's apparent need for respect and loyalty (can she trust him to be there for her?) and the perception that Simon is afraid of disappointing [competency] Natasha for fear she will be angered [reliability].

Understanding Cultural Issues

Our world is becoming increasingly globalized. One of the by-products of this is that most developed countries, and many less developed ones, are home to people from many different cultures, with correspondingly different mores, traditions, and ideas about appropriate behavior in a wide range of circumstances and despite cultural differences, relational needs are not bound to one particular culture or another. Providing therapy to couples from cultural backgrounds very different from one's own can be a challenge, and things can be even more complicated when both members of a couple are from different cultural origins. Let's explore an example.

> Siobhan and Igbe have been married for 2 years and live in Dublin, Ireland. Igbe, an accountant, works in computing for a big American multinational in the city. He moved to Dublin from Nigeria, via London, and he is very much the global citizen, at ease in most respects in most cultures.
>
> Despite that Igbe has moved to Europe, he remains in close contact with his family at home, communicating with his parents and siblings most days by email and at least once a week by telephone. Igbe is also an active member of a local cultural group that meets every 2 weeks to enjoy Nigerian food together and to arrange cultural events.

Figure 5.1   Things are not always what they first seem to be.

Siobhan is a pediatric nurse. Aside from a trip to Nigeria to meet her in-laws shortly after the couple married, she has traveled from Ireland only to visit Spain on vacation.

Both partners explain that they are very happy together but that now that Siobhan is 5 months pregnant and they know their baby is going to be a boy, they have run into some problems.

"It all started," Siobhan explains, "when Igbe mentioned that 'of course' the baby was going to be circumcised. I said, 'No bloody way; over my dead body,' and he just went mad. Then it was like the floodgates opened. He keeps finding things wrong with the way I do things, just because I'm not his mother. This is Ireland, and I don't see why I should know how to do things like her. After all, we're from different cultures. I don't even like plantains. Look, I'm not saying that their culture is any worse than mine, but it's different. Well, I suppose I think that maybe my culture is better in some ways. Here, we don't circumcise boy babies. None of the hospitals would do any such thing. It's considered mutilation. I don't want to chop pieces off my perfect new baby."

Igbe tries to adopt a patient expression, but he is clearly exasperated by what he considers to be a profoundly unreasonable approach on Siobhan's part. "OK, first things first," he says. "I've been a really patient guy. I'm not Catholic, but I agreed that the baby would be baptized in the family robes—the whole deal. And have an Irish name too, although nobody in my family is going to be able to pronounce it and despite that our family tradition is for the first son to be named after the grandfather. That's all OK. But in Nigeria, a baby boy is expected to be circumcised. If he isn't, it's seen as dirty. We're going to be going to Nigeria to see my family every year. They'll be shocked if I don't do it. She doesn't seem to understand that it's so important. And it's true what she says: since our first argument, we've been finding more and more little differences between us—the way we do things, think about things, see things. We really love each other; that's not the problem. But did we underestimate what a big thing all these little cultural differences would turn out to be? And what else lies in store for us?"

Here it seems that issues around loyalty and respect are extant for Igbe [feeling betrayed that the importance of the circumcision is being marginalized by Siobhan] while competency and reliability are core topics for Siobhan [he will not acknowledge that she knows what's best for the child and becomes emotionally disconnected by virtue of his anger towards her when he feels she is wrong]. Igbe appears to be offended that Siobhan does not respect his cultural beliefs and those of his family in Nigeria, and Siobhan seems upset that Igbe appears to be putting conditions on their relationship and also to be disrespecting her cultural ideals. As well, there is the possibility that Igbe feels betrayed by someone he thought he could trust, whereas Siobhan feels that her thoughts on what would work best in their new world have been denigrated. Both the couple and the therapist may benefit from a general exploration of the cultural differences between Siobhan and Igbe's family, before moving on to a more specific discussion of their personal grievances with each other.

Conclusion

Although every couple is distinct and unique, human beings experience emotions and develop behavioral patterns on the basis of a relatively limited palette of important relational needs. The focus in the Needs ABC model is on relational needs and the emotions they predict, their origins in childhood, and coping strategies that emerge from them. A good understanding of all of the implications of this focus is essential to the effective implementation of the Needs ABC approach, and this, consequently, is where we will turn next.

6

Unconscious Factors and Relational Needs

Couples who present for therapy usually do so because the dysfunctional behaviors that have arisen in their dyad are causing difficulties for them, are ensuring that they are not as happy or content as they would like to be or as they feel they could or should be, or are even leading them to behave in ways that may be seriously physically or psychologically damaging for them both. Often, they fear that these unresolved problems may be leading them inexorably toward the end of their relationship, regardless of how strongly they may feel that they still have the potential to be happy together. It may be that these problems always existed on some level or, more likely, that a change in couples' circumstances, such as the birth of a new child or a new working situation for one or both members of the couple, have caused underlying tensions and unmet needs that were always there but that heretofore did not cause significant disruption to couples' relationship. Often, the difficulties causing couples such distress are also creating unhappiness and confusion for members of the larger family, in particular any children couples might have. As such, they may well be setting up a self-renewing cycle of damaging behavior that could be perpetuated throughout generations if nothing happens to halt it.

In most cases, both couple members are very aware of the importance of "fixing" whatever has gone wrong, although typically couples begin therapy with a focus very much on each other's behavior and specifically on the aspects of each other's behavior that they do not like and that they feel are damaging to themselves personally and to their relationship as a pair. For this reason, most couples begin to attend therapy in a crisis or, at the very least, highly stressful situation; frequently, high levels of antagonism, bitterness, regret, and anger are demonstrated, often to the point where any meaningful communication has become impossible. Reaching a stage where couples can discuss their feelings and needs with each other at home and together with their therapist without becoming distraught, enraged, or detached is essential. In fact, it is one of the most crucial steps that can be reached because the alternative is, quite simply, no meaningful dialogue at all.

The description of these self-same dysfunctional behaviors by each partner, discussed in conjunction with the identification and analysis of the feelings that accompany them, contains the key to discovering their relational needs. Understanding the underlying relational needs that have been having such a significant impact on their behavior and on their relationship with each other will help them to find a way to work with them in a manner that is productive for the couple. It is essential for couples to understand that, unless unmet needs are identified and explored and unless a new, better way of meeting them can be found, difficult behaviors will not simply disappear. Therapists who use the Needs Acquisition and Behavior Change (ABC) model will find that they are generally able to identify the underlying need in clients' narrative, as it will most frequently arise when problematic behavior is discussed with references to a less useful emotion. For example, a man might say that he is "pissed off" at his partner, because it is easier to admit to than, "I'm afraid that Joyce doesn't care about me." In this case, anger is the less useful emotion, and fear is the more productive one; the client's underlying need is for reassurance that he is important and valued.

While couples frequently present for therapy because of dramatically problematic behaviors that are threatening the well-being or even the continuing existence of their relationship (e.g., violence, substance abuse, emotional abandonment), the Needs ABC approach maintains its focus on needs rather than behaviors, *regardless of how unpleasant the dysfunctional behaviors may be*, assuming that (in the absence of serious mental illness or another such counterindication), once needs are identified, understood, and addressed in a healthy way dysfunctional behaviors will no longer seem necessary or, at least, will be easier to isolate, discuss, and deal with rationally. (It goes without saying that, if one or both members of the couple face a risk to their physical well-being in the home, as in the case of a violently abusive spouse, this situation must be dealt with on a practical level before couples therapy can commence). Equally, however, couples who are not presenting with any seriously damaging behavior but who are making each other deeply unhappy anyway can also be effectively treated using this method.

One of the important aspects of this approach is that, by and large, it bypasses the unhelpful emotion of shame often provoked by a focus on less than appropriate behaviors and allows couples to discuss and problem solve around what they, as individuals, need from each other to become and remain a functioning, healthy couple. With this in mind, therapists will need to use their reserves of empathy and, in each instance, to consider, "If I were my client, what would I be thinking right now?" They must also remember that more than one label can be given to a specific situation and that individuals can be feeling more than one emotion and experiencing more than one relational need at the same time while, in fact, the emotions that they feel able to discuss earlier frequently represent the more socially acceptable, but less useful, element of their feelings.

It is also essential to bear in mind that it can take time for couples to find the right vocabulary to express an emotional component adequately and to identify which relational needs are the most important and which emotional components are the most useful. Not every couple will—or should—progress at an identical rate to every other couple or along an even trajectory. Just as each couple's relationship is unique, so will be each couple's progress through therapy.

Therapists who listen, in the context of therapy, to couples expressing their relational needs can validate and acknowledge what has been stated by verbalizing in their own words what they have heard and by using an emotion-focused, needs-based statement to do so: "Rob, it sounds to me as though it must be pretty scary to feel that you might be seen as expendable by Theresa when you tell me that Theresa makes decisions by herself that affect the whole family and presents you afterward with a *fait accompli*. I guess it's sad to think that, at times, she feels that your opinion just doesn't matter at all." Therapists can also maintain focus on clients and their life experience, recognizing that clients' needs can be met in various different ways as long as this occurs in a manner that is meaningful to them while also being respectful of the needs of their partner. For example, in a situation where a stay-at-home mom has recently seen her youngest enter high school, the therapist might reflect, "Alyssha, I know that George seems to be a tough act to follow, always traveling for business, a successful one at that. But George's success certainly doesn't diminish any of your own very real achievements. Perhaps now that you have more time for yourself, you could do something outside of the home that would make you feel more needed since both you and George both feel that your relationship is going well now." Here the therapist, anticipating the possibility that Alyssha's need to feel competent and respected might resurface and impinge negatively on her marriage unless she finds a way to meet this need, asks Alyssha to consider something outside of the relationship that will be fulfilling now that her children are less dependent on her. George had felt that it was up to him to fill that gap but could not completely do so because of practical reasons—work. They did negotiate more time together, and George agreed that he should give up some responsibility for running the home. By helping Alyssha find a feeling of competency outside of their relationship, she might feel more confident that she has a "fallback" position relative to her children's developmental stage: separation and individuation.

Projection

Projection, or *projective identification*, is another important consideration that Needs ABC, and other therapists, should consider when working with couples systems. Therapists, while assisting clients in their understanding of which emotions are extant in their narratives, should also bear in mind what they represent in the context of their relationships and their personal life histories. Normally, we define projective identification as the process whereby an individual projects his or her emotions, beliefs, and thoughts onto another (Klein, 1946).

The Needs ABC model identifies three types of projection concepts within the aforementioned rubric:

1. Needs projection. This assumes that we all want from others what we give to them. For example, individuals who are extremely loyal and trustworthy want their partners to be the same. In other words, they want to have their need for loyalty met. Or, if they are considering betrayal, their partner's disloyalty may also be suspected. Similarly, if individuals accept their partner unconditionally, the same would be expected in return, whereas if they placed the conditions on their relationship, the complaint would arise that their partner cannot be trusted, and so forth.

2. Empathic projection. This is an ancillary treatment goal, which involves taking comfort in the understanding that individuals in another's position would feel the same way and, consequently, would behave much as the other is behaving. For example, if an individual's partner is going through a tough time at work and seems to be less tolerant in general and more needful of personal space, rather than becoming upset at her distancing tactics or lack of warmth, he might think, "I don't blame her for being uptight. I remember how I felt when my boss gave me a poor evaluation." With this in mind, individuals can achieve a greater degree of objectivity and become less likely to react in a way that would compromise the relationship.

3. Vindictive projection. In this case, people might want retribution for what they have not been able to acquire from their partner by behaving just as their partner does. If they feel marginalized or ignored, they might instigate a game of "who can ignore the other the best." Needless to say, this "tit for tat" power struggle will most certainly drive the couple farther and farther apart. This mode of behavior is essentially a *passive aggressive* way individuals can express sentiments they personally find unacceptable, abhorrent, or feelings that they find difficult or impossible to talk about in relation to themselves. Let's look at an example.

Sophie and Armand have been living together for 5 years. Sophie is a fashion buyer for a large department store with branches all over North America, and Armand is a sculptor. He has enjoyed some success, but the nature of his work means that his income comes in fits and starts. Still, he is both grateful and proud that he is in a position to earn a living from his work, without having to teach or perform another day job, as so many artists do. Both Sophie and Armand have to travel quite often for work—she to international fashion shows, clothing showrooms and warehouses and branches all over the continent and he to sculpture competitions and art galleries. Over the course of the last year—a period of time in which both of them turned 30 and in which they began to discuss the possibility of having a child—problems have begun to emerge in their relationship.

"He never calls me when he's away on one of his trips," Sophie says. "And when he does, it's usually at 2 in the morning or something, when I'm trying to get some much needed sleep. I worry artists think their so-called artistic temperament excuses anything. So when he's away I just sit and think about how he could be doing anything with anyone. There are all these chicks who like artists because they think they're cool, and he has been featured in the *New York Times*. I suppose the bottom line is that I just don't trust him to be faithful; I don't know whether he's telling the truth when he says that he is, and all of that makes me wonder if he's really able to be a father yet or if he's just too immature."

"Always the same story," Armand retorts. "Sophie goes away more than I do. She's usually busier than I am. She works in the fashion industry, which is not exactly known for its Puritan culture; she's always hobnobbing with male models and designers.

"They're all gay, anyway," Sophie mutters sulkily.

"They're not all gay. And the point is that I've just as much reason to distrust you as you me, if not more. But I *do* trust you. And it really upsets me when you make accusations based on nothing, accuse me of being immature when I've told you that I'm prepared to work part-time for a few years to be a parent, because my career is more flexible than yours, and when *you* are the one who always picks the arguments. You just don't get it, do you?"

Listening to both partners talk, their therapist develops the hypothesis that Sophie is, in fact, torn between the couple's apparent desire to start a family and the excitement and temptations that her job in the fashion industry offers. She's very stylishly dressed and clearly enjoys her well-paid career. Why not? She has every right to. While she also has every legal entitlement to maternity leave, it is not unreasonable for her to feel conflicted about all the things she may have to give up, and it seems likely that she is projecting her own anxiety about getting out of touch with the glamorous circles she moves in and the flirtation, excitement, and stimulation her career offers her onto Armand who, as he has pointed out, has already proposed that he take a few years "in the slow lane" to concentrate on family life.

In couples therapy, projection can pose a challenge insofar as the individual members of a couple may ascribe their own deeply felt emotions and beliefs to their partner. This, however, is not an obstacle to the effective use of the Needs ABC model, as the clients' narratives will still describe and discuss the underlying relational need. Listening to clients' narratives and isolating the more useful emotions embedded therein is an important first step toward understanding the lacking emotional and relational needs. Helping clients understand which emotions are more useful in problem solving than others is another important step toward acquiring an understanding of how to get these needs met appropriately.

Less useful, or less productive, emotions are often more socially acceptable—such as Sophie's expressed fear that Armand may be partying too hard to be ready for adulthood, with the suggestion that he might be unfaithful [loyalty], rather than admitting to her own anxieties about the possibility of motherhood [competency] and taking on a more responsible, "staid" role in her life and in her marriage although they tend to create problematic behaviors. Armand, for example, might feel that Sophie is not able to accept him as he is [reliability] and doesn't respect his intentions to build a family life in the future. Because more useful emotions are often more difficult to express, Armand is showing his "anger" toward Sophie for not meeting his needs rather than the sadness he feels, which would be more representative of the emotion linked to his representative unmet needs.

In a functional couple, partners typically have similar relational needs that are being met, because we usually want from others what we give, or feel we give, to them. In a poorly functioning couple, partners typically have different relational needs because they are not getting what they feel they are giving to the other. As we each have a unique experience of childhood, when underlying relational needs are not met we each reach adulthood with a unique set of needs and coping behaviors that we fall back on when our needs are not currently being met. For example, as we have already suggested, if one member of a couple is very trustworthy, he or she will want similar loyalty in return and will be dismayed and even baffled if this is not received. If one is dishonest, he or she will suspect the partner of similar behavior and possibly will even create a scenario whereby this is confirmed; meanwhile, the partner may feel as though "I'm always getting yelled at for things I didn't even do, so why should I even try?" In the case of Sophie and Armand, it seems quite likely that when Sophie appears to accuse Armand of living life too much in the fast lane, she is in fact saying much more about herself than she is about him.

This form of projection will still point to clients' unmet need (needs deficit) by defining their respective relational concerns. Problems, then, arise when important, individual relational needs are not being met, especially when there is a problem of communication between members of the couple and especially when the needs deficit is not adequately understood.

Helping Clients Identify Relational Needs

All disciplines come with a certain vocabulary that individual practitioners adapt to their own needs and experience. In my experience, relational needs tend to revolve around certain key issues, and in Chapter 3, I have proposed a number of primary and secondary needs that can serve as a useful starting point for therapists seeking to integrate the Needs ABC model of therapy into their practice. Of course, their own experience of therapy and of life may well bring forth other primary and secondary needs; my list is not intended to be finite or exclusive.

Good therapists do not impose their views onto their clients or tell couples what they should be thinking or feeling in any given situation, although they will feel comfortable stating what they feel or think about the given situation. Rather than imposing a personal view, effective therapists will help couples find their own solutions to their own problems and will assist them in the often painfully difficult process of unearthing and coming to understand their own unmet needs.

> Antoinette and Richard have been doing very well in therapy, which they have been attending for several months. They initially began attending sessions because life had become stressful in their household since

they had both retired—Antoinette from her position as a chartered accountant and Richard from his role as an architectural engineer. They are an affluent couple, relatively young in their late 50s, with a healthy relationship. Antoinette and Richard have three grown children, all of whom are healthy adults. They had never suffered any serious relationship difficulties before, so when they found themselves increasingly caught up in bitter arguments just months after taking early retirement and starting what they thought would be an exciting new phase of their lives, they very sensibly decided to intervene before matters escalated and found a nearby counselor who was available to take them on as clients.

Both Antoinette and Richard have made good progress discussing their emotional development in childhood, the ups and downs of their relationship through the years, and the relational needs they feel characterize them. However, they report that their arguing continues.

"It's just one thing after another," says Antoinette. "We'd agreed that we were going to go away for a year in the sun, maybe to Mexico, but Richard keeps putting it off, and he won't tell me why, so we argue about that."

"Well, she keeps getting irritated because I want to go on a golfing trip with some friends, and she says, 'Oh, so you've time for that, but not to do the things that I would like to do too,'" interjects Richard.

"I'm sure that you're both equally capable of being annoying," says Natalie, the counselor, having grown to know the couple well enough to risk this sort of humor. "But it seems likely to me that the issues that are really lighting your fuses are deeper ones than matters of how and when you are going to sort out your trips. There might also be some practical issues of communication here with regard to how to more effectively meet the relational needs we have been discussing. Do you find that you are communicating in different ways than before?"

"Well, over the last 10 years, we've actually discussed a lot of the nitty-gritty of our plans by email," says Antoinette. "I guess that gave us time to think about what the other person was saying calmly without reacting off the cuff. Speaking for myself, I've never been a very spontaneous person. I do appreciate some time to think about things my way. I don't really remember how we did it before email."

"I think," Richard says slowly, "that Antoinette is voicing something about what we discussed before—how power is a big button for both of us and how we both have to feel that we are in charge of a situation. I know that she feels disrespected, but I can't seem to get her to understand how upsetting it is to feel that unless I comply with her wishes to the letter she's not happy with me as a partner. Now that we're both based at home, maybe we feel a little like loose cannons—and talking through every idea as soon as it comes into our heads means that maybe we sort of overreact to things we used to be able to think through because we didn't have to give an immediate answer to every suggestion."

> "So," says the counselor, "it seems that you are still pushing each other's buttons by not meeting those relational needs we discussed earlier in our work together. I guess you agree that Antoinette feels as though you are still ignoring her at times and that if you had more time to think about your response you might do a better job at acknowledging her wishes. You also seem to be saying that your reaction to feeling abandoned again in these conversations causes you to respond less objectively than you used to—and maybe even that Antoinette might not act so viscerally if she had more time to think as well."

Here, the therapist is making an observation for the couple to consider. It is presented to encourage thought, agreement, or rejection. Like an "open question," clients can agree, disagree, or elaborate on the therapist's statement.

Helping Clients Stay Focused

The mandate of couples presenting for therapy with a Needs ABC therapist is to identify the triggers to their dysfunctional behaviors, to unearth the origins of these triggers and behaviors—usually, as we have discussed, in childhood—and to become able to understand the origins of "difficult" behaviors, to find alternative ways to meet the unmet needs that are at their root, and to create new, healthier, behavioral patterns that will serve as an alternative default reaction to what were once stressors in the relationship. Even still, couples will often wander off-focus, often at least in part as a less-than-conscious way of avoiding possibly painful or difficult issues. There will also be times when an off-topic discussion can serve a useful purpose in the context of a therapy session, diffusing tension and allowing couples to regroup for a moment. However, discussions can all too easily wander seriously off-track, removing the emphasis of the conversation from the problems at hand and introducing issues that have a flimsy relationship, at best, to the underlying issues facing them. When this occurs, as invariably it will, it is the therapist's job to gently but firmly lead the discussion back toward more pertinent matters. For instance, when Dan seems to prefer to discuss his in-laws rather than his relationship with his wife, the therapist might respond:

Dan, it is interesting that you find it annoying when Eloise's parents overstay their welcome, and perhaps we can discuss appropriate boundary setting with them in a minute or two. I am wondering, however, if it might be more beneficial to your relationship to continue to discuss the way you have set boundaries with Eloise—the way she gets so upset when you seem to be distancing yourself.

The Importance of Emotional Safety

Problems arise between couples when they feel like they can no longer be open and honest with one another or when, with varying degrees of awareness, they play complex psychological games with one another, again with varying degrees of awareness of what they are doing, to avoid the real issues that are troubling them. These are situations in which emotional safety does not prevail. In therapy, couples can take their first tentative steps toward complete honesty with each other, practicing this difficult skill in the safe, enclosed environment of the therapist's office before venturing into the wider world. It is therefore imperative that couples know and feel secure in the knowledge that the therapist's office is a venue in which they can really feel free to voice their innermost thoughts, without fear of recrimination (Watson & Greenberg, 1994, pp. 164–166). This does not, of course, mean that they will always feel comfortable with the topics being discussed, because therapy inevitably means that many difficult and, often, unflattering issues are going to have to be discussed with searing honesty. What it *should* mean is that clients feel safe to voice any feelings they may have within the context of the therapist's office. Let's explore an example.

> Gilles, whose body language had gradually begun to imply discomfort with Lucie's discussion of her "undying loyalty" toward him, finally said after what appeared to be a long silence, "You know, I've been meaning to say this to you for quite some time but didn't have the courage to do so at home: as loyal as you say you've been over the years, I still sense that somewhere down the line you've cheated on me."
>
> Now, using the safety of the counselor's office and the expertise of the Needs ABC therapist, the couple can discuss this seemingly difficult subject in the spirit of collaboration—not denigration.

Supportive Challenges

When a therapist and, ideally, a client's partner relate with empathy rather than criticism to disclosures, a sense of being connected develops (Bachelor & Horvath, 1999, p. 142; Linehan, 1999, pp. 384–387). Also, in the course of expressing empathy, partners may also be demonstrating that they have found an outlet for some of their own emotions and anxieties. Let's look at the case of a couple that has decided to have children but is facing some difficulties as both members are experiencing serious anxiety around the fact that this would certainly impact their successful careers.

> "It's understandable that, working in such a cutting-edge environment, one such as yourself might be worried about the sort of changes that will be created by becoming a mother and taking on a new set of responsibilities," says the couple's therapist, Ingrid. "Anyone would find that scary, and I bet that Andrew can relate to at least some of what is worrying you."
>
> "Of course I can," agrees Andrew. "I go through a lot of similar feelings every day. But I guess it's maybe easier for me in a lot of ways because, most of the time, I'm working on my own in my office. I don't really have to consider how other people in my professional life are going to react to the changes I am undergoing, so it's one less thing to get stressed about."
>
> "Yes," says Fiona, "there is no question that I do have some concerns as to whether I am up to the task of being a parent. I know I will be sacrificing a lot, but I love family and want so badly to have one with Andrew."

Where Therapy Leads

Effective therapy helps clients to find themselves in a situation where they feel in control of their environment—in charge, to some extent, of the therapeutic process and able to access and discuss their emotions, including negative emotions, in a way that does not lead to dysfunctional behavior and distress to both them and their partner. This issue of control and the related topic of power—how it is distributed and experienced in the context of the couple and how individuals can feel confident that they wield power in their own sphere—is where we shall turn to next.

7

POWER AND CONTROL IN COUPLES THERAPY

Everybody typically appreciates feeling in control of their arena, without uncertainty and doubt about how they and those they care about will react to what is going to happen to them and around them and about how the people around them will react in turn to the things they say and do (Greenberg & Johnson, 1988, pp. 66–70). They also need to know that their areas of competence are respected and understood and that their opinions are valued and taken into consideration by the people in their lives—especially by their spouse or partner in life, who is almost invariably the one whose oversights or insensitive attention will be felt most deeply. Power is an important issue for everyone and, in one way or another, we all seek to have power in our own sphere, in the context of our relationship. In a healthy relationship, power is granted and ceded voluntarily by both parties to the couple. However, when both partners of a couple's respective relational needs are not granted, and when dysfunctional coping strategies have been allowed to develop in response to unmet needs, a bona fide struggle for power can occur.

It is easy to associate aggression, be it verbal or physical, with power. Clearly, those who lash out, yell, or attempt to physically or otherwise compel a partner to do what they want are trying to obtain as much power for themselves as they can. Aggressive behavior of this sort can be terribly damaging in the context of any relationship. However, passive-aggressive behavior, albeit less "obvious" and difficult to pin down, can be just as damaging to the relationship and both the object and the subject of the behavior, in varying ways.

In a relationship that functions well, both parties in the couple will be able to negotiate for their own space and to collaborate in achieving a situation in which both feel satisfied that their personal need for power within their own sphere has been respected. I refer to this situation as "power asking" as opposed to "power taking."

Of course, all couples have a different balance of power; while both parties need to feel confident that their own sense of power is real and is respected, this is not to say that each decision made by and for the couple must be shared on a 50/50 basis. Some couples will collaborate more than others in all areas of life. Some will have highly distinct areas of competence. What matters is that each feels respected within his or her own sphere.

Feeling in control of one's own life and decision making and one's place in a personal relationship is, for most people, a prerequisite for fulfillment and happiness. This is especially true in the context of the couple, a domestic and emotional situation that can be tremendously rewarding but in which one can feel especially vulnerable when or if things go wrong, as they so often do.

Chris, age 34, and Erin, age 32, have been married for 10 years. They have three children (Jacob, 8; Steven, 7; and Jillian, 4 1/2). Chris and Erin came into Alfonso's office describing that they were in a state of crisis and that Erin was considering leaving the relationship because of Chris's controlling and emotionally abusive behavior. Chris admitted that he was controlling and that he "had to have a say in everything she did." He also admitted that he was jealous and untrusting in general and that, even though he loved Erin very much, always felt somewhat distrustful of her motives and loyalty. He stated that he agreed to come in for help when he discovered that she had "stolen" the money he had put aside for her for emergencies and that, because they have not had sex for almost 6 months, he was worried she was having an affair. Erin immediately piped in, saying that it would be almost impossible for her to have an affair—that he was always either with her or calling her. She stated that she had taken the money because she was tired of being "told off" every time she needed money for "a bottle of shampoo." She said that she was generally tired of his criticisms and directives and that, in a sense, she had "given up."

Erin, the youngest of six, grew up in a family where her father drank and abused her mother and her two older brothers. She stated that "when all hell broke loose" she would run over to her girlfriend's house. She said that she had not spoken to her father since she left home at the age of 16 and before then would not have spoken to him unless she had to for fear he would "beat the heck out of me too." She said that the only person that she ever felt close to was her mother and that they were even closer since her father died about 6 years ago of cirrhosis of the liver.

Chris described his parents as extremely critical and "selfish." "Everything had to be on their terms," he declared. "I also left home at 18 to get away from their constant nagging and complaining about whatever I did." He went on to complain that his mother was "never really interested in being a mother" and that "she was always busy doing everything but being with him or his younger brother." Chris went on to describe that he and Erin had experienced an extremely tight financial situation after his business went under and that, even though he was optimistic about the future of his present business venture, "stealing the money was like sticking in the knife and turning it as well."

Alfonso suggested to the couple that what had inadvertently happened is that they both had recreated their worst nightmares from their families of origin. Chris had become violent and controlling as his father had been, and Erin had become Chris's mother with regard to her aloofness ("running away") when he became upset. Erin agreed that when she felt Chris was attacking her she would become "the ice woman." Chris also agreed that he became very upset when he felt his wife pulling away from him and that he felt inadequate as a husband, especially because of the bankruptcy.

The trio continued discussing their relationship, past and present, and Alfonso described the following relational needs deficits to Erin and Chris. He suggested that competency was a "huge button" for Chris—that his anger actually represented his fear that he could not measure up and that his "jealousy" was about feeling that because he was not "good enough" Erin might leave him, a prospect he found truly horrifying.

Alfonso's hypothesis was that Erin's need was to have emotional reliability versus *abandonment* and that Chris's "triggers" were around *competency*. In fact, in support of this notion, Erin had stated that when they first met she had "tested" Chris by trying to provoke him into violence but that he never made her feel unsafe. Chris admitted that Erin had looked up to him, and now it seemed that, no matter what he did, he always "messed it up with her." Chris emphatically stated that he did not want to lose Erin and would do whatever he could to "get her back."

Alfonso asked the couple to consider the following plan of action. Even though they both had behaviors that could be improved, it would be difficult for Erin to change her behavior in light of the violent nature of Chris's behavior toward her. Alfonso asked Chris to consider that he would have to take the first step in showing Erin that she could, once again, be safe with him, even when he was upset. He agreed, and Alfonso offered some behavioral tactics such as "time-out" and logging and encouraged them to see how it would go between this and the next session. When Alfonso suggested that eventually Erin would have to consider not giving him the "cold shoulder," she shook her head, saying that she was not prepared to do too much until Chris "did his part."

Before the session drew to a close, Alfonso asked Chris and Erin how they felt it had gone. Both agreed that in understanding what their relational needs were they would be able to consider ways of communicating

when they were not being met. Chris confided that he had never considered how powerful his aggressive behavior was, especially considering the
problems that Erin had had to confront when she was growing up. Erin was
thankful that she understood Chris's powerful reaction to her behavior considering his financial problems but reasserted that she was not prepared to
look at her part in this until he could regain her trust.

Many problems in couples arise from behaviors that are, in reality,
attempts to achieve a modicum of power and control over a situation
that seems to have acquired a life of its own. Paradoxically, of course,
couples typically sabotage their relational needs when they try to get
them met by using dysfunctional strategies, as was clearly the case
for Chris and Erin, and the scene is set for the escalation of their difficulties as each stressful interaction appears to prove what they are
coming to believe: "We just don't seem to be able to make each other
happy the way we used to."

Therapy for couples is about learning why these dysfunctional strategies are chosen and where they come from and devising ways to bypass
them and create, instead, a better, more functional, more useful, and
more rewarding way of interacting with one's partner. Helping clients understand what the needs behind their behaviors are and which
emotions function better than others in the problem-solving tasks at
hand will help them move toward better solutions, which positions the
therapy in an "answer-finding" mode.

Using the Needs Acquisition and Behavior Change (ABC) model,
therapists can help their clients understand how they are looking for
needs fulfillment within the presenting relationship, how to meet
these needs more constructively, and to appreciate how some of these
needs might also, or alternatively, be found elsewhere, at least for the
time being.

Although, in a functioning couple, much emotional fulfillment can
be found within the relationship, understanding the role and impact of
other relationships—with, for example, close friends, family members,
colleagues at work—is not just rewarding but also relieves couples of
the pressure of feeling that they should somehow be "everything" to
each other. Regardless of how much partners may love each other, it
is too much to expect any one individual to take sole responsibility
for meeting his or her partner's relational needs. Indeed, this situation

will inevitably lead to animosity, to frustration, and eventually to dysfunctional problem-solving strategies. Some form of the social sphere independent of couples will allow each part of the dyad to take responsibility for needs getting outside of the relationship and might even produce productive strategies that can be brought into couples' relationships.

In addition, if someone's relational needs cannot be met within a particular relationship, getting them met outside of the relationship will be the therapeutic task until such time as a new relationship can be negotiated, with the same or with a different partner. An example of where needs cannot be met would include the case of a female survivor of domestic abuse. Needless to say, when her partner is not prepared to take responsibility for his behavior, when the relationship has been terminated, or when she still cannot trust him to provide the physical and emotional safety she deserves, need must be acquired elsewhere.

Let us take the example of a woman whose needs are competency and respect. She has been in a relationship in which she has been told that she is inadequate and has been treated as valueless and unimportant. In this scenario, joining a photography group, joining a gym, or doing volunteer work might be the "ticket" to feeling important, respected, and validated for her accomplishments. Another example might be a man who is frustrated in the workplace because nothing he is doing seems to be good enough and because it seems like every time he is promised a promotion or change of venue "something always comes up." By sending out his curriculum vitae and doing research into options outside of his present situation he will be able to feel less "stuck" with the betrayal and conditions placed on him in his present situation. This is because relational needs are universal and exist in every domain in which we function relationally; the more important the relationship, the more powerful the emotional component.

Some of the approaches therapists can take to reduce defensiveness and anxiety include prompting clients to discuss the identities each developed in childhood and adolescence and how these identities helped them as they matured and grew to obtain their relational needs from those around them. By remaining focused on needs in the early phases of therapy, more difficult emotional components can be introduced gradually, as clients gain confidence in the therapeutic context.

By supporting clients' attempts to communicate and affirming positive needs-getting actions, therapists can promote useful behavior during therapy. This can be as simple as "rewarding" useful behaviors by making remarks such as, "What a great way to get noticed," or, "It must be really nice feeling so connected this way," or, "Bet you feel competent now."

When couples become able to collaborate in therapy, their relationship as a unit is also affirmed, and it is easier for them to rediscover the bonds of affection that lie behind their decision to seek therapy rather than find a more destructive solution to their problems.

Sustaining the Therapeutic Process and Eliminating Barriers

Therapy is a gradual process; even after couples have managed to achieve significant breakthroughs in their relationship, they will need to be assisted, over a period of time, to validate their personal discoveries about their relational needs and to practice, in the context of their sessions with the therapist and at home, the new skills they are bringing to bear on their relationship with each other (Jacobson & Margolin, 1979, pp. 109–124; Johnson, 2004, pp. 271–274). Understanding on an intellectual basis why and how one should adapt one's behavior does not necessarily mean that it will be immediately easy to make the necessary changes in one's personal life. Let's explore an example.

> Sean and Cynthia have made considerable progress in therapy toward understanding each other's needs and learning new ways of communicating these needs to each other.
>
> Cynthia grew up in a troubled family in which she suffered considerable physical and emotional abuse as a child. Her father, who had always been a physically violent man prone to dramatic mood swings, left the family home when she was 8 years old. As well as leaving, he cut off all contact with his former wife and children and, before too long, any financial contribution as well. Cynthia has always felt that her mother blamed and punished her for this, mostly by being "cold" but also by occasionally beating her daughter or making a point of withdrawing all physical affection from her. What is incontrovertible is that, once her husband had left, Cynthia's mother found herself in financially straitened circumstances and had to work "all the hours God sent" to keep her family going, often leaving her small daughter with babysitters for lengthy periods. For Cynthia, abandonment is understandably a major issue, and she has learned how to discuss, in the context

of their sessions with the therapist, how when Sean seems to ignore her needs or fails to be there for her she is plunged into the uncertainty, fear, and trepidation that marked her very unhappy childhood.

Conversely, Sean's major issues seem to revolve around reliability; in particular, he places great emphasis on the importance of feeling that her affection for him is conditional, especially when she reacts to her feelings of abandonment by lashing out.

In therapy, Sean and Cynthia have learned how to talk openly about their family backgrounds, have become accomplished at using a needs-based vocabulary, and have acquired a pretty good understanding of the concepts behind the Needs ABC approach. Cynthia has become able to identify how when she gets angry and yells it is often because something that Sean has done has reminded her of how she felt when, as a child, her mother withdrew from her, making her feel that she was being abandoned by yet another parent and also has triggered the memory of how, as a child, she always suspected that it was her fault her father had left, which her mother in no way tried to alleviate. However, these realizations do not always translate to changes in the dysfunctional behaviors that affect this couple on a daily basis.

Sean and Cynthia's therapist can help them to break out of their negative behavioral cycle by helping them to first work within the context of the therapeutic domain and by validating the meaningful progress they have been making in therapy with statements such as:

So, I guess you both now understand that Cynthia has the tendency to take on too much responsibility for what goes on in your marriage, sort of like what her mother attempted to foist onto her. Cynthia, you have also picked up on the fact that you remind Sean of his parents, who became very angry with him when he didn't drop what he was doing to do what they wanted. I'm impressed, Sean, by your understanding of how you might make Cynthia feel that you have abandoned her emotionally, just as her parents did, when you avoid listening to what she has to say when she is angry. Now I guess we can discuss what you would each find helpful in preventing the pushing the other's relational buttons in the future. If either one of you feels that your buttons are beginning to be pushed, ask for a break for now and reconvene later to discuss what the buttons were. I know it sounds silly, but you can blame this "time-out" on me. So when you begin to get that uncomfortable feeling in a conversation you are having with each other just say, "Caplan said to take a break when we feel uncomfortable so I would like to if you don't mind."

Helping Both Parties of the Couple to Join

It can often occur that one member of a couple finds it a great deal easier to discuss his or her emotions, behaviors, and needs than the other. This can happen when one individual has instigated therapy or sees therapy in a more positive light, while his or her partner might view therapy as intrusive, punitive, or embarrassing. However, it can also occur when both members have expressed their willingness to engage in therapy; some people simply find it easier to access words to express what they are thinking and how they are feeling than others.

However, the very reason for being in couples therapy is to enhance the quality of the communication and interaction between both elements of the couple (Gottman, 1999, pp. 105–110). Silence on one person's part may be reflective of a larger dynamic in his or her personal relationship or of fears or reservations about therapy in general or about its usefulness in particular. Either way, effective therapy cannot occur without input and interaction from both members of the couple. The couples therapist is in an excellent position to help the recalcitrant individual join in by avoiding stressing their apparent reluctance to speak and instead using linking interventions such as, "Wow, Timothy seems to have had a really hard time getting his voice heard at home when he was a kid. I wonder if you, Wendy, had any similar experiences?" There may, however, be occasions when one member of the couple *does* need to be gently asked to allow his or her partner more room to speak: "Angela, you're doing a great job of talking about why you feel you need the things that you do, but I'm a little concerned that we might not be giving Ben the room he needs to speak. Perhaps, today, we can try to focus on the issues that are of particular concern to him."

Let's explore another example.

Alessandra, a high school teacher of Italian origin, presented for therapy with her husband, George. The couple has two sons, both in late adolescence. Alessandra reported a history of both physical and emotional "delicateness" and a close family background. The reason for coming to therapy, according to her, is that she recently discovered that George, with whom she has been since high school, has had a number of affairs in the course of their marriage, which she had always assumed to be "as solid as a rock" and built on a foundation of romantic love and mutual respect.

George, a strikingly good-looking man who works in a blue-collar job and appears to be demonstrably less articulate and "smart" than his wife, states that his father has never been supportive of him, that his criticisms continue to the present and still contribute to his achieving less than his potential. In his job as a plumber, George meets a lot of women, mostly stay-at-home housewives and, with his good looks, is often presented with the opportunity to enter into an affair. The first time this happened was 7 years ago, and since then there have been some thirteen or fourteen. George also admits to a number of "encounters" with prostitutes. He also mentions a few instances when men "came onto him," although the extent to which he returned their interest is not clear, and he seems reluctant to discuss the topic in any detail, at least for now. He insists that he has been faithful to his wife for the past 2 years, that he is guilty and horrified by what he has done, and that he is prepared to "do anything—whatever it takes" to keep her. A year before, the whole family traveled to Tuscany in an attempt to become close again, but it was a "complete disaster" as Alessandra and George fought the whole time, making themselves distraught and embarrassing and disturbing their teenaged sons, who eventually refused to dine with them in restaurants for fear that yet another very public scene would ensue.

While Alessandra's horror at discovering her husband's affair is understandable, her reaction to one woman in particular has been rather over the top; she spent 3 months stalking one of the women with whom George became involved, including making harassing phone calls and even going to the woman's home once to harangue her at the front door. George was aware of Alessandra's activities and, far from trying to dissuade her, seemed to be encouraging. As things escalated, eventually charges were pressed against her. Although George has sworn never to be unfaithful again, Alessandra finds it impossible to trust him, and there is every risk that this sort of profoundly unhelpful behavior will surface again. At home, she "nags" George obsessively. By now, he feels that his mental health is being affected.

Although things are clearly not good for this beleaguered couple, they do seem to be determined to find a way through their problems. This is the fourth time they have sought professional help, and this is latched onto now as indicative of their conviction that they can find a solution to mend their damaged relationship, despite the many challenges they face.

Sian, the couple's therapist, identifies competency and reliability as important needs for George and respect and loyalty as major factors for Alessandra. She also acknowledges that the rebuilding of a trusting relationship seems to be a monumental task at this point because of the extent of the betrayal Alessandra has experienced. Turning to Alessandra, Sian says, "You know, Alessandra, considering what has happened with regard to George's affairs, I am surprised that you even want to try to rebuild your relationship." Alessandra replies, "Well, I don't know what the children would do without him; he's a good father, you know. Before I found out about the affairs, things were pretty good. I guess we could have had more sex recently, but I haven't been feeling very well—very tired. They have reduced the staff at our school, and I have had to do the work of two teachers. I come home burned out. Maybe it's partly my fault, but that one woman—what nerve. She's also married; how could she do such a thing?"

"And George, what about you?" Sian asked. "Since you've had so many affairs, I have to wonder why you would want to reconcile, especially after your description of the way you have been feeling in the relationship?" George responds by explaining, "I was so angry at Alessandra. All she ever seemed to do was put me down. When I married her she didn't seem to care that I was 'just' an assistant mechanic and never went to college. She thought I was great anyway. Now, nothing I seem to do is right. On our recent trip to Italy, anything I said about the kids was either wrong or stupid. She also needs to control everything. She can't just let things be. The problem was that even though the sex was fun I wasn't in love with these women. I was in love with Alessandra and couldn't seem to have her. Like she just said, she was either too tired or too angry at me to get close. She wouldn't even cuddle."

"Well, it seems you both want to have that relationship that brought you together in the first place," says Sian, "but it looks like a bit of a steep hill to climb. Let's begin by having you both start to log your behaviors every day at home. When you feel that the other person is doing something positive, please make a note of it and what was going on at the time. When you feel the other has relapsed into the old behavior pattern, log it in the same way. Let's meet again next week to see how it goes."

As therapy progressed, Alessandra and George, with the help of Sian, were able to deconstruct their difficult moments and validate their successful ones. They were to examine how and why their buttons were pushed in their relational interactions and understand how family-of-origin issues exacerbated their ability to problem solve effectively. This therapy took almost a full year because of the lack of emotional safety that both George and Alessandra had created. After meeting once a month, the following dialogue transpired in the final session.

Sian opened by commenting that it seemed that generally things had been going well and that she was curious as to why Alessandra and George felt like they were ready to terminate their treatment at this point in time. Alessandra began by saying, "I have to admit that I still find it difficult to back off from trying to control or criticize George even though he has demonstrated that his loyalty is to me and to no one else." George jumped in and added, "It's really easy to show you my devotion when you're not picking at me all the time. At least you agree to cuddle even when you're not in the mood for sex." Alessandra stated, "You know, Sian, we have had some difficult moments even lately, but those meetings you suggested to discuss what we felt was going on around our relational needs seem to be working out OK. I know you said that these were strategies to use during the therapy, but George and I think we might continue to use them. I hope you don't mind getting some of the blame even after we've finished." (All laugh.) "Yeah," says George, winking at his smiling wife, "at least I get a chance to complain, and she doesn't ignore me."

Helping Couples Take Responsibility

Making Sure Couples Remain Focused on Their Mandate   Since couples attending therapy invariably have to address very stressful issues, and at times even to explore issues and incidents from their past that may be immensely painful, it is easy to understand how tempting it can be to deflect tension or avoid direct confrontation with difficult memories by discussing issues that are tangential to the presenting problem or generally wandering away from the issue at hand. The therapist's role is to help clients, not to discipline them, so assisting couples in staying on track is best done with a gentle hand. Here's one example.

Frank and Kate are attending therapy for problems that both have with substance abuse and attendant behaviors of violence, fighting, and generally destructive behavior that at times overflows their small apartment and causes their neighbors to call the police. Their two small children, aged 3 and 18 months, are in foster care, although their parents have visiting rights and hope to regain custody soon; this is one of the reasons they are attending therapy. Both are also attending an outpatient clinic and a 12-step group (separately) to help them get control of their substance abuse.

"We've been clean for a couple of months now," Kate reports, "but I just know that Frank is going to get tempted and go back on the hard stuff. It's difficult for me, but it's worse for him. He's weak, and he's never been able to resist temptation."

"I know it's frightening to have to learn to live without the substances you've used in the past," says John, the therapist. "But as a couple and as a family, if you want things to work out for you all, you've got to stop playing the blame game and start looking at ways you can support each other, both in overcoming the problems you have had with drugs and alcohol and also in relating to each other in a mutually helpful, respectful way. What are some of the things Frank can begin to do to help you to trust him? And what can help you to support his competencies rather than focusing on what you perceive to be his deficits?"

Here, with a firm but supportive challenge the therapist moves the discussion from a nonproductive one of behavior back to the relational needs still not being met.

Giving Couples Information About Their Behavior   While remaining at all times empathetic and nonconfrontational, therapists are of little use to couples seeking help if they cannot provide couples with insights into their own behavior. The Needs ABC approach stresses the importance of understanding the origin and nature of unhelpful behaviors, and keeping a focus on this element is very helpful in avoiding blame or harsh criticism. At the same time, clients will sometimes have to receive information about unproductive things they might be doing. Let's revisit Frank and Kate.

> After John's intervention, Frank interjected, saying, "I am sincerely trying to stay on track. I just don't know where Kate sees the temptation she is talking about. I know I certainly don't. I am aware of my triggers, I go to meetings, I read my daily affirmations, I do everything I can. What's the deal?" Kate replies, "This is not the first time we've been through this. I am feeling really good about our relationship, staying clean and all, and then WHAM! You're not coming home when you promised, and when you do arrive you're drunk and smell like hell."
>
> "It's always something," says Frank. "Why can't you just believe that even when I do things my way they might work out OK."
>
> John jumps in with the following explanation: "It sure looks like we are back to the same old, same old. Remember we discussed your relational needs in the first few sessions and how they were created when you were growing up in your families? Just like in the first session when Kate agreed that she had found it hard to trust you and that Frank had agreed that Kate was always challenging his competency, we also learned that Frank's parents were very critical and that Kate felt that she couldn't trust her family members since they would agree to one thing and then do something else entirely. Well, it's the same discussion all over again. When one of you has a relapse, it's my feeling that this is most probably the result of the feelings that arise with this same cycle of criticism and distrust. Let's look, instead, at potential successes—ways you can validate each other and rebuild the trust you have lost."

Facilitating Dialogue   Problems with the way couples communicate are fundamental to the reasons therapy can be helpful. In the safe environment represented by the therapist's office, couples can learn how to talk about difficult or painful subjects with honesty and respect and can learn the skills they will need to bring to their personal life and their future together. By "training" couples how to access the Needs ABC concepts and vocabulary, primarily by introducing the topic of potential unmet needs and using modeling to demonstrate how these can be discussed, couples can be usefully taught how to bring these skills home and can base future discussions of needs, feelings, and emotions using them as was evident to Alessandra and George.

The Importance of Metaphor

As we have already made clear, the therapist's role is not to provide solutions for couples that present with problems but to help them find their own solutions. In therapy, one of the most effective ways to open avenues so that this can happen is to provide a vocabulary and mode of expression that couples can use to communicate their unmet needs to one another. One of the most powerful ways this can be done is the effective use of metaphor in conversation (Thomas & Caplan, 2004).

Metaphors tap into powerful symbolic language that can elicit a strong, visceral response when an important connection has been made.

> Fred has always felt passed over for promotions at work. Two days before meeting with his counselor he received word that Julius, a junior colleague, was just given the promotion Fred had been hoping for.
>
> "He sure knows how to kiss up to the higher-ups even though his abilities are questionable," Fred said. "I sure was angry and depressed too." Fred went on to say that on the way home in his car when someone suddenly cut him off, despite his feelings of sadness and lethargy, he felt a rage build up inside of him to the point that he had to pull over and get out of his car "for fear that he would do something he might regret." It seems the metaphor extant in feeling "passed over" by others rekindled the anger and fear that he was in a "dead-end job."

Metaphors in our daily lives can be responsible for behavioral relapses akin to this example. For example, at one in-patient substance abuse treatment facility where I had worked for a number of years, a client had returned for his third treatment. I was appointed as his case manager in this particular instance and met with him shortly after he had settled in. The client reported that he couldn't understand why he relapsed *again*. He had been doing everything he was supposed to: going to meetings daily, seeing his sponsor on a regular basis, reading "the Big Book," and saying his daily affirmations. It seems that he had gone to one of his usual Alcoholics Anonymous (AA) meetings and admitted he was feeling "pretty good." He left the meeting as usual, after spending some time speaking with other members, only to find that, on the way home, he had inexplicably walked into a neighborhood variety store and picked up a case of beer. "The rest was history," he said. "I proceeded to go through three cases of beer until I passed out and then went on a 2-week bender. Now here I am." After further discussion of what else had transpired in the week prior to his relapse it became evident that a situation reminding him of his worst childhood nightmare had occurred. A friend of his, who had recently separated from his wife, had confided in him that his wife had refused to let him see his children until custody arrangements had been finalized. This brought back memories of his father's separation from his mother when the client was 12 years old. Apparently it had been a bitter divorce, and his father would have nothing to do with him for years because of the animosity he had for his mother. He had been very close to his father and could not understand why he was put between his mother and father in such a way or how his father could abide to be without him, as he missed his father so very badly. He stated that "this was the most horrible time of his life" and that, in high school, he began to drink beer before coming home to alleviate his sadness and anxiety about feeling that he lost his father. In fact, in this recent relapse, he was reliving his childhood feelings of abandonment and betrayal through his friend's predicament and replicated his childhood behavior to deal with these negative childhood memories.

As well as recognizing metaphors in our experience of the emotional landscape, we all use metaphors every day to describe how we are feeling: "I'm between a rock and a hard place"; "We're just going to have to grab the bull by the horns"; "I was like a deer in the headlights of an oncoming car"; "It's as if we'd been hit by a freight train." In therapy, the metaphors clients use can provide astonishing insight to their worldview and their needs and also give an excellent starting point for dialogue around their current situation, their unmet needs, and what they require from their personal relationship to be happy and fulfilled. Folk tales, well known or otherwise, can often serve as valuable sources of metaphoric information. Selekman (1993) discusses how he uses Native American tales in his work with adolescents, for example. Well-known tales from clients' traditional backgrounds can also be useful, as they are rich in descriptive metaphors for difficult circumstances; just think of the powerful symbolism in the familiar tale of Hansel and Gretel, for example.

Richard Royal Kopp (1995) studied the use of client-generated metaphors in psychotherapy. One of the points he makes on this topic is that, especially when discussing a traumatic event or events or feelings or emotions that are difficult to broach, people often find it easier to access and vocalize metaphors rather than "plain speech." Symbolic language makes it easier to discuss painful topics without evading the situation at hand. By responding in kind, using metaphors to describe difficult, testing emotional environments and circumstances, therapists can facilitate clients' discussion of their presenting problems. Metaphors are also highly expressive ways of communicating emotion and make it possible for one to say a great deal while using few words; there is a good reason the use of metaphor is one of the main building blocks of effective poetry.

Rather than attempting to force clients to state their issues in plain language, embracing the metaphors they find easier to access can be much more productive, while at the same time effective use of metaphor can reveal many more layers of meaning than a simpler use of words. They allow people who are suffering psychologically to discuss the cause of their suffering at a slight distance, often making it possible for them to voice insights that more direct language would render difficult or impossible. However, accepting the use of metaphor does not mean that a therapist cannot explore clients' personal issues in depth. Instead, this can be done without leaving the relative safety of the metaphoric discussion. When a client says, "I would really be like a fish out of water!" a response might be, "And would that feel like you might drown?" or "I guess that being out of your element might make you feel inadequate" alluding to competency as the relational needs deficit. Indeed, exploration of metaphor is important because, whereas commonly used metaphors have effectively universal interpretations, personal metaphor use may incorporate more idiosyncratic understandings of the metaphors being used, and in an intercultural context understanding metaphor can become complex indeed. In addition, what the clients bring into therapy, the way they present their concerns or dialogue with each other, even the issues at hand can be metaphors for what they need from each other and in the world. In fact, these metaphors can cause problematic reactions to situations that are seemingly benign. Now let's look at a couple in which one is a recovering alcoholic who, as in the previous example, relapses without any apparent knowledge of what caused his powerful urge to drink. Again, a thorough exploration while working with the couple would probably uncover a situation that reminded him of some emotionally difficult situation from the past. We will explore an example of how to use a metaphor in the context of discussion with a marital therapist to bring about insight as to how to resolve the couple's relational issues.

> Gloria and Rick have come to therapy because, they say, they have serious communication problems and are beginning to wonder if there is any point at all in continuing with their relationship—if they wouldn't both be better off without each other.
>
> "It's pointless trying to talk to Rick about anything deeper than baseball," says Gloria. "I've tried engaging him, but I'm just beating my head against a brick wall."
>
> "I'm not the only one who has trouble getting stuff across," interjects Rick. "If you try talking to Gloria about anything more important than how she felt when I forgot to notice her new dress, it's like, 'The light is on, but nobody's home.'"
>
> "So," says Isobel, the couple's therapist. "You're both telling me something interesting and giving me some insight into the frustrations you are feeling when you try to engage with each other. It seems to me, Rick, that even when the bases are loaded you can't seem to bring anybody home. You keep striking out."
>
> "That's one way to look at it," Rick grumbles.
>
> "Well, perhaps it's because you are trying to hit the ball from behind that brick wall Gloria says you are putting up?"

As well as using a metaphor to work with couples' narratives, or purposely in discussion with clients to make a point, so to speak, other situations can be metaphors for what is actually happening within the couple dyad. For example, understanding how clients view, for example, intimacy, sex, hobbies, attire, or planning an event can illuminate the unmet relational need that is extant in the relational power struggle.

The Schmooze: When and How to Go Off Topic

There will always be times when a therapist deduces that clients might need a break from the intensity of therapy. For example, when a couple has been actively engaged in problem solving, a situation may arise where it seems evident that one partner is beginning to lose interest. Often, rather than directly drawing attention to this problem, the situation can be more aptly dealt with by applying what I have come to refer to, rather informally, as *the schmooze*, a Yiddish word for "light-hearted conversation." Let me give you an example.

> Eleanora has become visibly frustrated after a lengthy monologue in which she attempted to express some of her thoughts about her family background but without apparently breaking any new ground. At the same time her partner, Jack, has disengaged significantly from proceedings. While it is clear that Eleanora does have information to get across, and while this couple has a great deal of work to do, for now (speaking of metaphors) the phrase "flogging a dead horse" comes to mind, and it is obviously time to facilitate a shift in topic. Wishing to avoid making Eleanora feel that she has been wasting time, the therapist, Albert, says, "Forgive me for changing the subject, but I couldn't help noticing that you, Eleanora, are wearing a rather interesting Celtic motif brooch, while Jack has a fine Aran cardigan. May I ask if you've been on holiday in Ireland recently, or if you're making a statement about your cultural identity?"
>
> "Actually," Jack says, brightening up, "they're gifts from our son, Patrick. He's an exchange student in at the university in Galway."
>
> "Yes," says Eleanora. "We've promised ourselves we'll make a trip before his scholarship runs out. We've always wanted to go to Europe, and it looks like a fine place to start."
>
> "I guess the items struck my eye," Albert says, "because just last week I was reading a tourist brochure about the Galway oyster festival. Well, that's a coincidence. Small world."

While the schmooze has taken the couple clearly off topic, it has enabled both partners to "recharge their batteries," permitted Jack to reenter dialogue, enabled Albert to help Eleanora to refocus on the task at hand, and provided a change for them both to bond with their therapist and, by discussing their vacation plans, with each other. Another benefit of this technique is that it helps clients feel "human"—that they are more than "just clients" but also special in their own way. Finally, it models validating the value of others—that there is more to a relationship than getting what you want but that knowing what you have is also important.

Look at what clients are wearing or carrying for insights into their personality and interests. A sports bag could be an opener for a brief conversation about the football season this year; ethnic clothing and visible tattoos can be revealing of issues of personal identity. Understanding a bit more about what they do at work is another possibility for schmoozing.

Examples of Needs-Based, Emotion-Focused Statements (Made as an Observation or an Invitation to Problem Solving)

A feeling often experienced by those presenting for therapy is shame, a sense of guilt, embarrassment, unworthiness, or disgrace associated with behaviors that are intended to obtain individuals' needs but that do precisely the opposite. A crucial element is helping the client recognize that the behavior was inappropriate or personally damaging, quite apart from anybody else, and to find the motivation to deal better with solving the problem. Feelings such as shame are often associated with issues of inadequacy as a "problem solver" in general, as people often experience shame and guilt in circumstances in which they recognize that their attempts to solve the problem were more destructive than productive.

For example, if a woman says to her partner, "You had a big tantrum when I forgot to call you back, as I had promised," focusing on the tantrum will not be useful, whereas maintaining focus on the underlying need, respect, will be useful. Once the need is illuminated, it is important for the partner to get his needs met productively by understanding that his "fear" of being unimportant is more productive than his "anger" at her forgetfulness and by communicating this need to her in a way she can listen. Here the counselor can say, "From my perspective, it seems that you were feeling invisible in your relationship, and that would be scary for me. What do you think would work better for you in telling your partner if you ever felt that way in the future?" This might, for instance, encourage the client to say, "I can't help feeling frightened when you don't come through with your promises, because it seems that maybe I'm not really that much of a priority for you." On the other hand, the counselor could suggest the following to the woman: "It seems that when your partner gets that angry it only makes you feel criticized, abandoned, and alone. Do you think it might be a good idea to explain this to him when the smoke has cleared?" Here, the woman, with the understanding that her partner's need is for respect and acknowledgment, might challenge her husband more productively when confronted by his anger by saying, "I love you very much and you're very important to me, but responding the way you do is frustrating and only makes me feel inadequate and alienated."

Another experience often expressed is grief or mourning of a lost way of life, as problems presenting in the couple can challenge the individual in terms of a loss of identity, perceived status, or adequacy, often expressed in remarks like the following: "I used to be self-sufficient, but now I need to ask for help," or "I used to box as a hobby, but now I need a walker," or "I used to get it right all the time, but now all I do is keep making mistakes," or "I keep remembering the days I could walk into a store and buy something without looking at the price tag." Here the client usually seems like he has given up and is unable to do much of anything, as if he were paralyzed and his problems are utterly beyond his control. The focus here would be to not encourage movement for a time but to continue to brainstorm scenarios couched in a "whenever you feel you are ready" context. For example, in a couple where the husband has had to leave his dental practice because of an accident affecting one of his hands and the wife explains that she "just doesn't know what to do with him because he sits around and mopes or gets in the way of what I am doing," the couple could examine relational needs acquisition outside the sphere of finding other work to do and promoting mutual needs getting within the couple context.

When and How to Help Couples Split Amicably

The role of the couples therapist is to help couples that comes for help to find a new and better way of having their relational needs met within the context of their relationship. In many, or even most, cases the goal is to help couples strengthen or save their relationship, a goal typically seen as the ideal "happy ending" to therapy and that, for most couples, was the driving force that brought them to therapy in the first place. In some cases, however, couples will find after therapy that the only way they feel their relational needs can be met will be separately, and perhaps with other people. Such an outcome, while not the "happy ending" most couples attending therapy dream of, is not necessarily a *bad* outcome; we have all encountered former couples who maintain friendly relationships and even raise families together in a spirit of cooperation and mutual respect. This too can be a happy outcome, especially when it is compared with the alternatives: a couple grimly "sticking it out for the sake of the children" and making everybody thoroughly miserable in the process; a bitter separation and acrimonious divorce, accompanied by the deeply distressing and damaging process of battling over custody; or the gradual removal of one parent from the children's lives, possibly forever.

Because it can be frustrating for therapists to feel that couples' decisions to stay together or separate is inappropriate, it is important to continuously remind yourself that your mandate is to help couples reach an informed decision about their relationship—about whether it is possible, under the circumstances, for them to continue to want meet each other's relational needs on an ongoing basis.

In the case of couples who eventually decide or realize that they are no longer likely to be happy together, the therapist's job is to help them to find a way to engage in meaningful dialogue with one another, to separate in a respectful way, to collaborate, if they have children, toward finding solutions to potential problems relating to child custody and support and to the inevitable stresses their children will experience, and to assist them in avoiding the damaging acrimony and blame that all too often result from separation and divorce. When couples with children do separate, they need to be able to accept that they will always be bound to each other by their children and that they will need to find their own way of co-parenting, even if they are not all under the same roof. While accepting that a parental split does not have to be a disaster for the family unit, there will always be practical dilemmas that need solutions, and there will frequently, if not invariably, be considerable distress on the part of most family members surrounding the period of separation. Individual members of a couple may have to accept that their plans to move to another city or country are unfair to the family they created with their one-time partner and will inevitably have to embrace the fact that, if they have children, they will always (or at least until their children grow up and no longer need parenting, as such) have to cooperate and collaborate with one another. As well, as couples go through the process of coming to accept that their journey through life together is largely over, they should remember what their important relational needs are and how not meeting those needs has affected their relationship. This will be important for at least three reasons. First, if members of the couple dyad decide to form another significant relationship, they will not be as vulnerable to making the same mistakes they have made in the past and will be more tuned in to how their less useful emotions can predicate poor problem resolution. Second, since these relational needs apply to all relationships, the couples work they have carried out together can prove very useful at work, at the gym, at family functions, and so forth. Third, if these issues do crop up in their attempts to co-parent their children and to maintain a civil or, hopefully, friendly relationship, they will understand what these negative feelings are all about and will use more appropriate strategies, some gleaned in the previous couples work, so that the children will not be caught in the cross-fire of the parents' issues. Ideally, the respectful and useful dialogue they have become able to engage in, thanks to therapy, will remain a feature of their relationship even now that they are separated.

At this point, we'll move our focus to the family, which is usually formed in the context of a couple, and the identity, issues, and problems that so often spring from the unresolved tensions between the original pairing.

8
LIFE STAGES AND COUPLES

Although raising a family is not an essential quality of couplehood, sharing what can often be a particularly joyful burden is one of the most common uniting characteristics for many couples. A majority of couples, including many same-sex couples, form at least in part for the purpose of having and bringing up a family, a period that occupies a significant proportion of one's active life, as children grow from baby-hood through childhood to adolescence and beyond and eventually, in a majority of cases, becoming parents themselves. This means that a large proportion of couples are not a discrete unit but a subset of the larger unit that is a family, especially because creating children and working together to help them grow to adulthood often enhances or complicates the ties between the adult members of their couple and their own parents, siblings, and wider family group. Because mak-ing the shift from couple to family means taking a huge step into the unknown, it is not surprising that rifts and tensions between couples so often emerge—for example, when a couple decides to try for a baby, around the birth of a first or subsequent child, or when children reach their own important life stages, such as starting school, entering ado-lescence, or leaving home.

While most parents are delighted to be joined by a new family member, parenting brings with it a host of potential stressors and difficulties that can create problems for couples where there were no problems before or brings to the fore issues that previously seemed minor. In parenting, we typically revert to the models we know best: those we learned from our own mother and father and from the wider culture in which we grew up. As each family is different, the variety in parenting skills and styles is immense.

Becoming the heads of a family can be an enormous challenge to any couple and a challenge that begins even before the first child is born. While the new mother is confronted early in pregnancy with the reality of the situation in the form of the physical changes she is experiencing and the new responsibilities and challenges that are already presenting themselves, such as the necessity of trying to abstain from smoking and consuming alcohol, for the father these changes are primarily represented by alterations in his partner's behavior and may be more difficult to assimilate. Equally, when children are small and are very dependent on their mother—often even for their sustenance in the form of breast milk—fathers can feel isolated and left out to the point of feeling irrelevant. As parenthood continues to present challenges to couples' integrity, it is more important than ever that they find a way to clearly and respectfully express their relational needs to each other.

The Needs Acquisition and Behavior Change (ABC) model is easy to apply to couples with children, to families with older children and adolescents, and to adolescents and can be readily adapted to therapists' own style and clients' particular circumstances. With children who are in less verbal stages of their development, therapists might need to use more "projective" techniques within the range of therapies for children, which could include play therapy (Lambreth, 2002) or drawing (art therapy; Hogan, 2001) to ascertain their relational needs as well as to work with them. In other words, while the Needs ABC model, in my experience, has been most commonly used with more verbal clients, it can also be used with younger, less verbal clients if the therapeutic interventions are appropriately modified to accommodate them. While there is not a fixed guideline as to precisely at what age the Needs ABC model can begin to be usefully applicable to children, such clients do need to be either sufficiently verbal or intellectually aware to engage in the therapeutic process, a prerequisite that eliminates infants and preverbal children in general.

Let's explore an example of how one couple's failure to meet each others' needs impacted on their whole family.

John's performance at work had been under par for quite a while. One morning, after he had arrived late several mornings in a row at the paper mill where he worked, his foreman laid into him without even bothering to step out of earshot of John's fellow workers on the shift. When the bell rang to announce the end of the afternoon shift, John headed not home but straight out of the paper mill and into one of the local bars, where he knocked back several large whiskies before staggering out. John had always enjoyed drinking, but it was only a year ago or so that drinking had become a problem for him. He used to get drunk with the boys once in a while; now he is doing it several times a week and is drinking at home as well. This is eating into the modest budget that John's work provides for his family and is also threatening his relationship with his wife, Mary-Ellen.

Mary-Ellen, John's wife of almost 9 years, was upset about her husband's new drinking habits but felt there was little she could say to him—although she could think of plenty to say when she was on the phone to her mother or her sisters. She was really worried about him, but she was angry as well. She knew that something was bothering John—he had never drunk like this before—but she didn't know what and couldn't think of how to ask. Besides, she was busy with the kids, who were occupying more and more of her time as they grew up. Mary-Ellen had worked as a manicurist before her marriage and was now doing temporary work as a clerk at Walmart. Goodness knew they needed some help when the holidays came around, and this Christmas was going to be a nightmare because the way John was going on it didn't look like there was going to be any Christmas bonus this year, which meant some serious difficulty paying for the toys the children would expect and the lavish Christmas dinner that was just part of the whole thing. Walmart didn't pay a lot, but the earnings were better than nothing and the shifts were flexible. The three kids were close in age, and taking care of them demanded a lot of attention. While Mary-Ellen was working, the two little ones attended a daycare center. Jonathan, the oldest at age 11, let himself in with a key and waited an hour or so until his mom got home. He was supposed to start doing his homework; usually, though, the television in the corner of the living room posed too much of a temptation, and he ended up watching that instead. John was supposed to watch only the cable children's channel, but Mary-Ellen knew that he was tuning in to wrestling shows and who knows what else. She didn't want to think about it, because she knew that there probably wasn't a whole lot she could do about it anyway, and she didn't feel ready to sit down and start a discussion about why certain channels just weren't appropriate for a kid his age. In the meantime, John had started coming home from work a couple of hours late on a regular basis. "At least," Mary-Ellen thought to herself, "he's out with friends and able to let off steam about the things that are making him tense. I know how he is feeling. I'd like to get out more often myself." Even though John was often coming home a little worse for wear, she hoped that staying out with the boys was a way for him to let off steam; she didn't know that, increasingly, John was drinking on his own after his friends had returned home to their wives and families.

Shortly before the violent incident that finally brought Mary-Ellen and John into therapy, John "calmed down" after work with three beers and then knocked back a few whiskies when his crowd showed up after 5 p.m.; he had left work an hour and a half early after yet another warning from his supervisor. One thing led to another and one drink to another. At 10 p.m., John finally headed home. He wasn't able to take the bus, let alone drive, so he blew $20 he could ill afford on a taxi.

At home in their two-bedroom apartment, Mary-Ellen had no time to worry about John or the dinner getting cold on the table. Their three children needed all her attention and patience. It had been their bedtime several hours ago, but this had been one of those days. Helena, age 3, was in bed at last but was still crying and feverish with a sore throat. Mary-Ellen was afraid she might also be coming down with chicken pox—it was going around the school and was probably inevitable that her kids would pick it up—but had not had time to check for spots. Jonathan had been glued to the television since coming home from school and at least claimed to have done his homework. But the real problem was Willie, age 6. Mary-Ellen didn't seem to be able to do anything with him anymore. Helena acted spoiled and Jonathan was turning into a surly boy, but Willie seemed to be completely out of control. As John came in, Willie was sitting on the floor, banging his head against his blocks and screaming, as he had been for the last hour. He had soiled his trousers as well but had refused to let Mary-Ellen do anything about it. He was obviously embarrassed but was dealing with it by getting mad. Nothing she could say or do would calm him down, and she was afraid to restrain him physically in case she hurt him. The daycare center where the two smaller kids spent their afternoons had called that afternoon and asked Mary-Ellen to come and take Willie home. He was fighting with the other kids, and had been caught scribbling on the walls in the boys' bathroom. Mary-Ellen had gotten permission to leave work early and had been trying to cope with Willie's tantrums ever since. She was terrified she might lose her job. The teachers in school—the daycare center was attached to the local grade school—were finding Willie just as difficult as she was, and she knew they might refuse to take him the following term. The guidance counselor had suggested in May that Mary-Ellen have him tested or get counseling before first grade started in September. She suggested that he might have attention deficit hyperactivity disorder (ADHD) or maybe Asperger's syndrome. Mary-Ellen had tried discussing the suggestion with John, who had been outraged.

"I'm not letting any shrinks get their hands on my son," he had said emphatically. "There's nothing wrong with him. He's just high-spirited, like I was when I was his age, and I turned out just fine. Besides, it'll probably cost money, and money is not something we have a lot of these days. Anyway, don't you read the papers? ADHD isn't real; it's just a scam to sell drugs."

Now, it took a minute before Mary-Ellen heard John's pounding fists over the noise of the television, Willie's screaming, and Helena's crying. When Mary-Ellen opened the door at last, one word led to another, and it didn't end there. Mary-Ellen told John that he was a poor excuse for a man; John retorted that if she did her job like she was supposed to and kept the kids under control he'd be more inclined to come home early. Mary-Ellen said she should have married Shane Willis when she had a chance. He had his own shop now, and she was sure he was nice to his wife and kids. That was the final straw. John had yelled at Mary-Ellen before; he had even shoved her once. This time, however, he pushed her up against the wall with his hands around her throat and dug his knee into her belly. Somehow Mary-Ellen managed to free herself and lock herself in the bathroom, where she called 911 on her cell phone. The police came and took John to jail, where he spent the night. He was charged by the police with domestic assault and told he could not have any form of contact with Mary-Ellen for the time being. During his hearing, the judge mandated him to domestic violence treatment. At the same time, the court social worker strongly encouraged the couple to attend counseling following John's treatment.

During the intake (screening) interview with the therapist, John admitted to what he had done. "I'll never drink again! It's that goddamn booze that screwed things up. It wasn't really me who hit Mary-Ellen; it was the guy I become when I drink. I don't know why I have to take your stupid course. All I ever needed to do was stop drinking!"

Even though there is no rationale for the use of violence as a problem-solving strategy, John's drinking and violent behavior are only symptoms of his unmet relational needs, needs that he has been unable to express in a mature and coherent manner. As well, it is universally understood that alcohol is not the cause of violence, though it does have a disinhibiting effect on the ability to set appropriate limits—in John's case, his ability to become frustrated or angry without acting out in a destructive manner. It appears evident that John has been unable to feel adequate [competency] at work in meeting the expectations of his foreman and, as a father and husband, unable to help guide his children toward more productive behaviors and to support his family adequately. When he faced the possibility of losing his job, John started to feel like he was not a "real man." In addition, John was probably thinking something like, "If I can't do better than this I will never gain my family's respect, and Mary-Ellen will have an affair and leave me" [reliability]. For her part, Mary-Ellen was probably feeling betrayed [loyalty] by John's drinking and the accompanying problematic behavior and marginalized [respect] with regard to her need for getting John to help her care for three young children, who require attention from their father as well as their increasingly harassed mother.

As we have seen, the Needs ABC model is strongly focused on the universality of experience; the fact that the emotional landscape can be described using a vocabulary that allows every listener to tap into the issues being discussed. In practical terms this means that, rather than examining only individual client needs, the counselor's role is to involve couples in discussing the unmet needs of both members, to relate to their experience, and to collaborate in finding ways forward that may enable them once and for all to break out of the loop in which they have been stuck. In the case of John and Mary-Ellen, John needs to find a more effective way of meeting his need to feel competent and reliably connected to Mary-Ellen. At the same time, he must be able to help Mary-Ellen regain her trust for him and to feel respected by him. While John's treatment relating to domestic violence is mandated, the couple is provided with the details of a couples therapist and is asked to make contact when the time is right. At this point, John is living on a temporary basis in a hostel, but he and Mary-Ellen are on speaking terms and are both hoping that they will be able to get back together again soon, despite Mary-Ellen's anxiety about John's potential for violence. John asks Mary-Ellen to make the call, as she is "better at that sort of thing."

When Mary-Ellen rings, the therapist—with the understanding that Mary-Ellen has confirmed that John has made sufficient progress in his own therapy to proceed with couples work and that she feels safe to proceed—affirms her bravery by saying that he knows it takes courage not to give up: "You and John are both taking a big step forward, and that can be only a good thing." They agree to meet in the evenings, when John has finished work and when the children can be left with a neighbor for an hour or so.

John and Mary-Ellen came to therapy regularly on a once-weekly basis for seven sessions. In the first session, both are quite subdued, almost accepting of the possibility that things would never be the same again, that their relationship had been destroyed forever. Mary-Ellen states that she has already discussed with her mother how they might share child-care duties if she and John split up and she has to return to work full-time. Both seem to agree that John's drinking was problematic, but John seems to have a bit of trouble "owning" his responsibility entirely for what he has done while "under the influence." He says, "I know my drinking was out of control and I shouldn't have hit her, but when I drink I lose control," as if to say that the alcohol might have been responsible for his violence against Mary-Ellen and that he is all but powerless to do anything about it. Rather than pursue challenging John at this point in time about this difficulty, the focus is not put on the behavior at first, especially because John is not currently living with his family. He also agrees to continue with his domestic violence group until it has been determined that he no longer needs intervention of this sort. In the context of the couple's therapy, the initial focus is on an examination of individual relational needs in the relationship. The first session, therefore, illuminated John's need to feel connected to his wife unconditionally [reliability] as well as his need to feel adequate [competency] as a husband

and father. Mary-Ellen feels that John doesn't value her role in the family [respect] and seemed to choose alcohol and his friends over Mary-Ellen even though he had promised her time and time again that he would be there for her [loyalty]. Both feel encouraged by the first session, as it seems to clarify what was causing them to operate as they had.

In the second session, the therapist examines their developmental history, specifically with regard to how they saw their relationships with their parents. In John's case, the therapist helps him uncover the origins of his destructive behavior. John grew up the youngest child in a large family. His parents both worked outside the home, and he felt like he never got any consistent attention from them, loving or otherwise. Because he was by far the smallest, the sense he got was that he was "holding everybody back." His older brothers and sisters were usually charged with the tasks of getting him washed and dressed every day and "out of his mother's hair." John had never really done anything for himself, not because he was not encouraged to be independent but because it would take longer than if his siblings just did it for him. John always felt that nobody really believed that he could do anything on his own. To make matters worse, John's parents both drank and seemed to become inaccessible emotionally when they did. "They changed," he said, "into zombies. When I saw Michael Jackson's *Thriller* video for the first time, that's what I thought of: mom and dad."

Mary-Ellen's father, on the other hand, left her family home for the first time when she was just 5 years old. Over the course of the next 10 years he had "come and gone" as he pleased and never seemed to have to accept responsibility for anything he did. When he came he was "treated like a king," and when he left the family just got on with things. Her mother, Sandra, was an unskilled woman who had her first child before she turned 16. Because she felt that she had little to offer prospective employers, she had never looked for serious work and had put up with whatever her errant husband dished out, feeling like she had no choice since she was financially dependent on him. Mary-Ellen had resolved as a child that she would never put up with this sort of thing. She had trained as a manicurist, feeling that this profession was good, flexible, and gave her the potential to earn relatively good money. Most of all, she had always longed for a man on whom she could depend for love and practical and emotional support. When John failed to live up to his side of the bargain she felt they had agreed upon, she felt bitterly betrayed and very disinclined to trust him again, because "that's what Mom did, and look where that got her." However, she continued to accept his erratic behavior until the violence escalated and was observed by one of their children. When Mary-Ellen understood with greater clarity her own and John's needs, she was able to appreciate how difficult it initially was for her to set appropriate limits with John. Now she was able to begin to challenge her own "demons" and become more assertive with regard to her relational needs. By making it clear that drinking to excess and being abusive were not acceptable, she was able to meet her own need to insist on being respected by her partner.

Knowing that John was finally clear on what was acceptable and what was not, she was able to ask for his help and advice with the children, validating him as a father and a husband.

In this session Mary-Ellen and John were able to get a clearer understanding of where they learned to do what they did with regard to "survival" in their relationship. As well, they appeared to more clearly understand how their relational needs had developed. John seemed to understand that he had always been fearful of "never making the grade" and acknowledged that Mary-Ellen's taking over the role of principal decision maker in the family because of his drinking only exacerbated his fears that he was not respected as the head of the family, since he felt he should be. Mary-Ellen realized that she, almost without thinking, would take charge of her family whenever she felt abandoned by John. She admitted that her anger at John prevented her from including him in her decision making.

In the third session, the couple's individual challenges to improve their relationship are discussed. John has to remain emotionally available and demonstrate that he values what Mary-Ellen does for him and the family. Mary-Ellen has to try her best to include John in decisions she makes, as long as he is doing his part. As well, she is encouraged to validate his successes. Toward the end of the session, John still appears to have difficulty with the concept that alcohol is not an excuse for his behavior, so it is suggested that they each log their negative emotions and report back with regard to their perceived successes and failures in dealing with difficult feelings in their relationship.

The fourth session begins with an examination of their "behavior/emotion" log. Mary-Ellen acknowledges that, even though he was never threatening, there were a few dicey moments when John appeared to be "taking things for granted." Rather than alienating him as she has done in the past, she is able to discuss this with him (as she was encouraged to do when the logging began). John admits that at times he has had thoughts about drinking and that he has become quite angry at Mary-Ellen on one occasion, when she told him "he didn't know what he was talking about." With this incident the therapist is able to "convince" John that alcohol is not the issue but that his unmet relational needs are. John states that he understands that his anger is generally not about Mary-Ellen but instead about feelings from his childhood that come up for him when Mary-Ellen does certain things. As well, he agrees that alcohol exacerbates the potential for him to lose control but admits that earlier on in their relationship he "lost it" without alcohol being in the picture.

In the fifth, sixth, and seventh sessions, both partners continue to examine how their emotions are affected by unmet relational needs on a day-to-day basis. They continue to use the logs, and, even though their therapist suggests that termination of treatment can be done after the sixth session, they state that they want to have "just one more session in about 4 weeks just to be sure we are able to continue successfully without the therapist."

The seventh and final sessions proved to be positive. By this point, John and Mary-Ellen were able to describe how their development impacted on their negative emotions without a therapeutic interpretation. John stated that understanding where his needs came from made it easier for him to examine his behavior more objectively. He also shared that understanding how Mary-Ellen's behavior was impacted by her own history made him more sensitive and motivated to meet her needs.

Engaging Adolescents in Family Therapy

Parents of adolescents face a particular set of challenges when they suddenly find themselves living with an individual who is as physically big and powerful as they, who challenges their assumptions, and who tests their patience and parenting skills to the limit. At the

Figure 8.1   Adolescents.

same time, adolescents need a different sort of parenting approach than what may have served them very well to date. They need more freedom and the capacity to make and learn from their own mistakes, although the extent to which they should be allowed to do so is a matter of great debate. When children reach adolescence, parents' views and assumptions about almost everything are likely to be challenged: sexuality, politics, acceptable behavior in social contexts. If adolescent children are perceived by their parents to be behaving in a less than ideal way, parents may adopt blame situations and attempt to accuse their partner for what they believed to be their children's limitations or failings. The constant presence of individuals who are young, vibrant, and about to embrace life can also be a daily reminder to parents that they are now in a process of having to "let go of" their child—that they will soon no longer have any control over them—and they may feel like dreams, aspirations, and hopes they may have once held for their offspring are no longer likely to be fulfilled.

We are all aware that adolescence occurs along a continuum; it does not automatically begin with puberty and end with one's 18th birthday. It is a period when individuals begin to withdraw from the extraordinary intimacy of the family, to test boundaries, to challenge assumptions of parental omnipotence, and to start striving toward becoming the adults they wish to be. As a result, engaging an adolescent in the process of family therapy can be even more challenging since it could be considered a further threat to their independence and autonomy, which they are in the process of "fighting" for.

When adolescents come for therapy, it may well be that their problems stem from a wider dysfunction in the family in general or from problematic behaviors the parents may be modeling. Initially, however,

> I usually meet with parents first to find out their perspective of the child's history and pertinent developmental concerns such as a diagnosis of learning or attention problems and then suggest that their "problematic" child come in alone to tell his or her side of the story.

we need to apply the Needs ABC approach specifically to *their* concerns and needs while remaining alert to the tensions and undercurrents of their wider family circle. It is crucial that they not see the therapist as one of "them"—just another authority figure who doesn't get it and who is trying to impose his or her own standards without really thinking about what that means. Furthermore, adolescents tend to be particularly sensitive to "labeling" and appreciative when they are seen as individuals with legitimate needs and desires. As Selekman (1993, p. 20) writes, "...The labels given to ... adolescents and their families had a stigmatizing effect and made their situations worse." By the time adolescents reach the stage where they encounter a therapist, they have often experienced months or even years of conflict with their parents or other figures of authority, such as teachers. Therapists will have to work carefully to ensure that they are not viewed by the adolescent as just another oppressive adult who will be quick to assume that the situation can be easily summed up.

Once a useful working bond has been established, the scene is set to supportively challenge the young persons and help them work toward negotiating a better relationship with their parents. In forming this bond, it is helpful to understand that the therapist may have to act as parent, nurturer, and teacher from time to time while offering empathy, support, and insight. Both adolescents and adults like to know what is going on. In my practice, I find it helpful to offer my interpretations of what may underlie presenting behaviors and needs "up front" rather than relying on cryptic statements or rationalizations.

It is worth a reminder that, in all therapies, it is important to give clients a feeling of "control" over the therapeutic process. Before challenging the dysfunctional behavior, joining with clients in a meaningful way must be accomplished. The same is especially true for adolescents, especially if you want the outcome to be productive sessions with the rest of the family. By first allying with the relational need and examining the emotion associated with it, clients can feel that the therapist is on their side in understanding their predicament. Selekman (1993, p. 82) says:

> ...If the therapist joins well enough with the adolescent, the youth may
> be willing to do whatever the parents and the therapist request.... Most

adolescent clients tend to cooperate with therapists that pay attention to what their goals and expectations are, not just what the parents want.

Once the therapeutic alliance has been affirmed, therapists can go on to collaboratively discuss the pros and cons of the strategies they have used. It is important not to take adolescents' side "against" their parents, the system, and so forth but only to demonstrate an empathic perspective—an understanding that even if the behavioral strategy seems "crazy" they are not.

Let's look at a case study.

> Briana, who is almost 17 years old, has agreed with great reluctance to attend therapy together with her parents.
>
> "I don't want to be here," she says frankly, but not impolitely, to the therapist, Allison, during the intake interview. "But sometimes it's easier to say 'OK' just to get them off my back."
>
> Briana is a very bright high school student who plans to go to university. She gets good grades in school and has never been in any serious trouble of any kind. She also has very idiosyncratic views about life in general, is not afraid of airing them, dresses in full-blown Goth, and pronounces herself to be a Trotskyist, although it's not clear whether she really under-stands the implications of her declaration. As a child, both she and her parents report, they all had an excellent relationship; however, this has been deteriorating over the course of the last 2 years, and communication between Briana and her parents has all but broken down.
>
> "It's not that she does anything actively mean," her mother, Mary, explains. "But she's so—I don't know—cold and indifferent. She treats us like we are idiots, never wants to do anything with the rest of the family, won't even come to Christmas Mass with us. She won't even eat with us. She just takes her vegan mush from the fridge and shuffles upstairs with it to eat it in her bedroom. She says she can't stand the smell of meat, but she used to love hamburgers. When she goes away to college, what then? She'll just disappear?"
>
> "And I don't trust these so-called Goth friends of hers, either," inter-jects Steve, Briana's father. "What's with the black makeup and the stupid jewelry? She looks ridiculous. I don't even recognize my little princess anymore. I don't know if she's taking drugs, but surely that's the logical next step. Isn't it? And then her life will be basically over. I've seen a few people go down that road before, and they don't generally come back up it again!"
>
> Listening to her parents talk about her, Briana is plainly exasperated and makes little attempt to hide it.
>
> A few things about Briana and her family are apparent from how the family presents in the therapy room and from some additional exploration

of the family's *modus vivendi*. As well as the generational difference, there is a rather pronounced class and educational imbalance between the girl and her parents. Briana's mother and father are both bright people from poor backgrounds who left school early and have worked hard ever since. They have never had the time or the inclination to sit down and read anything other than the Sunday papers. Realizing that their daughter was bright and fully cognizant that she would benefit from educational opportunities not offered to them, they have always encouraged her to study, and their efforts seemed to have been rewarded when Briana was given a full scholarship to attend one of the most prestigious private girls' high schools in the city. However, an unforeseen result of this has been that Briana has already acquired a much higher educational level than her parents and a rather ambivalent view toward them and their background. From the lofty height of junior year in high school, they seem to her to be provincial and small-minded. In her self-confessed Trotskyism, Briana seems to be attempting to express some loyalty for her working-class roots, whereas in her evident reluctance to engage with her parents and family socially, to the extent of refusing to eat with them, she seems to be expressing more than the common teenager's attempts to exert autonomy and independence. It seems that she is torn between loyalty for her family members, whom she genuinely loves very much, and for her "tribe," represented to her by the well-educated daughters and sons of her city's elite.

Briana's parents also seem to be sending some mixed signals. When she was a bright, independent child, they supported and encouraged her in everything she did and were always delighted by her originality and talent, but now that she is a bright, independent young adult, Briana's father, in particular, worries frequently and audibly that she is "getting into drugs," even though there is no evidence to suggest any such thing, and complains about her "weird" sense of fashion, which, although flamboyant, is modest and harmless and would seem to most onlookers to be a perfectly ordinary adolescent form of expression with no particular associations with a drug culture. Certainly, it's unlikely that Briana would be continuing to do so well at school if she were dabbling in self-destructive habits.

Having long been rewarded for her independence of mind and spirit, Natasha now feels that she is being punished for displaying these same qualities.

Allison, the therapist who is helping Briana and her family, makes a few observations about relational needs for both the parents and Briana. She understands that a focus on Briana's behavior would most probably alienate her and make her feel that she was being "teamed up against." Allison first speaks to Briana to make sure she understands that there are two sides to the story—that her feelings may be justified. She will work with Briana in individual sessions not to provoke shame and resentment that could cripple the therapy from the start.

"Boy," says Allison, "you must be a little confused. First you feel that if you live up to certain expectations [reliability] everyone will be happy. Now that you seem to have succeeded in doing so well at school I guess you feel that your parents are still not satisfied that you are doing the right thing [competency]."

Allison then quickly turns to her parents, adding, "I guess you guys are feeling a bit frustrated that, from your perspective, Briana is not honoring your value system [respect]—that she has, unexpectedly, turned into someone you can't understand [loyalty]."

Now the family is able to have a discussion around their needs without pointing a finger at what each person has done to upset the other. Allison is careful to bring the discussion back to needs and emotions when one of them tries to bring it back to the power struggle that brought them into therapy. Briana seems to feel more included rather than alienated, and Allison suggests that she meet with Briana a few times to understand more clearly what is happening with her. She suggests that when they are ready to do so she will reconvene a family session to go over the issues at hand. In addition to a discussion of confidentiality, Allison also inquires as to whether Briana would be OK about her having a session with only her parents if the need arises to clarify some of Briana's concerns. All seem to approve of the plan, and an appointment is made to begin some individual work with Briana.

Some of the behavioral goals that Allison could discuss with Briana and her parents, once Briana feels more inclined to collaborate, could include that Briana not isolate herself and eat with her family rather than alone upstairs, provided she is free to restrict her diet to the vegan meals she prepares for herself. At the same time, Briana's parents could be asked to consider being more supportive of Briana's successes and try to stop complaining about their daughter's choice of clothes and to stop nagging her about drugs in the complete absence of any proof that she has ever taken any. Later, Briana and her parents are asked to think of an activity that all enjoy and to set aside some time for it every so often.

Embedded in Allison's treatment of Briana and her parents is the assumption that they, as a family, will be able to make the necessary changes for happiness to return to their relationship. In general, therapists should always assume that positive change is not just possible but that it *will* happen provided clients are willing to explore their own needs and behaviors. In the case of adolescent clients, in particular, therapists will benefit from demonstrating that they do not consider them or their needs to be subsidiary to the presenting problem as described by the parents. Therapists must strive, as Selekman (1993, p. 90) puts it, to "capitalize on the strengths and resources of the adolescent and help foster a cooperative therapeutic relationship"; to be an "effective intergenerational negotiator for the family" (Selekman, p. 96).

Let's turn now to the case of a very different adolescent.

Jeremy is a 16-year-old boy who was spending a year and a half at a Juvenile Detention Center for uttering death threats to a classmate at his school. He and his 13-year-old brother Lionel have been raised mostly by their father since Jeremy was 6, at which point his mother, who had been a heavy drug user, left the family without explanation. Richard, the boys' father, is a 41-year-old technician at an auto parts manufacturing facility. After his wife left, he took on a second job "to make more money to be better able to give my kids what they need." Because of the pressures of work, Richard left his sons with their grandmother (his mother), whom Jeremy described as "an old woman who thought she was in the 'old country.'"

Bob, the therapist, initially met with Richard, who told him about Jeremy's history and that he had been placed on time-release methylphenidate (for attention deficit disorder) since elementary school. At high school, Jeremy started to cause problems, which included refusing to take his medication. He had been compliant since "serving his time," and it did seem that the medication helped somewhat with Jeremy's impulsivity, although it would not be adequate in terms of providing a long-term solution to his difficult behaviors.

When Jeremy arrived for his first session, his initial comment was, "Let's get this over with so I can spend some time with my father." Bob used empathy for Jeremy's feelings and allied himself with Jeremy's point of view by initially focusing on how he must have felt about being sent away, despite that his threats to his classmates were a serious matter. Jeremy responded by becoming able to recount how his mother had remained almost absent from his life and, somewhat tearfully, how much he wanted to be with his father and brother and how badly he had missed them when he was "put away." He related that his mother never seemed to have time for anyone and was either "stoned" or "missing in action." Jeremy was often tearful in discussing his relationship with his younger brother and how his father always tried to get them the things they wanted. As the initial meeting progressed, Bob suggested to Jeremy that family was very important to him and that he probably missed his father now, as he had always done when he was with his grandmother. Jeremy burst into tears. When he had calmed himself, Bob commented, "It must feel awful to feel so unimportant that your father would get a second job and leave you with your grandmother instead of spending time with you and your brother." Jeremy looked up wide eyed, thought for a moment, and said, "Yeah, and I'm glad he has only one job now."

Bob continued to ally with the feelings that had caused Jeremy's behavior, and the youth became able to engage in an exchange that would eventually expose his relational needs. It was apparent that he felt abandoned and marginalized by those he loved and that his perception was that he was defective. He admitted that his feeling was that since no one cared enough to spend time with him he must be "bad" and that as a consequence he might as well make no effort since he was just living up to others' expectations anyway.

A favorable indication for Jeremy was that Richard, his father, was prepared to do whatever it took to be with his children as much as possible. In fact, despite worries about money, he had quit his second job just before Jeremy was referred to therapy. Jeremy was obviously happy about his father's decision and said that Lionel was as well. As Jeremy and Bob ended their session, they agreed that the whole family would come to therapy so that they could talk together about what would make them all happier so that *everyone* could be heard.

Adolescent Couples

The Needs ABC model is applicable, as we have discussed, with any groups composed of individuals who have sufficient verbal and intellectual skills to engage in dialogue with a therapist or with individual clients who fit into this category. It is, therefore, an excellent therapeutic model to use in providing individual or group therapy to adolescents. In the case of very young parents or adolescent couples or co-parents, the Needs ABC model can be of great assistance in enabling them to face their unmet needs in the context of the considerable challenges they face in a society in which to be an adolescent and a parent is no easy task. While all that we have already stated about the Needs ABC model is valid for adolescent couples, we are highlighting this demographic here, as such individuals do have to deal with additional pressures compared with their older counterparts and because adolescents generally have not left their own natal family unit, practically or emotionally (Erikson, 1959).

Adolescence is also, of course, the period when the body comes of age, and individuals who were so recently children are suddenly equipped with full reproductive capacity and with a full range of sexual and emotional feelings that are quite new and can be difficult to process, especially in societies, such as the predominant societies in the West, that send young people very mixed messages about how they should be behaving related to their sexuality and emotional lives (Esman, 1975). On one hand, young people are encouraged by the media to dress "sexy" and to strive to make themselves attractive to the opposite sex. On the other, they are exhorted to not actually engage in sexual behavior, or at least not to procreate, until they are well into their 20s, if not later.

In traditional societies today, and certainly in times gone by, it was customary for girls and boys to marry much earlier than is nowadays the case. However, when marriages did occur involving couples of which one or both could be as young as 14, the social environment into which the young couples were welcomed was very different from today. Typically, they would live with paternal or maternal parents, and any children born into the relationship were raised in the context of a wider family that generally shared the work of bringing them up. For most people, educational and career options were limited and were thus not hampered by the presence of offspring at such a young age. Nowadays, everything is different. For almost all middle-class families and for most families in the West in general one of the constant battles of the parents of adolescents is the prevention of pregnancy until the young adults in question have reached an age deemed appropriate by their social milieu for reproduction—typically, at least 10 years after reproduction has become physically possible and often in fact beyond the years of optimum reproductive health. Increasingly, educated couples often wait until they are well into their 30s to start a family. While the drawbacks of this approach are well known, the benefits are manifold, such as more freedom to study, to develop a career, to travel, to "become oneself." Frequently, however, the system breaks down and, very often—with considerable degrees of national, regional, and ethnic variation—adolescents become parents, despite the widespread availability of reliable forms of contraception and abortion. The degree to which they succeed at this new role depends on many factors, including, of course, the level of support they receive from their families and societies and also the degree of success with which they manage to delay additional pregnancies or continue their education or training.

It is well known that, statistically, the children of teenaged parents are less likely to do well in school and are more likely to be badly nourished or dangerously overweight. But statistics are of very limited use in individual cases. With appropriate interventions and help, adolescents can use parenthood as a time in which to continue to grow and mature while also providing a secure home for their children.

This is easier for everyone when both parents remain involved in the child's life, even if they do not remain together, and when extended families are in a position to provide tangible, especially emotional, support. Early intervention with teenaged fathers, in particular, can help them to identify with their child, to accept their new status as parents, and to remain involved with their offspring even when or if both they and their mother have developed new relationships and responsibilities away from each other.

With appropriate help and support, even 17-year-olds can be good parents and can fulfill their potential, whether together or separately. Any therapist encountering adolescent parents in practice will need to be aware of a few salient issues. In the case of unplanned pregnancy in adolescence, it is not untypical for men to still want to be adolescents, for example, while women might "grow up" suddenly in the course and aftermath of their pregnancy, with the understanding that one cannot be a mother and a child at the same time. Men do not share the impact of childbirth to nearly the same extent as women, because they do not personally experience birth giving and the initial connection and attachment to a child the way women do right after birth. They also do not experience pregnancy in the same way, having not had the physical feeling of something growing and developing in the same way women do. In other words, for most women, giving birth can be a powerful wake-up call, whereas for some men—and especially very young fathers—it can be just a nuisance, with an incomplete understanding of all of the implications.

Whether adolescents choose to have children or just happen to become parents unexpectedly, several challenges face people at this developmental stage, one being the concept of commitment. Here, there often can be a sense of ambivalence as to whether to "close the door," so to speak, to experimentation with different partners and become a unit committed "till death do us part," a daunting prospect even for much older partners. Here are two examples of the sort of situation adolescent couples might bring into the therapy room.

Bob and Laura are aged 19 and 17, respectively. Bob is a trainee mechanic, who intends to settle down in the small town where he grew up. He is good at his job and feels confident that he will do well. Bob comes from a stable family background; his parents married young, and he seems to feel confident that settling down early is something he would like to do. In many ways, Bob seems to be a very mature young man. It's true that his horizons are quite narrow—he has never dreamed of leaving his home town—but there is nothing wrong with that.

Laura says that she loves Bob and respects him and that she wants to have her baby, but she is also afraid that becoming a mother and settling down will limit her possibilities. She's a reasonably high achiever in high school and expects to be admitted to Art College next year: "I've always wanted to be a painter. I know it's hard to make a living, but if I don't at least try I'll never know if I can make it." Like Bob, she comes from a happy family background. Her parents were very disappointed when she became pregnant, but they like Bob; now that the pregnancy is advanced they feel that Laura should give up her dreams of attending Art College and instead take a more vocational training, such as a secretarial course, so that she can work part-time when the baby is small and in the fullness of time help Bob to run his own mechanic's workshop.

In her 6th month of pregnancy, Laura has panicked and announced that she wants to "give the baby up for adoption," that she loves Bob but "doesn't know if she is in love with him," and that she fears she will resent her whole family, including the as yet unborn baby, if she ends up "stuck here in Hicksville forever where nothing ever happens."

At Bob's insistence, the young couple arranges to attend therapy, in the hope that they can reach a satisfactory position. Both adolescents' parents feel strongly that the baby should remain within the extended family rather than being given up for adoption.

"I know that Laura is smarter than me," Bob says. "That's one of the reasons I always liked her. She wasn't like the other girls. But I'm not stupid. I graduated high school, I'm good at my job and I'm really ready to settle down, even if we are young. It's not the end of the world. Hey, we could even be grandparents before we're 40."

"Bob just doesn't understand," says Laura. "OK, so I got myself into this situation, I do love him, and I'm sure I'll love the baby. But I always thought I'd get out of here. There was an art school in Chicago that liked my work. What if I never get a chance to do the things I think I can? My art teacher says I really have talent and that I could make it. I just don't want to stay here getting fat and bitter and disappointed—just like so many of the women in this damn town."

Another couple, from a middle-class suburb outside a city in the southern United States, is also expecting a child rather unexpectedly.

"We actually met at church camp," says Brad ruefully. "Kind of ironic, huh? I don't think either of us thought we'd end up like this—and neither did our parents."

"Yes, but what happened happened," says Linda. "Not the right way, but our parents have forgiven us, and they've all promised to stand by us as we have this baby and finish high school. Even before we get married."

"*If* we get married," adds Brad.

"Look, it's not the baby's fault," shouts Linda, with a flash of anger, "that we weren't able to resist temptation. Now I'm like this, and we've got to do the right thing."

"It's just really hard," says Brad. "I mean, we were each other's first boyfriend and girlfriend. How can we ever know if we really love each other or if we're just settling for, well, if we're just doing what we think we should?"

The reality of adult responsibility, and all that goes with it, is an important challenge to someone who may feel up to the task but in fact may be ill prepared for this developmental stage. Here are some examples of how a therapist might help adolescent couples cope more functionally with their reality.

Lillian, age 17, and Jacques, age 21, are not married but have been living together for 2 years. They have a 16-month-old son, Julius, who was a "happy accident" according to the couple. Lillian came in complaining that Jacques, who was a very good father to Julius "when he wanted to be," did very little to support her in general with "the less pleasant parenting tasks" such as preparing Julius's meals, cleaning the house, and giving Julius a bath. Lillian angrily stated that it was a good thing her parents were around to "sit" for Julius when she worked at her part-time job at the local library. She said, "I feel like I have two children, not one, and if I can manage to hold down a job and take care of the home, how difficult can it be for Jacques to take over a bit when he comes home from work?" Jacques worked in a blue-collar job driving a truck for his municipality. He stated, "She knows I work a long day to support her and the baby; I do as much overtime as I can—usually 12-hour days—and I'm zonked when I get home at night. I do what I can, but she's only working part-time and only from 8:30 to 4:00 at that. It's easier for her to do that stuff. I try to do whatever I can but it's never enough for the 'slave-driver.'"

"Yeah," Lillian snapped back, "and what about those 'slow' days and weekends when you want to play hockey with the boys? You seem to have time for that. Why don't you just grow up?"

Before Jacques could add any more fuel to the fire, Jon, the therapist, interjected, "So Lillian, it sounds like you feel that when you ask Jacques to do something it goes in one ear and out the other [respect]—that his friends are more important than his family [loyalty]. And Jacques, you seem to feel that you can never win no matter what you do [reliability] and that even when you do something it is wrong [competency]."

   In the subsequent session, an examination of their developmental history revealed that Lillian felt like she was the least favorite of all her siblings—that her parents, especially her father, seemed to "brush her off" when she asked for something and that, when they did listen, never followed through on their promises. Her father worked long days as well and had also seemed to have no time for her on weekends when she was a child because he was too busy with the other children. Things hadn't changed at all since she became a mother. Lillian understood that having a special needs brother took a lot of her parents' time—her younger brother Jake has Down's syndrome and needs a lot of attention—but felt they could have split up their time more equitably between her and her older sister. It had always seemed to her that she got "the short end of the stick." Lillian's mother was described as a fiercely independent woman who "wore the pants in the family" and ran the house "like an army base."

   Jacques, on the other hand, came from an extremely "traditional" family. His mother was a stay-at-home mom who also "ran the house." His father was the breadwinner and never lifted a hand around the house except to clean his golf clubs for the weekend. He described his mother as being extremely critical and said that she would blame things on him and never on his sister, who was 2 years younger and his only sibling.

   This information supported the hypothesis Jon had described in the first session, but there still seemed to be something missing. Why did Jacques seem to focus so much time on his friends when his child needed his attention, especially since he had expressed that "right now he [Julius] is my only joy in life." Given Jacques's own experience, it would seem that he would want to spend more time at home with his son and that by doing so he would inadvertently address part of Lillian's relational needs deficits.

   In the third session Jon explored this reality by examining the couple's decision to have the child even though the pregnancy had not been planned. It seems that when they first met at a party it felt like "love at first sight"; both agreed that they had never sensed this kind of connection and that they had each had begun to have committed relationships earlier than most—Lillian at 14 and Jacques at 16. This one just seemed special. When Lillian became pregnant, Jacques was not convinced that he wanted to have the baby, but Lillian persuaded him otherwise. Finally, Jacques thought, "Why not; we get along so well, and I always wanted a family. We can work this out." Jacques admitted, however, that he was never truly convinced that he had made the right decision. "I sacrificed a lot for her, giving up my freedom to settle down. I was really hoping to go away to school, get a good job, and then get married. She knew I liked to play hockey with my friends, and she knew my work schedule. Now all she does is raise the bar higher and higher, and if she doesn't like what I am doing, she tells me she hates my guts." Lillian immediately retorted, "I don't tell you, 'I hate your guts,' and we discussed the responsibility you would have to take if we decided to keep the baby."

   "Yeah," said Jacques, "but even when I try to help you give me heck."

Jon stated his concern that both of them had been "forced" into becoming a couple sooner than they had expected to be and that at their age it could be difficult to deal with the reality of becoming a parent before it's time. He then explained the dynamics of what he felt was going on: Lillian needed to feel that she and Julius—rather than his bachelor life—were Jacques's priority, and Jacques had to be reassured that he was being given credit for his efforts and could take a break from time to time from the stress of parenthood and have an opportunity to connect with his friends. Jon suggested that this was not an easy task but worth trying to negotiate for now, as both young people were very attached to their child. Both Jacques and Lillian agreed to try, and both acknowledged that they would be willing to attempt to accommodate the other more to see if that could bring them closer to the family Lillian wanted while relieving some of Jacques's anxiety about becoming a father so soon.

Another young couple had to deal with the issue of substance abuse and the impact that this was having on their relationship with each other.

Louise and Norman were both 18 when Louise became pregnant. They had met in middle school in their small, rural community. Now, they lived together and would often joke about "how neat it was to be roomies." Norm worked on his father's farm and struggled in school though he excelled at farming, something he enjoyed immensely. "I love working with my hands, and it's great working with my father and uncles," he said. Louise worked in a local video store, which she really enjoyed, although her parents both felt that she would have been capable of holding down a more skilled job. Now that she was pregnant, both agreed that they would take their relationship to another level—even marriage. She and Norm had gotten pregnant before but had gotten an abortion because of pressure from both their families.

"You both are too young to start a family; you have your whole lives ahead of you," their parents said. This time they both agreed to keep the child "no matter what." The couple often frequented their local public house for "drinks and snacks" with their friends. Once Louise discovered she was pregnant she would join Norm and "the gang" as usual but would end up nursing one beer until they left. At first Norm didn't say much, but one evening after having a few pints himself, he began to badger Louise: "Aw come on now, why not just have one more. What's wrong with you? You're no fun anymore." Louise said nothing but the next day appeared visibly sad and withdrawn. When Norm asked what was going on with her, she burst into tears, exclaiming that "you can't be a kid anymore. We can't party like we used to. We have a big responsibility to deal with. Why don't you just grow up?" Norm was taken aback. What was the big deal? They only went out two to three times a week, "so what if he got a little bombed every once in a while?" A few days later Norm said, "I'm going out with Jill and Pete; want to come?" Louise declined, explaining that now that she was further along in her pregnancy she needed to rest more because her energy levels were low.

As time went on, Norm went out with the boys more and more often until Louise didn't know whether to be furious that he "didn't get it, they were going to be parents," or concerned about his safety when he used farm equipment while hung over. Finally, with just 2 months to the birth of their child, Louise couldn't take it anymore and told Norm she was moving into her parents' place until he decided "to grow up and act more like a husband and soon-to-be father."

Cyrus, a certified marriage and family therapist, welcomed them into his office and was told by Norm that he had reluctantly agreed to come to couples counseling because of the ultimatum Louise had given him. Louise explained the situation and stated her concern that "not only is he drinking more and acting like a kid, but it's also like I am not even there. I'm the one who's pregnant, and he doesn't understand that I need support even before the baby comes. I'm feeling more and more alone and like I'm the one who will be left holding the bag after all is said and done."

"I know it's a difficult time for her," Norm responded, "but she is taking everything so seriously. How are a couple of drinks going to hurt? I'm not asking her to get drunk—just to have a good time, relax a bit, chill out."

"Chill out?" Louise exclaimed. "How much chilling out can you do? I get tired easily now and lately spend nights all by myself because you want to go out with the boys. That's why I moved in with my mother; at least I'm not alone."

Cyrus was encouraged that both partners seemed, despite their difficulties, to be allied around the birth of their child and still cared for one another deeply. He mentioned this, and they seemed to agree that the impediment to their relationship was that Louise was concerned that Norm was not taking the pregnancy seriously and that Norm was concerned that "his days of fun might be over."

As their therapy progressed, Cyrus was able to help the couple to recognize how Norm's behavior was linked to his fear that he wouldn't succeed as a father [competency] and that Louise would hate him for that [reliability]. Louise was surprised by that admission and told Norm that she felt betrayed by his preference about "partying with the boys" over her [loyalty] and that this behavior made her feel like she and the pregnancy weren't important to him [respect]. Cyrus also helped them to understand how these needs had evolved and why they created emotions that predicted less than functional ways of behaving toward each other. Finally, because of their commitment to each other, the three of them were able to brainstorm strategies that would allow Norm some freedom to unwind with his friends after work but would give Louise the support and encouragement she needed. Overall, they seemed to feel that they could reconnect around the reality of their decision to have a family.

Another very young couple also presented with issues surrounding commitment.

Samantha, age 18, and Keith, age 17, came to Tracy's office after Keith, an only child, had called her in a state of great agitation. Tracy had worked with Keith on and off for years around his relationship with his parents. Now he was in what he described as an extremely important relationship with his girlfriend of 13 months, and "things seemed to be falling apart." Both of Keith's parents were quite a bit older than most people of his age, having married later in life, and his father, now retired, was a very rigid and demanding man who had "old-time values and ideas." His mother was a criminal lawyer who had little time for the family during the week and, as a result, often disappointed Keith when she failed to be available for family outings at the last minute or called him apologetically because she could not meet him as promised because of a court case. Samantha stated that she had been eager to meet Tracy because "it was neat to finally meet someone Keith could trust." Samantha's parents both worked but always seemed to have time for her and her younger sister when she needed to speak with them and always had a way of "making me feel good even when I was bad."

Keith was working at a local McDonald's, having barely scraped through his final year of high school. He was in what they called a "technical" stream for people who "preferred to work with their hands rather than their heads." He was considering becoming a mechanic but needed some time "to see what else was out there." Samantha was in her first year of junior college with every intention of going to an arts school to learn how to be a graphic designer. She supported Keith in his dream to do something "with his hands like become a foreign car specialist or carpenter or something." She admitted that she was "not crazy about his decision to drop out altogether and work at McDonalds," but she trusted that he did want to do something more meaningful in his life and that he would move on "to bigger and better things" eventually.

Almost before he could sit down Keith began to speak: "Sam is driving me crazy. All I have ever asked her to do was to watch what she drinks when she goes out with her friends. I know she wants me to trust her, but when she has a few she loses control. Even when I'm with her she can do things that tick me off. Last week, we went to the pub and met a few of our friends there. About 2 hours later I saw her in Patrick's face—big Mr. Engineer. They used to have a thing going. How the heck am I supposed to feel? I know she was tipsy. What happens when she goes out with her friends without me and meets him?"

Samantha remained calm and said nothing until I asked her how she felt about what Keith had said.

"Keith," she said looking him straight in the eye, "I told you nothing has happened and that nothing ever happens. Do you want me to ignore all of my friends and act like a jerk? Yes, I went out with Patrick over 2 years ago; I suppose you didn't go out with Wendy?"

"Yeah, but I don't get so close that I have to use protection."

"You see," said Samantha to Tracy in exasperation, "that's what I always get. He knows all my girlfriends; don't you think that one of them would tell him if something happened?"

After some more bickering and accusations by one to the other, Tracy managed to break in by saying to Samantha: "I guess you feel that to have a caring relationship with Keith you have to follow certain rules?"

"You got it," said Samantha. "We're not married, and I have been with Keith through thick and thin—remember when your dad kicked you out because he felt you weren't keeping your room the way he liked it? Who convinced her mother to let you stay?"

"Yeah, I know," said Keith, "I trust you most of the time; it's just when you go out with your friends and start drinking. I don't think you always know what you're doing."

"So I need to be put on a leash now?" Samantha immediately replied.

Here, two issues presented themselves as the main topics for discussion. First, there were relational needs not being met and causing feelings that seem to provoke less than functional responses in attempts to solve them. It seemed quite clear that Keith had always doubted himself, especially with women, as being good enough to be with [competency]. When Samantha, a good-looking young woman who had dated some of the more sought-after men in his community, came along he always felt that this was too good to be true [loyalty]. Samantha, on the other hand, felt that he did not acknowledge her needs [respect] to be trusted and secure in her emotional connection with him [reliability]. The other issue was Samantha's ambivalence about committing to anyone at her stage of life. It seemed that, developmentally, Keith was ready to "settle down" and make a long-term commitment, whereas Samantha had thought about traveling after her graduation from junior college and maybe getting a job in a foreign country before applying to university or a school for graphic design.

Tracy addressed Keith and Samantha's issues over the next four sessions by first helping them to understand what their relational needs were and how they had evolved from their earlier developmental stages. Keith had been criticized most of his life by his father, and his mother seemed to choose her work over him. Samantha's experience was that of a family who loved her unconditionally and always acknowledged and supported her concerns. Tracy suggested that these needs would be there whether they stayed together and encouraged them to examine these needs deficits as possibilities when they became frustrated in this or other relationships. Tracy also gave them some techniques with respect to communicating to each other when they felt these needs were not being met and how to use a more productive emotion in communicating their needs to one another.

The second part of the therapy was in acknowledging that Keith felt powerless in his efforts to get Tracy to make a definitive decision about their relationship despite the fact that she had always been there for him as a therapist and that Samantha did not seem ready to take on the responsibility of a committed relationship at this point. She also helped them understand the importance of their reality—that they both seemed to be on different tracks and that it might not be the moment to make a realistic long-term commitment. Samantha needed to understand that, if she wanted to show Keith her loyalty even if "just for now," she would have to temper her tendency to appear unattached in social situations. Keith, on the other hand, had to understand that the more he tried to keep Samantha on a tether the more she would feel trapped and need her space.

Tracy heard from Keith about a year later. He told her that the work had been helpful toward his understanding of his own buttons and that things had improved for the pair after their meetings, while Keith's doubt as to the extent to which he could trust Samantha had never completely dissipated. In any case, Samantha had felt unable to offer him the sort of commitment he wanted and had in fact gone to study in Italy. Keith had decided to investigate the possibility of taking a degree in mechanical engineering and has just been accepted at the local university after successfully completing his prerequisite courses. Now that Keith had a clearer idea of where he was heading, he was less upset about being with Samantha, following their amicable parting, which had occurred when Keith decided to go to summer school to study some of the courses he needed to complete prior to attending university.

While the reality is that many young couples in adolescence will find that life takes them in different directions, couples therapy using the Needs ABC model can be enormously helpful to them in achieving a respectful, productive relationship with each other during the period of their relationship and in co-parenting any children they might have, with profoundly useful and felicitous results for the future emotional health of their children and their eventual partnerships. Notwithstanding the relatively limited experience of adolescent clients, no substantial changes need to be made to the Needs ABC model in clinical practice with them, while therapists should bear in mind the particular importance of behaviors such as allying with clients, who are especially likely, because of their age and social standing, to be at risk of viewing any adult in a position of authority as a potential adversary. In brief, treating adolescents who are in a position of adulthood as adolescents rather than as adults will only propagate their fears of being inadequate in taking on the adult responsibilities they have acquired and will only sabotage the work to be done.

9

ADDITIONAL TECHNIQUES

Developing and Using Emotion-Focused, Needs-Based Statements

Tools and Techniques That Can Help

Central to the Needs Acquisition and Behavior Change (ABC) model approach to couples therapy is that, although it is not always necessary, dysfunctional behaviors can be treated more easily when the origins of these behaviors are properly understood and dealt with. At the same time, however, couples need to learn some pragmatic ways to circumvent behavioral patterns that have been less than helpful to them in the past. Many of these tools are simple in concept and, if they are used, can also provide couples with some much needed space in which to calm down before reacting to what promises to be a stressful moment. These tools can be used in therapy and the lessons used therein brought home where, tentatively at first and then with gradually increasing confidence, couples can start to implement them into their daily lives.

Feelings Chart It is often difficult to express one's own feelings succinctly, even for those of us who, like me, make a living dealing with feelings. After all, just look at the great effort we can all make to avoid confronting our deeper sentiments or admitting that we feel vulnerable when we are sure that we should be strong. Putting our real, useful emotions into words makes them seem more "real." It makes us feel more vulnerable and as if we are somehow laying ourselves bare to the outside world. It makes us worry that we might be exposing too much of ourselves and laying ourselves open to ridicule or further hurt. Why else do human beings develop such a complex and, at times, almost bizarre array of behaviors that seem to have been developed expressly to avoid dealing explicitly with the feelings that are at the root of our problems? I have already mentioned a couple of examples of the frequency with which men and women often find it difficult to express, respectively, sorrow or fear and anger.

Rather than asking clients to use an emotional vocabulary they may not be ready to access, therapists can use a feelings chart that displays a range of stylized facial expressions associated with various emotions. These facial expressions are universal and innate; even children who are born blind display the same fundamental expressions of joy, disgust, and so forth, on feeling the relevant emotions (Galati, Miceli, & Sini, 2001). In other words, everyone can view the images in question and understand what they mean.

Clients can be asked to point to the expression they feel best illustrates how they are feeling "right now." The opportunity offered to them by using the simple black-and-white drawings to project onto

Figure 9.1   Examples of "feeling faces."

rather than having to explore their psyche for words that are likely to be less than welcome can provide liberating access to the more useful emotions that lie beneath the easier-to-express, less useful emotions they feel able to discuss verbally. Gradually, it will become easier to verbalize feelings and emotions that have previously been unwelcome.

Role-Play Role-play is a time-honored technique in psychotherapy, and in other types of therapy, that is often used to very good effect by individuals working from various theoretical backgrounds (Constantine, 1986; Jacobson & Margolin, 1979, pp. 175–176). In couples therapy, it offers both members of the couple a degree of removal from their own feelings by encouraging them to try to see and to put into words the sentiments of their partner. Let's look at an example of how this can work in practice.

> Abel and Simona are attending therapy in the wake of Abel's discovery that Simona had an affair about a year ago. The affair, with a co-worker from the office, had lasted for about 3 months and, Simona said, "hadn't really meant very much." She added that Abel had not been supposed to find out and that if he hadn't been snooping around in her email account he would never have been the wiser and they would both have been better off. Simona's air is one of defiance and reluctance to admit that she has really done anything wrong at all, whereas Abel maintains a dejected expression and appears to be resolute in his victim role with little interest in exploring how things have gone sufficiently astray in his relationship with Simona that she felt the need to seek attention and comfort elsewhere.
>
> On discussing things in some more detail, Scott, the couple's therapist, discovers that Simona engaged in her affair following a lengthy period of depression on the part of Abel and not long after a rather half-hearted suicide attempt—"his third; he doesn't seem to think that I'm getting the message"—that had necessitated Abel spending 3 days in the hospital after having had his stomach pumped. Abel took the overdose just half an hour before Simona was due home from work. He has been offered individual therapy and has been strongly urged to take up the offer, but has resisted it thus far, on the grounds that he had just suffered a "moment of weakness" and that he didn't want "some shrink telling him what to do." Scott also finds out that Simona's father abandoned the family home when she was only 8. Abel's depression has stabilized now, despite his refusal to engage in individual therapy. He is taking medication and attending a support group and has been able to return to his accounting job. However, he remains significantly emotionally withdrawn from Simona and states, "I don't know if I will ever be able to trust her again, now that I know what she

is capable of—sticking a knife in my back when I am at my most vulnerable and twisting it."

Having spent a little time with the couple, Scott has developed the hypothesis that Simona's affair was symptomatic of the couple's deeper problems rather than a causal factor. She was already dealing with a deeply depressed husband at the time of her romance and, in the absence of a more positive outlet, had embarked on a risky relationship with a co-worker—who was also married at the time—in a rather desperate attempt to seek the attention she needs and the support that Abel did not seem to be able to give her.

"Abel," says Scott, "I think you remember that in one of the earlier sessions Simona described a family background in which her dad left the family when she was just a little girl. We all agreed that this has left Simona with some pretty serious issues around abandonment, and you mentioned that she often 'just wanted to sit beside you' while you read the evening paper. Perhaps you, Abel, can 'be' Simona for a while and try to talk about why you think you were tempted to have an affair. You, Simona, could try to respond as Abel."

At first, it is difficult for Simona and Abel to get into their roles. Abel struggles to be Simona and continues to minimize his part in all of this. With some coaching from Scott, after a few minutes and some exasperated comments from Simona, they seem to finally relax somewhat and make a serious effort to access the other's emotions and feelings.

"I think," says Abel, speaking as Simona, "that when my husband psyched out on me and spent a few years being depressed, it was almost as if he wasn't even there. Maybe he was there *physically*, but he was never there for me. He wasn't interested in me, in how I looked, in anything. He didn't pay me any attention or give me any compliments. I suppose, in a way, it was a bit like he had gone off somewhere. Maybe that made me feel insecure and made it easier to get involved with someone else."

"I guess," says Simona, rather tentatively, speaking as Abel, "that finding out that my wife had been fooling around when I was already having major problems with self-esteem and stuff anyway just seemed to confirm all the negative feelings I was having about myself."

Abel and Simona do still have a great deal of work to do, but by using role-play in the context of therapy, with Scott's help they have started to understand just what it is like to be the other and to gain some insight into the emotional triggers that prompt their partner to engage in behaviors that damage them both as a couple.

Therapist Self-Disclosure   Disclosure by the therapist can be a powerful tool indeed (Johnson, 2004, p. 89; Teyber, 1997, pp. 29–30) in modeling for clients ways they can discuss their emotions, in providing vocabularies they might be able to use in discussing their feelings and their needs, and in demonstrating that therapists are not distant characters whose views are uttered from a position of superiority but are instead human beings who have also experienced weakness, vulnerability, and personal problems and who are capable of understanding such issues not just from an academic standpoint but also as people who have known heartache, despair, and frustration in the course of their personal lives. Far from detracting from therapists' authority, timely and appropriate self-disclosure can open new avenues for discussion, can illuminate difficulties couples may have been having, and can facilitate the flow of empathy between therapists and couples, creating a bond of understanding that will be invaluable as the therapy progresses. Let's examine an example.

Adam and Aine have been attending therapy for several weeks and have made some progress in discussing what they need from their relationship and how they might be able to help each other to achieve these needs. However, they do find themselves constantly revolving around the theme of the amount of time Aine spends on her postgraduate thesis, when Adam feels that she should be more available to him. Since Aine works full-time and is studying nights for a master of arts in media studies, she feels that she "needs all the time she can get" and admits that she devotes most evenings and a great deal of time at the weekend to her studies.

"Adam knows that this degree is important to me," Aine says, "and there's only one more year to go. I don't see what the big deal is."

"We always come back to this," says Adam, wearily. "It's not a big deal to *her*, maybe. But what about me? Don't I count for anything? I'm the one left on my own in front of the television night after night, bringing her supper up to the office so that she can eat in front of the computer and going off to bed on my own for the umpteenth time. I honestly don't know if I can cope with another year of this. And who knows if it will take only a year? Last year, she said, 'Just another 3 months.'"

Paul, the couple's therapist says, "Aine's determination to succeed in achieving her goals is certainly impressive. I remember when I was finishing my research degree—I wish that I had had that much dedication. But I did find that, at times, working too hard was counterproductive—for the degree and for my personal life. Eventually, my partner cracked. She said, 'Look, you're just going to have to set aside a couple of evenings a week when we can be together—and no more dinners in front of the computer!' So I think I can really identify with Aine here. At first I resisted it, but I could see that Alice had a point in feeling second best to my work—and even a little betrayed. So I did as she asked, and we picked two evenings that would be just for us and also ate together every evening. That was good for us, but one unexpected bonus was that spending a little more time away from my studies gave me a clearer head and actually made it easier for me to concentrate the rest of the time. Not rocket science, huh? Even my professors told me to take a break every hour, but I thought I knew best. Also, I reminded Alice that she didn't have to sit around waiting for me all the time, as if she wasn't allowed to have fun just because I was busy. She could go out with friends, go to the movies, whatever—as soon as we reached a compromise and she didn't spend every night watching TV waiting for me to turn up, we were both a heck of a lot happier."

The close parallels between Paul's past situation and Aine's current one has given him a chance to make some practical suggestions for ways she and Adam might start working on spending some quality time together. Paul has also successfully modeled a way contentious issues can be discussed calmly and pragmatically and without resorting to blame. The scene has been set for becoming able to probe the issues of abandonment and trust that seem to be so important to Adam and Aine, respectively, without constantly returning to practical issues that seem to trigger these emotional buttons.

The "One-Time Negotiation"   While one of the aims of therapy is to establish a set of behavioral norms that allow both members of the couple to express and seek their needs in a safe environment, sometimes rules are made to be broken, albeit only with mutual consent and with the understanding that the rules still stand for all default purposes. The "one-time negotiation" is used when couples need to negotiate to problem solve with the understanding that the proposed solution is for the particular circumstances that they are facing at the current time. This technique can serve to reinforce couples' potential to negotiate and collaboratively problem solve by supporting relational

One way to self-disclose appropriately would be to use a fictitious client as the example. So, instead of saying, "That reminds me of the time when I...," you could say, "That reminds me of a client I once had...." It is important to link clients' relational needs with the example you are sharing.

flexibility. If there is a feeling that the solution will not work in the longer-term or if it is an exception to the rules that they have decided on in the past, they can decide to leave it to one side in the future with the agreement that they will go back to their original plan or can always try something else another time and that they can keep trying until they have found a viable solution that works for them both more consistently. In other words, they agree a certain stratagem to deal with the presenting problem, with the understanding that a precedent is not being set and that they will renegotiate the next time this or a similar issue presents itself.

Time-Out, Logging, and Business Meetings   A "time-out" provides clients with a concrete technique that gives them a mechanism that they can use to break their dysfunctional behavioral patterns and to strive toward calm and places them in a position in which a rational response to the given circumstances is possible. As a skill that they learn in therapy and bring home to their personal lives, it can help their partners to feel safe in their company while providing both elements of the couple with breathing space so they can identify their presenting emotions and work on using a viable alternative to their default behavior. Couples are taught that they need to discuss this tool with their partners so they can instigate it as a new element of their behavior. This technique consists of simply leaving the scene of stress and triggers to inappropriate behavior and taking some time to calm down, to acquire some perspective, and to arrive at a new approach for reentering the potentially stressful situation. For example, this technique can be used to excellent effect in the case of domestic violence on the part of a man toward his partner. It can also be used in less dramatic or potentially dangerous situations where the men in question are taught to recognize that they are responsible for their own problematic behavior, to recognize when they are nearing a risky situation and liable to do or utter something that will be less than helpful, and to become able to say something like, "Excuse me, I have to go outside for a while," so they can take the time they require to calm down and, ideally, think about why they have grown so angry and how else they might be able to deal with the situation or behavior that has triggered this anger.

Again, inasmuch as people are responsible for what they do and must learn to become able to own their own behavior, something I have found effective in couples work is what I label the *mutual time-out*. The women or the men in this scenario must understand that if they feel that they may be in a vulnerable situation, and especially if it is suspected that they might revisit the behaviors that brought them into therapy in the first place such as violence or other unconstructive behavior, one partner has the right to tell the other partner that a time-out must be taken. This right is not dependent on either partner actually being upset, angry, or liable to lash out but is purely at the behest of the person who is usually the recipient of the inappropriate behavior. This position gives the ones asking the other for space a sense of being in control of their environment—a sense of emotional safety with the understanding that their needs are being acknowledged and that their partner is prepared to listen to them. It also can indicate, assuming the other complies, that they are working together in earnest to resolve their relational differences.

"Logging" is just what it sounds like. Couples undergoing therapy are encouraged to note down the circumstances when they feel that they may start to display the dysfunctional behavior that has brought them to therapy. For example, in the case of a couple in which the woman tends to "yell" and the man runs away, both are asked to log times when they did or did not engage in the typical behaviors. Similarly, "mutual logging" can prove to be effective in helping clients to collaborate on improving their behaviors. For example, in the case of the man who tends to "run away," both he and his partner can log whether they think he is doing better or worse in the circumstances in which he usually absconds. Table 9.1 is provided to assist with this task.

Couples who have been taught by their therapist to use "time-out" and logging skills can combine these tools with "business meetings," in which couples agree to discuss, at a specified time and place and in as calm and level-headed a manner as possible, for example the findings they have made in relation to the needs they are attempting to express as well as ideas that they may have about how each might be able to modify behavior in response to these needs. For example, a client who has fears associated with abandonment or loyalty issues

Table 9.1 Logging Behaviors

DATE, TIME, AND PLACE	WHAT WAS HAPPENING	WHAT DID YOU DO?

might feel badly when her partner promises to be home on time for a special anniversary dinner but shows up late, having apparently forgotten about the celebration. This may not be the right moment to discuss the situation, as she may be feeling deeply angry and bitter. Instead, they can arrange another time when they can get together and meet, with the specific agenda of "going over" the things that are disturbing her. In this case, once she is calm enough to "make the appointment" for the meeting, she could suggest that they meet in the dining room after the children are in bed to discuss her concerns. Ideally, this meeting should be held in a room not normally used for leisure activities (e.g., the dining room). As well, the couple should be seated facing each other a comfortable distance apart. The reason for this physical configuration is twofold: (1) since we all tend to experience our situation as being more vulnerable when seated (as opposed to standing) the situation is less likely to become chaotic; and (2) this will frame the situation as a "problem-solving session," helping each to remain, as much as possible, on their best behavior with the focus on collaboratively rectifying what has occurred.

Prefacing her statement with a reminder that this is part of the "homework" suggested by their therapist, a woman client could tell her partner, "I was pretty upset the other day when you did not show. I was feeling alone and abandoned, much like I did when I was a kid and my parents didn't throw me a birthday party when they promised they would." Here, the client recognizes that dealing with the feelings that she has are *her* responsibility and not the responsibility of her partner, but she is also reminding him that reliability is important to her because of her unhappy childhood experiences and is tacitly suggesting to him that he bear this in mind in his interactions with her. As well, this helps her partner to be more objective about her statement to him by understanding that he is not primary to her experience of abandonment but that reliability is his responsibility in being a good partner to her.

Understanding the origins of our needs and the coping behaviors we have developed to deal with them is central to the main goal of the Needs ABC model. At one and the same time, the model strives not only to deal with the presenting problems *now*—although that is certainly important—but also to provide the couple attending therapy with the understanding that the lessons they have learned and the tools they have acquired can bring them into a better, happier future in which they have become enabled to cope with understanding and reason with situations in which their buttons are pressed. However, exploring our relational needs and the issue of where they come from can be difficult, and clients will need both practical and emotional support as they proceed to explore their own and their partners' backgrounds and emotional landscapes and work together to create new ways of relating to one another.

10
After Treatment

Reaching the end of a period of therapy is a big step, and, like any rite of passage, it can be associated with considerable stress, which can be manifested in a variety of ways and which can represent a significant challenge to even the experienced therapist. Helping clients end their relationship with their therapist and to broach the world and their relationship with their partner and family on their own needs to be respected is an important and often difficult event, and many people will need considerable help and support throughout this period if they are to emerge safely and successfully on the other side:

> Termination is an important and distinct phase of therapy that must be negotiated thoughtfully. Ending the therapeutic intervention will almost always be of great significance to clients. The way in which this separation experience is resolved is so important that it influences how well clients will be able to resolve future conflicts, losses and endings in their lives. It also helps determine whether clients leave therapy with a greater sense of self-efficacy and the ability to manage their own lives more successfully…. It holds the potential either to undo or to confirm and extend the changes that have come about in therapy. (Teyber, 1997, p. 315)

Possible Reactions to Planned Termination and How to Deal With Them: Some Examples

Sadness

Realizing that the time has come to bring a period of therapy to an end is a decision that can be as momentous as the one to embark on therapy in the first case. Often, feelings of mutual respect and even affection have grown between couples and their therapists, who have often been the only ones to listen to their most heartfelt feelings and to assist them in communicating with each other as never before. In some ways, therapists know more about couples than even their closest friends and family members, and it is unsurprising that sadness is one of the emotions most commonly accessed at this time; knowing that one is about to "lose" a therapist can feel a lot like losing a cherished friend. These feelings can be minimized by keeping couples focused as much as possible on the many real achievements they have accomplished and on the better future together than they have worked so hard together to attain. For example, a client might say, "Gee, I am really going to miss these sessions. They've become the only time in the week when I really get to talk about the problems I worry about, and Thursdays just aren't going to feel the same anymore." The therapist may answer, "I guess Thursday evenings may feel a little empty for a while, but with everything you've learned I am sure that you will be able to broach the topic of your problems on your own, too. How about setting aside a little time every week when you can both sit down and use the vocabulary that you've learned here to talk about any of the issues that have come up in recent days?"

Anxiety and Fear

Anxiety is a perfectly normal and understandable reaction to the termination of therapy. A couple or a family may think, "We can keep this up so long as we have our weekly sessions to keep us focused. But what will happen now that we are being tossed into the world again? What if we can't avoid falling back into the same old routines as before?"

Latter sessions can keep a focus on all the real, tangible progress couples or families have made so they feel reassured about their ability to continue their good work. At the same time, they can be gently reminded that, should it become necessary, attending therapy at a later stage is always an option. Presenting this possibility can be a delicate balancing act between assuring the individuals in question that they can and do have the ability to "make it" on their own while not suggesting that a future return to therapy would be a failure in any way. A client might say something like, "It's all very well remembering why we behave the way we do when we have you to talk to every week, but how are we supposed to remember all this stuff on our own? I think there's a real possibility we'll just slip back to the old ways of doing things."

Firstly, reassuring clients that such feelings are perfectly normal and understandable is crucial. Encouraging people to discuss their fears rather than "bottling them in" is important. Final sessions might provide a recap on skills that have been learned and abilities that have been accessed so that fear can become something that is accepted and then approached and dealt with rather than being the "monster beneath the bed" that can threaten the real progress that has been made throughout the course of therapy. A good response to such fears could be, "It's OK to be scared about coping on your own in the future, but I think when you sit down and really go through all you've learned and all the real progress you've made, you'll understand that you can do it on your own and that you've also learned when the time has come to ask for help."

Relapse

It is not uncommon for people facing the end of therapy to react by regressing to former, less than useful patterns of behavior. In so doing, they are not unlike children who, afraid of the change that starting elementary school represents, may revert to "babyish" behaviors such as thumb-sucking or bedwetting in an attempt to elicit the attention they feel they need. By returning to these behaviors, clients are making a powerful statement: "I am afraid of what the future holds and of my ability to cope with the problems that I will be presented with." Another possibility is that the stress of termination might add to their feelings of vulnerability and cause them to inadvertently make use of the older, more dysfunctional behaviors in dealing with their concerns. As in the case of more explicitly expressed fears and anxieties, clients need to be reassured by reviewing how their relational needs might have impacted on this emotional relapse, how their feelings have predicted the resurrection of less productive problem-solving behaviors, and which strategies they have learned can be implemented to deal with this retrogression. As well, they should be reminded that relapse is often an important part of moving toward remission and can help only to solidify their problem-solving skills by "learning from one's mistakes." They should be supported in the understanding that they have shown themselves, in the course of therapy, as able and effective in confronting the challenges that they will inevitably face and that outside help will always be available, when and if they need it.

Flight

It is not uncommon for clients who are facing the end of therapy to suddenly cease to attend, often without providing an explanation. When this happens, frustrating as it can be to the therapist, it is important to understand that it is occurring in the context of the stress, anxiety, and pain that can surround the end of therapy. When possible, they should be contacted and encouraged to finish therapy or at least reminded that, when and if problems reemerge, they will be welcome to return.

Unplanned Termination

Ideally, couples who attend therapy will remain with their therapist until they have learned how to understand the origins of their needs and dysfunctional behaviors, have adopted a more useful vocabulary and mode of discussing their situation, and have moved into a healthier relationship by taking the lessons that they have learned in therapy and applying them to their everyday lives. However, there are various circumstances in which an unplanned termination may take place. One or both members of the couple might have to move to another city for work, a financial crisis might make privately funded therapy unfeasible, or one or both members of the couple might decide that they have "had enough"—perhaps because of stressful issues that had begun to emerge and they did not feel able to deal with.

Whatever the cause of a sudden, unplanned termination, what is important is that clients know that the door is always open to revisit therapy at a later date. Even when couples do not engage directly with their therapists to inform them directly of their decision to cease attending, a follow-up phone call is useful to reassure them that therapy will always remain an option at a future stage and to offer clients the opportunity to express their feelings about any way they might feel that their therapy did not meet their specific needs.

Tools to Take to the World

Those facing the imminent termination of a period of therapy need to feel confident that they can put into practice the many lessons they have learned, abilities they have become able to tap into, and tools they have acquired in the course of therapy, and it is worth spending the final session or sessions recapping the insights that have been acquired into the manifestation and origins of their unmet needs and of their earlier, unsuccessful attempts to have them met and practicing the new techniques that they have learned to bring to bear on their personal relationships.

11
CONCLUSION

The course of our society in recent generations has changed a great deal. Social conservatives often point to the increasing numbers of "broken marriages" as indicative of, for example, a decline in moral fiber. The flip side is, of course, that people today are less than willing to remain in unhappy relationships. One of the reasons is because women are increasingly financially and psychologically independent. They, and their partners, are now freer to make decisions, including the decision to leave an unhappy relationship. Similarly, couples who are determined to stay together are much less likely to settle for an unsatisfying domestic situation. When things go wrong, as they can do for any couple even when there are no serious underlying problems such as domestic violence or substance abuse, there is increasingly the knowledge that professional help is available and that it is a reasonable option to take.

Despite the aspirations of some of the traditionalists among us, the higher bar that has been set for satisfaction in the context of one's personal relationship and family seems unlikely to change for the foreseeable future. While this may mean that levels of divorce and separation will stay higher than they were 50 years ago, it also means that couples are more likely to seek the help they need to be happy together or to find a way to separate respectfully with the minimum of psychological fallout for themselves and their families. All of this means that the scope for therapists to continue to help is certain to grow, now and in the future.

Psychotherapy and other therapeutic modalities have become sufficiently mainstream across the English-speaking world and elsewhere to the extent that the concept of therapy has become very much an element of popular culture and has, fortunately, lost a great deal of the stigma formerly attached to it. In all walks of life, there is now the consciousness that therapy, of one kind or another, is an option—and a valid, reasonable one—for people facing difficulties in their personal life. Furthermore, an increasing appreciation of the usefulness of therapy in helping individuals to cease damaging behaviors means that many therapists now work in sync with social workers and with the legal services as well as with, for example, schools and colleges.

All of this means that therapy has entered a very exciting stage in its development, with many possibilities for the growth in its relevance to clients in a wide range of ways. Academically, things are also flourishing, and access to new and exciting ideas is widespread. However, this is also a very challenging period for the discipline, and one in which the many therapeutic modalities offered can seem overwhelming, both to clients and therapists; how is one supposed to distinguish one type of therapy from another? If this can be tricky even for some health-care professionals, imagine how difficult it must be for clients. Are some approaches intrinsically "better" than others or just "better for me"? While some therapists will tend to cling to one or another orthodoxy, others may "pick and choose" among therapeutic approaches to find a system that seems to work best for both them and their clients. The problem with the former approach is that excessive rigidity in this area can be detrimental to clients whose problems or situations cannot easily be pigeonholed, whereas the latter can create a rather amorphous, directionless therapy that seems to go nowhere and lacks the structure and discipline that provide clients with a sense of security and safety within the therapeutic environment. While almost any type of therapeutic intervention can help couples and families in the short-term, what serious therapists need is an approach that will make their services redundant; that will help people to heal their own dysfunctional behaviors.

It is my intention that, by maintaining a strict focus on emotion and using the Needs Acquisition and Behavior Change (ABC) approach to help clients both to understand underlying relational needs and to work proactively toward creating healthy ways of meeting them, therapists can neatly steer a course between the often apparently contradictory requirements of flexibility and direction in providing meaningful help in a therapeutic context. However, this is not to suggest that the approaches described in this volume are intended to be a complete list of relevant relational needs and possible therapeutic approaches to the same. Rather, it is hoped that by providing the Needs ABC model as a sounding board, therapists can create models and means of working with clients that are uniquely adapted to their own and their clients' needs. In a world in which society is increasingly complex, multiethnic, and differentiated, the possibilities are endless.

The Needs ABC model rests on the understanding that all individuals have the capacity to improve their situation and to find a way to heal in a healthful way with the dysfunctional behaviors that arise from their unmet needs. It helps clients recognize their strengths, in terms of both their inner, personal resources and their interpersonal relationships in the wider world. A significant asset of this approach in the acquisition of this "curative insight" is that it is a *relational* model exemplifying appropriate empathic relationships through client–therapist interaction. I am convinced that therapies should be relational, implying a sense of connection. I am also confident that acknowledging and understanding the emotional component is "the royal road" (Freud, 1913) to behavior change (Greenberg & Johnson, 1988). Because we always expect from others what we give to them, modeling good relationship skills is a quintessential operative task of psychotherapy. As well, the integration of various psychotherapeutic models and strategies allows for a greater opportunity to connect with the client by being able to select from a broader base of strategic interventions. Keep in mind that clients can feel a sense of accomplishment only if they are the ones who achieve the success; self-esteem increases when they actually do the work—not just discuss it.

While the Needs ABC model recognizes that it is very important to understand how and why our relational needs developed as they did, from childhood through to adulthood, our approach is more a "doing cure" than a "talking cure" insofar as clients are urged to take transformative action in terms of altering the behaviors they have developed to have their relational needs met. Achieving an understanding of needs, behaviors, and strategies that can be used to change behaviors can always be done while using a vocabulary and series of metaphors that are accessible to the clients in question. Clients are provided both with practical tools, such as a feelings chart and time-out techniques, that will facilitate their behavioral modification and with a more refined intellectual understanding of themselves and their needs that will assist them in forging long-term change. In addition, using the needs ABC approach models a constructive relational approach that provides an opportunity for clients to feel allied with emotionally and supported in taking the responsibility for "figuring things out" and improving their quality of life—the very factors that have been shown to predict a positive outcome. At the very least, because the model helps clients concretely understand what they and their partner need, and because an informed decision is better than one made brashly, clients can decide whether to keep trying.

Above all, the Needs ABC model collaboratively searches for common ground in client differences among couples. That is, rather than illuminating and supporting only individual client needs, the counselor's role is to involve the couple in discussing and understanding the unmet needs of each partner, to relate to both partners' experience, and to agree upon appropriate methods to help each other acquire what each needs to sustain a healthy and hopeful relationship.

The following practice techniques can offer a successful therapeutic experience by giving support to those involved in understanding what is missing in their important relationships and acquiring their unmet relational needs within a spirit of mutual cooperation (Caplan, 2008a):

1. The awareness of client needs as described in the themes embedded in their respective narratives
2. The identification and exploration of these universal process themes descriptive of missing relational needs for individuals as well as for couples as a whole
3. The recognition of the emotional components of clients' narrative
4. The illumination of the most effective of these expressed emotions in addressing client and couple needs
5. The interpretations formulated from these techniques, reflected back to couples, to support the development of possibilities for them to meet their therapeutic goals

6. The organization of strategies to help needs acquisition both within and beyond the therapeutic setting

By focusing on client and couple needs rather than on behaviors, the Needs ABC therapeutic process provides a vehicle whereby social skills and appropriate behaviors in relationships are modeled and assimilated (Garvin, 1974). Implicit in this model is that challenging clients' maladaptive behaviors should be considered a goal rather than a technique. The aim is for counselors to support couples in challenging ineffective attempts to meet their relational needs by presenting objective observations about the themes and emotions perceived in their narrative. When the acquisition of these takes place in a functional manner, the maladaptive behaviors will gradually be extinguished. Overall, the Needs ABC model suggests that, in all forms of therapy, clinicians are expected to be participants, observers, mentors, and teachers.

What, then, are the possibilities for this model outside of those already mentioned? In fact, early on, Sugar (1974) espoused "interpretive psychotherapy" for children of the age of latency (Erikson, 1959). Reminding us that it is important to have an understanding of "the specific aspects of latency children's type of thinking, psychosexual level, and typical defenses, as well as experience with individual child therapy" (Sugar, p. 648). Sugar states:

Interpretive group therapy takes place in a specific, constant, and stable setting—the usual playroom—which is designed to facilitate the demonstration of conflicts, defenses, and fantasies through verbalization and play. The therapist's activity is interpretive in a relatively nongratifying group setting where it is possible for the child's feelings to be understood through observing symbolic or representational behavior in the playroom. (p. 648)

Needless to say, because of this focus on emotions and behaviors, play therapies can be used to interpret a preadolescent child's needs through the "narrative" of their play and the emotions they display at various times during their various activities.

Behavioral treatments such as substance abuse, gambling, or violence—especially spousal abuse—are well suited to this model, which evolved in the first instance in the context of behavioral treatment for domestic violence at the McGill Domestic Violence Clinic. Whether clients are in group or individual treatment, when they say, "I don't know how much longer I'm going to be able to hold out in this program. I was doing OK in meeting the program goals so far, but I'm really getting concerned that, like so many things in my life, I'm going to screw this up," wouldn't it be better to examine ways of dealing with competency issues in their life rather than promote an emotion that will predict success rather than failure (in this case anger at the drug of choice rather than sad feelings of defeat)? Or if someone with a gambling problem acknowledges, "I don't know which happened first. Sometimes I think my family disowned me, and other times I think what a relief it was to get away from them. The bottom line is that when I get into a jam, I feel like I have only myself to count on, and I've never been that dependable," an examination of betrayal and reliability in the client's life might be in order as well as a more productive emotion. In both of these examples, rather than looking at gambling or drug use as the vile demon, which can put the responsibility outside of the client, an unmet need would help the client to concretize what is going on and give him some options to both get his needs met and change his behavior.

Needs ABC: The Flexible Model

At this point, I would like to show you an example that illustrates very clearly just how flexible the Needs ABC model can be. Bernard, a colleague of mine in Massachusetts, is a graduate of the Adler School of Professional Psychology in Chicago. He has been a fan of my model since its incarnation in my first book (Caplan, 2008b). Because Bernard often worked with inner-city youth, many of whom were teenage parents, I asked him to share his perspective on how he would have worked with the "Lillian and Jacques" case given in Chapter 8 (in the section titled "Adolescent Couples"). You will remember that Lillian and Jacques were young parents who decided to keep their child when Lillian became pregnant. Lillian felt marginalized [respect] and often let down [loyalty] by Jacques, much in the same way her parents had treated her. Jacques came from a traditional family where his father never lifted a hand in the household and his mother was extremely critical [competency] and blaming [reliability] of him. He felt that Lillian was never satisfied with his efforts and was constantly demanding more than he felt he could give. As he began to address this issue, Bernard reminded me of several Adlerian principles (Ansbacher & Ansbacher, 1967; Carlson, 2006). First, Adler and Adlerian psychologists believe in what can be called "the unity of the individual"—that all perception is biased according to clients' viewpoints and that their strategies to resolve their difficulties would also be chosen on that basis. He stated that the Needs ABC developmental history was akin to a popular Adlerian exercise called "early recollections," wherein clients were asked to remember situations that happened around the age of 8 years of age. He suggested that Lillian's inability [power] to feel important [respect] in her relationship with Jacques [power] as well as to have him choose her over others [loyalty] in his life would be made evident in both her developmental history (as it was in this example) and in her early recollections. He suggested that part of Lillian's dilemma was to be the independent woman her mother was while desperately needing to feel valued and allied with by her husband. Jacques, coming from a traditional background, probably assumed he was doing this by supporting the family financially and that that was sufficient—no more and no less. Another Adlerian principle is that of "goal orientation"—that clients are future oriented, striving for what Alfred Adler termed "superiority," or success (see Oberst & Stewart, 2003 and Carlson et al., 2006 for Adlerian terminology). Here, Lillian's goal was to succeed in getting her needs finally met in her marriage, although the way she saw success may have been somewhat unrealistic (Adler's "fictitious goal") given Jacques's need for independence. Jacques's goal was to remain independent despite his responsibility to his family, which also was unrealistic with respect to the way he pursued his "fictitious goal," since the achievement of this goal is guided by the goal as well as the way clients move though the world (Adler called this clients' "lifestyle" and was indicative of the way clients generally problem solved relationally).

With this in mind, Bernard stated that he would have focused initially on the couple's lack of autonomy because of both partners' decision to have their child. With regard to the way Jacques was attempting to meet his goal of being a competent father and husband, Bernard would help Jacques examine the extent to which he could be autonomous under the circumstances and how a show of altruism and support (Adler's "social interest") might actually give him greater emotional freedom. With regard to Lillian's apparent need for "unhesitating loyalty," he would connect her worldview to what he saw as her desperation to be valued and allied with and how an improvement in her negotiation strategies might make her life goals more realistic. Bernard suggested that this might, in fact, be an "intimacy" issue for Jacques as he describes both parents as emotionally aloof. Bernard went on to explain that the Needs ABC perspective was, in fact, "very Adlerian," in that clients' directions or goals are usually influenced by family values and hereditary factors such as personality (Ansbacher & Ansbacher, 1967) and that this "path" can be illuminated by examining birth order (another Adlerian tactic) and coping patterns through the aforementioned early recollections as in the Needs ABC brief developmental history. Finally, an understanding of the social context from within which clients, or couples, operate is important to the Adlerian counselor. Bernard concluded by saying that the use of the model's needs list was extremely helpful in his work because it gave the clients something concrete and understandable to work on with regard to their personal goal orientation. If they could negotiate and collaborate around the giving and getting of relational needs, then they could readjust their "fictitious goals" (Ansbacher & Ansbacher, 1967) to be more realistic. Bernard admitted that he did not do a lot of emotional work per se but addressed the emotional component as he felt necessary. Overall, he felt he now used a more integrated approach combining his Adlerian perspective with the Needs ABC approach; it gave him "a bigger tool box" with more strategies to choose from when doing treatment planning.

It will be interesting to see how practitioners with diverse ideological backgrounds and methods integrate the Needs ABC model into their practice, and I look forward to an active correspondence on these matters.

A Call to My Colleagues

Finally, for now, two groups for potential Needs ABC therapists to consider are people with intellectual disabilities and people with autism. With regard to clients with intellectual deficits, Hurley (2006, p. 465) reports that "patients with intellectual disability have limitations in verbal ability, and with increasing levels of disability may have an atypical clinical presentation." She goes on to say that mood disorders occur at a higher rate with this population. In addition, she says that these disorders are usually accompanied by problematic behaviors. Perhaps, in this case, examining client behaviors as well as listening carefully to what they are saying (despite their apparent limitations) to determine their relational needs might be a way of treating some of their mood problems or as an adjunct to medication. Suggestions as to how to devise more concrete needs-getting strategies that are easily comprehended by this population would be most certainly welcomed.

In *Bridging the Gaps: An Inside-Out View of Autism*, Sinclair (1992, p. 298), a 27-year-old autistic man, describes his experiences at a conference with a focus on autism:

> There are other gaps that I'm just beginning to notice, and other assumptions that I'm just beginning to explore. They have to do with interpersonal rather than intrapersonal processing. The assumptions are similar: that I have the same needs for relationships that other people have, that I know how to relate in ways that are considered normal, and that I don't relate normally because I have negative or uncaring attitudes toward other people…. But probably the most important thing I learned from it was that I am capable of making authentic connections…. That's a good thing to know. Since then I've learned a lot more about how I can make connections, and about what kinds of people I want to make connections with.

It is apparent that if connections can be made then relational needs can be illuminated and dealt with. Perhaps others can suggest strategies and techniques for working with autistic persons, but I feel that behavioral and verbal narratives can be used to uncover these needs and help these clients to improve their quality of life.

At this point in time, it would be interesting to see how the Needs ABC model can be implemented, used, or modified for use, in a wide variety of situational and cultural environments, and I would very much welcome feedback from my colleagues in therapy with respect to their own experience of this model in the therapeutic environment as well as any suggestions they might have with regard to modifications or amendments to those listed herein.

References

Ainsworth, M., & Bowlby, J. (1965). *Child Care and the Growth of Love.* London: Penguin Books.

Ainsworth, M., Blehar, M., Waters, E., & Wall, S. (1978). *Patterns of Attachment.* Hillsdale, NJ: Erlbaum.

Ansbacher, H.L., & Ansbacher, R.R. (1967). *The Individual Psychology of Alfred Adler.* Heinz L. New York: Harper and Row.

Asay, T.P., & Lambert, M.J. (1999). "The Empirical Case for the Common Factors in Therapy: Quantitative Findings." In Hubble et al., *The Heart and Soul of Change,* pp. 33–56.

Aylmer, R. (1986). "Bowen Family Systems Marital Therapy." In N. Jacobson & A. Gurman, *Clinical Handbook of Marital Therapy.*

Bachelor, A., & Horvath, A. (1999). "The Therapeutic Relationship." In Hubble et al., *The Heart and Soul of Change,* pp. 133–178.

Berg, I., Dolan, Y., & Trepper, T. (2007). *More than Miracles: The State of the Art of Solution-Focused Brief Therapy.* New York: Routledge.

Bohart, A.C. (2000). "The Client Is the Most Important Factor: Clients' Self-Healing Capacities and Psychotherapy." *Journal of Psychotherapy Integration,* vol. 10, no. 2, pp. 127–149.

Bowen, M. (1966). "The Use of Family Theory in Clinical Practice." *Comprehensive Psychiatry,* vol. 7, pp. 345–374.

Bowlby J. (1999). *Attachment and Loss: Volume 1, Attachment* (2d ed.). New York: Basic Books.

Cacioppo, J., & Patrick, W. (2008). *Loneliness: Human Nature and the Need for Social Connection.* New York: W.W. Norton and Co.

Caplan, T. (2008a). "Needs ABC: Needs Acquisition and Behaviour Change; An Integrative Model for Couples Therapy." *Journal of Psychotherapy Integration,* vol. 18, no.4, pp. 421–436.

Caplan, T. (2008b). *Needs ABC: A Needs Acquisition and Behavior Change Model for Group Work and Other Psychotherapies.* London: Whiting and Birch.

Caplan, T., & Thomas, H. (1995). "Safety and Comfort, Content and Process: Facilitating Open Group Work with Men Who Batter." *Social Work with Groups,* vol. 18, nos. 2–3, pp. 33–51.

Caplan, T., & Thomas, H. (2004). "If We Are All in the Same Canoe, Why Are We Using Different Paddles? The Effective Use of Common Themes in Diverse Group Situations." *Social Work with Groups,* vol. 27, no. 1, pp. 53–73.

Carlson, J. (2006). *Adlerian Therapy: Theory and Practice.* Washington, DC: American Psychological Association.

Carlson, J., Watts, R.E., & Maniacci, M. (2006). *Adlerian therapy: Theory and practice.* Washington, DC: American Psychological Association.

Carson, R.C. (1969). *Interaction Concepts of Personality.* Chicago: Aldine.

Christensen, A., & Jacobson, N.S. (2000). *Reconcilable Differences.* New York: Guilford.

Constantine, L. (1986). "Jealousy and Extramarital Sexual Relations." In N. Jacobson & Gurman, A., *Clinical Handbook of Marital Therapy,* pp. 173–195.

Couture, S., & Sutherland, O. (2006). "Giving Advice on Advice-Giving: A Conversation Analysis of Karl Tomm's Practice." *Journal of Marital and Family Therapy,* vol. 32, no. 3, pp. 329–344.

De Shazer, S. (1982). *Patterns of Brief Family Therapy: An Ecosystemic Approach.* New York: Guilford Press.

De Shazer, S. (1985). *Keys to Solution in Brief Therapy.* New York: W.W. Norton and Co.

De Shazer, S. (1991). *Putting Difference to Work.* New York: Norton.

De Shazer, S., Berg, I.K., Lipchik, E., Nunnally, E., Molnar, A., Gingerich, W., et al (June 1986). "Brief Therapy: Focused Solution Development." *Family Process,* vol. 25, no. 2, pp. 207–221.

De Shazer, S., Dolan, Y., & Trepper, T. (2007). *More Than Miracles: The State of the Art of Solution-Focused Brief Therapy.* New York: Routledge.

Deveny, E., Liaw, S.-T., & Pleteshner, C. (2003). "Understanding the Problem Is the Solution." In C. Simpson, *Proceedings of the HIC 2003 RACGP12CC (Combined Conference).* Brunswick East, Victoria: Health Informatics Society of Australia (HISA); Royal Australian College of General Practitioners (RACGP), pp. 137–143.

Doel, M., & Sawdon, S. (1999). *The Essential Groupworker: Teaching and Learning Creative Groupwork.* London: Jessica Kingsley Publishers Ltd.

Dryer, D.C., & Horowitz, L.M. (1997). "When Do Opposites Attract? Interpersonal Complementarity Versus Similarity." *Journal of Personality and Social Psychology,* vol. 72, no. 3, pp. 592–603.

Ellis, A. (1997). *The Practice of Rational Emotive Behavior Therapy.* New York: Springer Publishing Company.

Emerson, R.W. (1904). Letters and Social Aims. *In The Complete Works of Ralph Waldo Emerson:* Vol. 3. (p 313). New York: Houghton Mifflin & Co.

Erikson, E. (1959). *Identity and the Life Cycle.* New York: International Universities Press.

Esman, A. (1975). *The Psychology of Adolescents: Essential Readings.* Madison, CT: International Universities Press.

Freud, S. (1913). *The Interpretation of Dreams* (Trans. A.A. Brill). New York: Macmillan. (Original work published 1900)

Freud, S. (1960). *The Psychopathology of Everyday Life.* London: Hogarth Press.

Galati, D., Miceli, R., & Sini, B. (2001). "Judging and Coding Facial Expressions in Congenitally Blind Children." *International Journal of Behavioral Development*, vol. 25, pp. 268–278.

Gordon, R. (1999) "Demystifying Psychotherapy." Paper presented at the Inaugural Psychodynamic Psychotherapy Conference of the Goldcoast IMHS, Sept. 4, 1999, Currumbin, Queensland, p. 6.

Gottman, J. (1999). *The Marriage Clinic.* New York: W.W. Norton and Company, Inc.

Gottman, J. (2002). *The Relationship Cure: A 5 Step Guide to Strengthening Your Marriage, Family and Friendships.* New York: Three Rivers Press.

Gottman, J., & Silver, N. (1999). *The Seven Principles for Making Marriage Work.* New York: Crown.

Greenberg, L., & Johnson, S. (1988). *Emotionally Focused Therapy for Couples.* New York: Guilford Press.

Greenberg, L., Rice, N., & Elliott, R. (1993). *Facilitating Emotional Change.* New York: Guilford.

Greenberg, L., & Safran, J. (1987). *Emotion in Psychotherapy: Affect, Cognition and the Process of Change.* New York: Guilford Press.

Gurman, A.S., & Jacobsen, N. (2002). *Clinical Handbook of Couple Therapy* (3d ed.). New York: Guilford Publications.

Hazan, C., & Shaver, P.R. (1987). "Romantic Love Conceptualized as an Attachment Process." *Journal of Personality and Social Psychology,* vol. 52, pp. 511–524.

Hazan, C., & Shaver, P.R. (1990). "Love and Work: An Attachment-Theoretical Perspective." *Journal of Personality and Social Psychology,* vol. 59, pp. 270–280.

Hendrix, H. (2001). *Getting the Love You Want: A Guide for Couples.* Owl Books. New York: Holt Paperbacks.

Henry, W., & Strupp, H. (1994). "The Therapeutic Alliance as Interpersonal Process." In A. Horvath & L. Greenberg, *Working Alliance.*

Hogan, S. (2001). *Healing Arts: The History of Art Therapy.* London: Jessica Kingsley Press.

Horowitz, L.M., Dryer, D.C., & Krasnoperova, E.N. (1997). "The Circumplex Structure of Interpersonal Problems." In R. Plutchik & H.R. Conte (Eds.), *Circumplex Models of Personality and Emotions.* Washington, DC: American.

Horvath, A., & Greenberg, L. (Eds.) (1994). *The Working Alliance: Theory, Research and Practice.* New York: John Wiley and Sons, Inc.

Hubble, M., Duncan, B.L., & Miller, S.D. (Eds.) (1999). *The Heart and Soul of Change: What Works in Therapy.* Washington, DC: American Psychological Association.

Hurley, A. (2006). "Mood Disorders in Intellectual Disability." Medscape: http://www.medscape.com/viewarticle/542519. From *Current Opinion in Psychiatry,* 19(5):465–469.

Jansen, A., Nguyen, X., Karpitskiy, V., Mettenleiter, T., & Loewy, A. (1995). "Central Command Neurons of the Sympathetic Nervous System: Basis of the Fight-or-Flight Response." *Science,* vol. 270, pp. 644–646.

Jacobson, N. (1984). "A Component Analysis of Behavioral Marital Therapy: The Relative Effectiveness of Behavior Exchange and Communication/Problem-Solving Training." *Journal of Consulting and Clinical Psychology,* vol. 52, no. 2, pp. 295–305.

Jacobson, N., & Gottman, J.M. (1998). *When Men Batter Women: New Insights Into Ending Abusive Relationships.* New York: Simon and Schuster.

Jacobson, N., & Gurman, A. (1986). *Clinical Handbook of Marital Therapy.* New York: Guilford Press.

Jacobson, N.S., & Margolin, G. (1979). *Marital Therapy: Strategies Based on Social Learning and Behavior Exchange Principles.* New York: Brunner/Mazel.

Jacobson, N., Follette, W., Revenstorf, D., Baucom, D., Hahlweg, K., & Margolin, G. (2000). "Variability in Outcome and Clinical Significance of Behavioral Marital Therapy: A Reanalysis of Outcome Data." *Prevention and Treatment,* vol. 3, no. 1, pp. 497–504.

Jenkins, A. (1990). *Invitations to Responsibility.* Adelaide, South Australia: Dulwich Centre Publications.

Johnson, S. (2004). *The Practice of Emotionally Focused Couple Therapy.* New York: Brunner-Routledge.

Kitchen, K. (2005). "Beyond Therapeutic Models: Do Therapists Know What Clients Really Want?" *CrossCurrents: The Journal of Addiction and Mental Health.* Autumn 2005, vol. 9, no. 1, p. 17) Available at: http://www.camh.net/Publications/Cross_Currents/Autumn_2005/crosscurrents_autumn05.html. From Centre for Addiction and Mental Health.

Klein, M. (1946). Notes on some schizoid mechanisms. *Int. J. Psychoanal,* 27:99-110.

Kopp, R.R. (1995). *Metaphor Therapy: Using Client-Generated Metaphors in Client Psychotherapy.* Boca Raton, FL: Taylor & Francis.

Kurland, R. (2004). "Social Group Work: Five Key Components of Superb Practice." Association for the Advancement of Social Work with Groups. 26th Annual International Symposium, Detroit, MI.

Lambert, M., & Barley, D. (2001). Research Summary on the Therapeutic Relationship and Psychotherapy Outcome. *Psychotherapy,* vol. 38, no. 4, pp. 357–361.

Lambreth, G. (2002). *Play Therapy: The Art of the Relationship.* London: Brunner-Routledge.

Linehan, M. (1999). "Validation and Psychotherapy." In C. Bohart & L. Greenberg, *Empathy Reconsidered: New Directions in Psychotherapy.* Washington, DC: American Psychological Association, pp. 384–387.

Locke, K.D., & Sadler, P. (January 2007). "Self-Efficacy, Values and Complementarity in Dyadic Interactions: Integrating Interpersonal and Social-Cognitive Theory." *Personality and Social Psychology Bulletin*, vol. 33, no. 1, pp. 94–109.

Maslow, A. (1998). *Toward a Psychology of Being* (3d ed.). New York: Wiley.

McGoldrick, M. (1996). *Ethnicity and Family Therapy* (2d ed.). New York: Guilford Press.

Miller, W. & Rollnick, S. (1991). *Motivational Interviewing: Preparing People to Change Addictive Behavior.* New York: Guildford Press.

Nichols, M. (1987). *The Self in the System.* New York: Brunner/Mazel.

Nichols, M. (2007). *The Essentials of Family Therapy* (3d ed.). New York: Pearson.

Nichols, M., & Schwartz, R.C. (2006). *Family Therapy, Concepts and Methods* (7th ed.). New York: Allyn and Bacon.

Noel, S., & Howard, K. (1989). "Initial Contact and Engagement in Psychotherapy." *Journal of Clinical Psychology,* vol. 45, no. 5, pp. 798–805.

Oberst, U. E. & Stewart, A. E. (2003). *Adlerian Psychotherapy: An Advanced Approach to Individual Psychology.* New York: Brunner-Routledge.

Orlinsky, D. (1994). "Effective Ingredients of Successful Psychotherapy: Implications of 40 Years of Process Outcome Research." In *Psychotherapy East and West Integration of Psychotherapy, Korean Academy of Psychotherapists, Proceedings of the 16th International Congress of Psychotherapy.*

Orlinsky, D., Grave, K., & Parks, B. (1994). "Process and Outcome in Psychotherapy: Noch Einmal." In A. Bergin and S. Garfield, *The Handbook of Psychotherapy and Behavior Change* (4th ed.). Toronto: John Wiley and Sons, Inc.

Orlinsky, D.E., & Howard, K.I. (1986). "Process and Outcome in Psychotherapy." In S.L. Garfield & A.E. Bergin, *Handbook of Psychotherapy and Behavior Change* (3d ed.). New York: Wiley.

Packman, J. & Bratton, S. (2003). A School-Based Group Play/Activity Therapy Intervention with Learning Disabled Preadolescents Exhibiting Behavior Problems. *International Journal of Play Therapy,* 12(2), pp. 7-29.

Poon, V.H.K. (2007). "Model for Counselling People in Relationships." *Canadian Family Physician*, vol. 53, pp. 237–238.

Prochaska, J. & Di Clemente, C. (1983). "Stages and processes of self-change of smoking: Toward an integrative model of change." *Journal of Consulting and Clinical Psychology*, vol. 51(3), Jun, pp. 390-395.

Reeve, J., Inck, T.A., & Safran, J. (1993). "Towards an Integration of Cognitive, Interpersonal and Experiential Approaches to Therapy." In G. Stricker & J.R. Gold, *Comprehensive Handbook of Psychotherapy Integration.* New York: Plenum Press.

Roberts, J., & Prior, M. (2006). "A Review of the Research to Identify the Most Effective Models of Practice in Early Intervention for Children with Autism Spectrum Disorders." Report funded by the Australian Government, Department of Health and Ageing, University of Sydney and University of Australia.

Rollnick, S., & Miller, W.R. (1995). "What Is Motivational Interviewing?" *Behavioral and Cognitive Psychotherapy*, vol. 23, pp. 325–344.

Rowe, C., Gomez, L., & Liddle, H. (2007). In M. Nichols, *The Essentials of Family Therapy* (3d ed.). New York: Pearson.

Ruesch, J. & Bateson, G. (2006). *Communication: The Social Matrix of Psychiatry.* Piscataway, NJ: Transaction Publishers. p. 180.

Sager, C. (1986). "Therapy with Remarried Couples." In Jacobson & Gurman, *Clinical Handbook of Marital Therapy.*

Selekman, M.D. (1993). *Pathways to Change: Brief Therapy Solutions with Difficult Adolescents.* New York: Guilford Press.

Sexton, T.L., Ridley, C.R., & Kleiner, A.J. (2004). "Beyond Common Factors: Multilevel-Process Models of Therapeutic Change in Marriage and Family Therapy." *Journal of Marital Family Therapy*, vol. 30, no. 2, pp. 131–149.

Sinclair, J. (1992). "Bridging the Gaps: An Inside-Out View of Autism." In E. Schopler & G. Mesibov, *High-Functioning Individuals with Autism.* New York: Plenum Press.

Stricker, G., & Gold, J.R. (1996). "Psychotherapy Integration: An Assimilative, Psychodynamic Approach." *Clinical Psychology: Science and Practice*, vol. 3, pp. 47–58. Available at: http://cyberpsych.org/SEPI

Sugar, M. J. (1974). Interpretive group psychotherapy with latency children. *Am Acad Child Psychiatry.* Autumn; 13(4):648-66.

Teyber, E. (1989). *Interpersonal Process in Psychotherapy: A Guide for Clinical Training.* Pacific Grove, CA: Brooks/Cole Publishing Company.

Teyber, E. (1997). *Interpersonal Process in Psychotherapy: A Relational Approach* (3rd ed.). Pacific Grove, CA: Brooks/Cole.

Teyber, E. (2006). *Interpersonal Process in Therapy: An Integrative Model.* Pacific Grove, CA: Brooks/Cole.

Teyber, E., & McClure, F. (2000). "Therapist Variables." In C.R. Snyder & R. Ingram, *Handbook of Psychological Change: Psychotherapy Processes and Practices for the 21st Century.* San Francisco: Wiley, pp. 62–87.

Tracey, T.J.G. (September 2004). "Levels of Interpersonal Complementarity: A Simplex Representation." *Personality and Social Psychology Bulletin*, vol. 30, no. 9, pp. 1211–1225.

Wark, L. (1994). "Client Voice: A Study of Client Couples' and Their Therapists' Perspectives on Therapeutic Change." *Journal of Feminist Family Therapy*, vol. 6, no. 2, pp. 21–40.

Warzak, W., William, J., Parish, J., & Handen, B. (1987). "Effects of Telephone Intake Procedures on Initial Appointment Keeping in a Child Behavior Management Clinic." *Journal of Compliance in Health Care*, vol. 2, no. 2, pp. 143–154.

Watson, J., & Greenberg, L. (1994). "The Alliance in Experiential Therapy: Enhancing the Relationship Conditions." In Horvath & Greenberg, *The Working Alliance,* pp. 164–166.

Watzlawick, P., Beavin, J.H., & Jackson, D.D. (1967). *Pragmatics of Human Communication: A Study of Interactional Patterns, Pathologies and Paradoxes.* New York: W. W. Norton and Company.

White, M., & Epston, D. (1990). *Narrative Means to Therapeutic Ends.* New York: Norton.

Yalom, I. (2005). *The Theory and Practice of Group Psychotherapy* (5th ed.). New York: Basic Books.

Index